More Praise for the Second Edition of *Beyond Change Management*

"Once again, Dean and Linda have nailed it! *Beyond Change Management* is an extraordinary book examining the shifts in change management that have occurred over the years. This book offers real, practical solutions for change practitioners to become extraordinary conscious change leaders."

—Darlene Meister, director, Unified Change Management,
United States House of Representatives

"Entering the offices recently of a highly respected Fortune 500 company, I was stunned by the enormity of change they were facing and at the same time how ill-equipped they were to deal with the challenges that lay ahead of them. They had little *capacity* to lead and manage the change required. And, of course, consulting firms were swarming all over them. They needed this book by the Andersons to help them. In fact, Chapter Five alone on building organizational capability is worth the price of the book."

—W. Warner Burke, Ph.D., Edward Lee Thorndike Professor of Psychology and Education;
chair, Department of Organization and Leadership; program coordinator, Graduate Programs
in Social-Organizational Psychology, Teachers College, Columbia University

"*Beyond Change Management* is a must-read for today's C-Suite executives and those who lead organizational change. Change is a fact of life in all successful businesses. Based on this breakthrough construct, we now view our approach to transformational change as a strategic advantage. It is a way of thinking and organizing each critical systemwide initiative for our healthcare system."

—Alan Yordy, president and chief mission officer, PeaceHealth

"While the first editions were excellent to begin with, these enhanced second editions of *Beyond Change Management* and *The Change Leader's Roadmap* are even better with age. The additional years of experience deepen the author's articulation of the links between theory and practice. These books are outstanding resources for both organization change consultants and organization system leaders. Having a roadmap in common promotes the teamwork required for complex adaptive and continually evolving change efforts."

—Charles Seashore, Ph.D., Malcolm Knowles Chair of Adult Learning,
Fielding Graduate University, Santa Barbara, California

"Dean and Linda have broken the code by integrating the leadership of people and culture with business content to deliver results from change. They are unquestionably the experts in *leading* transformation in business. This book reveals their wisdom."

—Pete Fox, general manager, Corporate Accounts Microsoft US

"For today's leaders and managers, the promise of 'change management' seems to be everywhere, but unfortunately not how to achieve real change results. That gap is ably filled by the Andersons who use their more than sixty years of combined experience to clearly explain what is needed and how to do it. Their discussions of a multidimensional, process-oriented approach for achieving transformational results and what it takes to be a conscious change leader should be required reading in all OD and MBA programs."

—Robert J. Marshak, Ph.D., organizational change consultant; senior scholar in residence, MSOD Program American University

"In every generation there are creative and disciplined mapmakers who provide clear guidance to those whose paths will take them on similar journeys. Dean Anderson and Linda Ackerman Anderson are this generation's mapmakers. Their books are rich, resilient, comprehensive and innovative guides that enable change leaders and consultants to practice their trades with heightened awareness and skill. Their grasp of the multiple dimensions of leading successful transformation help us recognize both the practical and the wise."

—David S. Surrenda, Ph. D., author, *Retooling on the Run*

"The comprehensive and pragmatic thinking in this book has truly taken my company and myself beyond change management. This is a must-read for all consultants and executives who aim to master successful implementations in organizations—and who does not have that aspiration? This is not academia; this is the essence of many years of practitioners' experience. And it works!"

—Thomas Fischer, director COO, Valcon Management Consultants A/S

"Transformative times require transforming the way we change! This book challenges, equips and encourages leaders to understand how to deliver breakthrough results. It is not just about change . . . it is about YOU as a leader in these transformative times."

—Professor Todd D. Jick Columbia Business School
President, Global Leadership Services

"In *Beyond Change Management* and the *Change Leader's Roadmap*, Dean and Linda provide practitioners and executives not only the how (tools) but the why (concepts). If you are looking for a comprehensive treatment of the tricky journey of transformation, this is it."

—Christopher G. Worley, Center for Effective Organizations, University of Southern California; former director, MSOD Program at Pepperdine University

"Want a well-documented and valuable book for moving beyond change management–one that can reduce work and improve results? Well, this is that book. It's for those who are serious about their effectiveness in the face of change."

—Mel Toomey, LHD, scholar in residence for Master of Arts in Organizational Leadership Center for Leadership Studies, The Graduate Institute

"In today's dynamic business environment a vital competency every senior executive must bring to his/her organization is not just change management but change *leadership*. This book is a must-read for any such executive as it creates a comprehensive roadmap for change by offering key concepts, powerful insights, relevant examples and practical how to's."

—Richard Whiteley, cofounder, The Forum Corporation; author, *The Customer-Driven Company*

"*Beyond Change Management is* an essential book for anyone attempting to understand and manage complex change, especially today's health care leaders. The book offers a comprehensive and practical guide that will help you get change right the first time. It will significantly increase your likelihood of success and lower your risk of costly setbacks. We have used the Being First methodology successfully on a variety of difficult organizational change initiatives including major clinical quality improvement and safety initiatives, as well as technology implementations such as electronic health record and enterprise resource planning systems. Based on more than fifteen years of experience successfully managing complex clinical and operational change, I highly recommend *Beyond Change Management* and its companion text, the *Change Leader's Roadmap.*"

—John Haughom, M.D., senior vice president,
Clinical Quality and Patient Safety, PeaceHealth

"*Beyond Change Management* is yet another extraordinary resource from Dean Anderson and Linda Ackerman Anderson. There is nobody more qualified to teach organizational transformation to beginners as well as seasoned professionals. This book should be required reading for anyone engaged in change management!"

—Rayona Sharpnack, founder and CEO, Institute for Women's Leadership

"There is a powerful energetic force inside all of us that, once unleashed, can make any change a reality. *Beyond Change Management* captures that essence with passion and purpose."

—Richard Leider, author, *Repacking Your Bags* and *The Power of Purpose*

"*Beyond Change Management* and the *Change Leader's Roadmap* are the best sources I know to learn how to lead and excel at change and business strategy execution."

—Eric Dillon, chief operating officer, Servus Credit Union Ltd.

"Even the expert and experienced change practitioner will be humbled by this book. The leaders we support require us to transform our skill set so they can transform their organizations. This book brings together the totality of the most relevant and applicable approaches to advancing change successfully, but more important it fills the gap we all fundamentally need—how to move ourselves and our organizations to achieve transformative change."

—Polly Ragusa, director, Organization and Learning Development, Cisco

"This second edition of the pioneering book *Beyond Change Management* continues to break new ground in explaining what transformational change is all about, and what it takes to lead and make it happen. The authors present a straightforward account of transformational change combining relevant concepts and approaches with their own extensive experience helping organizations transform themselves. The book is highly informative, stimulating, and inspiring."

—Thomas G. Cummings, professor and chair, Department of Management and
Organization, Marshall School of Business, University of Southern California

"The Andersons have a proven track record in the field of Organization Development. This most recent contribution furthers and reconfirms their reputation for exceptional contributions. Their work provides us with a systematic integration of the most recent thinking and practices in OD—essential reading for both managers and OD consultants."

—Peter F. Sorensen, Ph.D., director, Ph.D. and Masters Programs in Organization Development, Benedictine University

"Dean Anderson and Linda Ackerman Anderson remind us that leading change continues to be a critical capability for organizations who want to thrive in the twenty-first century. They revive the solid wisdom of change leaders from years gone by and bring us up to date with the essential organizational and human dynamics we must consider as we transform our organizations for future success."

—Jackie Alcalde Marr, director, Organization and Talent Development, North America Oracle USA; coauthor of *Social Media at Work;* founder, Evolutions Consulting Group

"Linda and Dean are in a unique position to offer such comprehensive thinking, models, and tools for change because they have devoted over three decades working directly with senior leaders and strategic consultants in numerous transformations across a wide variety of organizations. By doing the work, studying the theory, and reflecting on outcomes, they have captured both the basics and the nuances of change and integrated them into understandable models, processes, and tools. These books are essential reads for change leaders as the authors have advanced the theory and practice of planned change to new heights. Kurt Lewin would be proud!"

—David W. Jamieson, Ph.D., practicum director, American Univ/NTL MS in OD Program; past president, American Society for Training and Development

"This volume contains the best guidelines anywhere for supporting organizational transformation processes. It provides the fundamental essentials for preparation to lead change."

—John Adams, Ph.D., emeritus professor, Saybrook University Organizational Systems Ph.D. Program

"Linda Ackerman Anderson and Dean Anderson bring their many decades of practical experience in supporting leaders in systemwide change to this book that makes explicit the relationships among mindset, leadership actions, project planning, and complex change. While it's never easy to accomplish this kind of change at an enterprise level, this book makes the change leadership process understandable, clear, and actionable—so you can succeed."

—Kathryn Goldman Schuyler, Ph.D., Marshall Goldsmith School of Management, Alliant International University

"Building a service culture requires the transformation of leaders' and employees' mindsets and behaviors and the continuous upgrading of an organization's processes and systems. This extraordinary book provides the insights, methods and tools you need to succeed in this challenging yet essential transformation. Study it thoroughly, apply it rigorously, and succeed brilliantly."

—Ron Kaufman, founder, Up Your Service! College; author, *Up Your Service!*

From determining the type of change effort to developing organizational and leadership capacities that increase the success of change initiatives, this book is easy to read and apply. It is written for a wide range of audiences including executives leading strategy, operations planning and executing change, learning and development groups, and anyone who wants to build long-term capabilities."

—Barbara Plumley, vice president regional operations,
HealthCare Partners Medical Group

"Quality outcome measures and evidence-based medicine will dictate how patients are treated in the future. This book comes at just the right time to guide health care professionals, physicians, and hospital administrators toward adopting such important but sometimes threatening changes. It provides a pathway to embrace the change we must all accept."

—Jim A. Youssef, M.D., founder, SpineColorado

"In this book, Dean Anderson and Linda Ackerman Anderson not only show you the most effective path for success in your change outcomes but also how you can revitalize your organization and people in the process."

—Christian Forthomme, CEO, RealChange Network, Inc.

"If you missed the Anderson's first editions, you may not know what a terrific contribution they are to the field of Organization Development. Now you have a second chance to read these excellent new editions from these gifted writers. These books are essential reading to those who want to become master practitioners in this field."

—Jane Magruder Watkins, coauthor, *Appreciative Inquiry:*
Change at the Speed of Imagination

"*Beyond Change Management* is a must-read for managers, consultants, and anyone else interested in the process of transformational change. It challenges conventional wisdom regarding change and offers an engaging and insightful alternative based upon the notion of 'conscious change leadership.'"

—Cliff Oswick, chair, Organization Theory; academic dean for Law
and Social Sciences, Queen Mary, University of London

"The definitive 'how to' guide for change leaders—the Andersons have taken up where the theorists left off, providing practical mechanisms and strategies to build change capability within organizations. They challenge all of us who call ourselves change agents to practice what we preach and build reflexive consciousness into all our change leadership efforts."

—Quentin Jones, Australian managing director, Human Synergistics International,
coauthor, *In Great Company—Unlocking the Secrets of Culture Transformation*

FREE
Premium Content
▼

Pfeiffer®
An Imprint of

This book includes premium content including worksheets and job aids that can be accessed from our Web site when you register at **www.pfeiffer.com/go/anderson** using the password *professional*.

Instructors are invited to download a free Instructor's Guide with materials and information for using *Beyond Change Management* (or *The Change Leader's Roadmap* in that book) in a workshop or college course. The Instructor's Guide includes PowerPoint slide shows, key points, resources, student activities, helpful teaching strategies, and other supplemental classroom aids. College professors may download the materials at **www.wiley.com/college/anderson**

Corporate trainers, please email **instructorguides@ beingfirst.com** to receive your copy for use in your executive and management development programs.

About Pfeiffer

Pfeiffer serves the professional development and hands-on resource needs of training and human resource practitioners and gives them products to do their jobs better. We deliver proven ideas and solutions from experts in HR development and HR management, and we offer effective and customizable tools to improve workplace performance. From novice to seasoned professional, Pfeiffer is the source you can trust to make yourself and your organization more successful.

Essential Knowledge Pfeiffer produces insightful, practical, and comprehensive materials on topics that matter the most to training and HR professionals. Our Essential Knowledge resources translate the expertise of seasoned professionals into practical, how-to guidance on critical workplace issues and problems. These resources are supported by case studies, worksheets, and job aids and are frequently supplemented with CD-ROMs, websites, and other means of making the content easier to read, understand, and use.

Essential Tools Pfeiffer's Essential Tools resources save time and expense by offering proven, ready-to-use materials—including exercises, activities, games, instruments, and assessments—for use during a training or team-learning event. These resources are frequently offered in looseleaf or CD-ROM format to facilitate copying and customization of the material.

Pfeiffer also recognizes the remarkable power of new technologies in expanding the reach and effectiveness of training. While e-hype has often created whizbang solutions in search of a problem, we are dedicated to bringing convenience and enhancements to proven training solutions. All our e-tools comply with rigorous functionality standards. The most appropriate technology wrapped around essential content yields the perfect solution for today's on-the-go trainers and human resource professionals.

www.pfeiffer.com

Essential resources for training and HR professionals

Beyond Change Management

HOW TO ACHIEVE BREAKTHROUGH RESULTS
THROUGH CONSCIOUS CHANGE LEADERSHIP

Dean Anderson
Linda Ackerman Anderson

A Wiley Imprint
www.pfeiffer.com

Published by Pfeiffer
An Imprint of Wiley
One Montgomery, Ste. 1200, San Francisco, CA 94104
www.pfeiffer.com

For additional copies/bulk purchases of this book in the U.S. please contact 800-274-4434.

Pfeiffer books and products are available through most bookstores. To contact Pfeiffer directly call our Customer Care Department within the U.S. at 800-274-4434, outside the U.S. at 317-572-3985, fax 317-572-4002, or visit www.pfeiffer.com.

Pfeiffer also publishes its books in a variety of electronic formats. Some content that appears in print may not be available in electronic books.

Library of Congress Cataloging-in-Publication Data

Anderson, Dean,
  Beyond change management : how to achieve breakthrough results through conscious change leadership / Dean Anderson, Linda Ackerman Anderson. —2nd ed.
    p.   cm. —(J-B O-D (organizational development) ; 36)
  Includes bibliographical references.
  ISBN 978-0-470-64808-7 (pbk.)
    1. Leadership.   2. Organizational change.   I. Ackerman-Anderson, Linda S., 1950-   II. Title.
  HD57.7.A527 2010
  658.4'063—dc22

2010032262

ISBN 978-0-470-64808-7; 9780470890967 (ebk); 9780470891131 (ebk); 9780470891124 (ebk)

Acquiring Editor: Matt Davis	Director of Development: Kathleen Dolan Davies
Production Editor: Joanne Clapp Fullagar	Editor: Julie McNamee
Editorial Assistant: Lindsay Morton	Manufacturing Supervisor: Becky Morgan
Printed in the United States of America	

PB Printing   10 9 8 7 6 5 4 3

TABLE OF CONTENTS

FIGURES, EXHIBITS, AND TABLES

PREMIUM CONTENT FOR *BEYOND CHANGE MANAGEMENT*

Available for download at www.pfeiffer.com/go/anderson

▶ Ten Most Common Mistakes in Leading Transformation
▶ Leadership Breakthrough: Topic Options and Methods
▶ Building Change Capability: Leading Change as a Strategic Discipline
▶ Upgrade Your Organization Development and Project Management Staff to Strategic Change Consultants
▶ How Developing Breath Control Can Make You a Better Leader
▶ How Command and Control as a Change Leadership Style Causes Transformational Change Efforts to Fail
▶ Identifying Project Briefing Questions
▶ Selecting the Best Change Process Leader to Oversee Your Transformation
▶ Ten Critical Actions for Leading Successful Transformation
▶ A Candid Message to Senior Leaders: Ten Ways to Dramatically Increase the Success of Your Change Efforts
▶ How to Use Decision-Making as a Tool for Successful Transformation
▶ Six Faulty Assumptions about Change Communications
▶ Elements of a Whole System Integration and Mastery Strategy

PREFACE

Our life's work has always been about change. Dean started his career in the field of personal change, and Linda in organizational change. In 1986, when we met, it became clear that our two professional specialties were meant to be merged into one unified approach to transforming organizations.

Dean was one of the first people doing deep personal mastery work in organizations, having created the Optimal Performance Institute to offer his approach to breakthrough performance (originally developed for world-class athletes) to people in business. Linda was one of the founding leaders of the Organization Transformation movement, focusing on teaching the process of organization change and transformational leadership to executives and consultants world wide. At the time of our meeting, Dean had realized that his personal and team performance models and interest in culture had to align with the complexities of larger organizational systems, while Linda had recognized that her work required more overt emphasis on personal and cultural change to fortify her large systems work. Both our interests and the requirements of successful large systems transformation were moving each of us toward the other's expertise.

In 1988, we brought our specialties, insights, and theories together to create an integrated approach to leading transformation and to form Being First, Inc. In our early years, we mentored and coached one another in our individual specialties; now, we each stand in both arenas—personal and organizational transformation—and consult to senior executives across industries, government, the military, and large nonprofits.

Individually, and then collectively at Being First, we have always considered ourselves thought leaders in the area of transformation, not so much because of what we know, but because of the cutting edges we are willing to explore and the continual learning and development we pursue. We are committed to pushing the envelope of thinking and practice for accomplishing tangible, breakthrough-level results. We created Being First—appropriately named for our bias toward the personal work required to transform individuals and organizations—to offer our thinking and advice to people and organizations around the world.

Being First, Inc. is a full-service change education, consulting, and change leadership development firm assisting organizations to maximize their business results from change, transform their people and culture, and build internal change capability. We provide organizational change capability and change strategy consulting, enterprise-wide breakthrough training for culture and mindset change, change leadership skill development for leaders and consultants, licensing of our change process methodology, coaching, personal transformation training, and transformational team development. We support clients to create strategic disciplines for change so that their organizations can embody masterful change leadership and increase their success from change. We are developing a curriculum for women leaders and managers and are planning a worldwide Change Leadership Institute.

Our style, based on our commitment to walk our own talk, is to co-create a personalized strategy for each client with the appropriate balance of consulting, training, and methodology, integrating personal change and organizational change. We are devoted to our own continuous learning and development through applying our own personal practices and true partnerships with our clients. Our personal and organizational work provides us the opportunity to develop, field test, and write about what we see is required to transform human systems successfully and consciously.

We released the first edition of this book and its companion volume, *The Change Leader's Roadmap*, in 2001. Much has happened since then—in the world, in organizations, and in us. The messages of the first edition are as relevant today as they were then, and in many ways, more so. The challenges of change leadership continue to increase. Transformations in organizations are ever more complex, the stakes are higher, and the impact these changes are having on people and culture are more profound now than ever. These challenges are requiring leaders and those that consult to them to advance their thinking and methods. As we develop and evolve ourselves, we see with ever greater clarity and distinction what is required to succeed at transformation—personally, organizationally, and globally.

To help meet these challenges and clarify the terrain of positive change, we have added five new chapters to this edition, further developed another one, and removed three that no longer seemed as pertinent. We have made these changes to integrate our insights and learning over the past decade. We have attempted to capture what is true for us in this moment in time in the evolution of change and leadership. This has been a challenging effort—a bit like trying to capture a river that keeps on flowing. The insights we explore here will continue to evolve—and have done so even as we have rewritten them. We explore ideas and theory at the conceptual level; offer strategies, actions, and tools at the pragmatic level; and attempt to bridge the two in the clearest and most useful way possible for you, our reader.

For three decades, we have thoroughly engaged in the debate of personal change versus organization change, change the people or change the structures, carefully plan change versus let it unfold, manage change versus consciously lead it, and focus on process versus outcomes. The debates continue, drive our investigation, and fuel the wisdom we seek to share.

In our writing, we have attempted to be forthright about what we see as true, while keeping our mindset and eyes open to what we do not yet understand. We have attempted to denote what we think is factual, what we believe due to our own experiences, and what we are still learning or questioning.

We invite you, our reader, into this exploration with us—into the inquiry—into our attempt to give language, guidance, and incentive to growing the field of *conscious* change leadership. We hope you will participate in the conversation about the issues and propositions in these books, and then put them to the test in your own conscious leadership of change.

Please read on with the spirit of inquiry. Read with your concern for the state of today's organizations. Read to contribute to our collective ability to transform organizations into places in which people love to work and feel regenerated, as well as add value to their customers and stakeholders. Read on with a concern for people and the world, and how to make our lives ever more healthy and meaningful as we collectively co-create a future of greater social justice and environmental sustainability. Read on while honoring how far the fields of organization transformation, change management, and change leadership have come from the first attempts to infuse the values of planned change and human development into organizations. And please read with yourself in mind as a leader or consultant of change. Our message is written for you, and we hope it benefits you personally and professionally.

Dean Anderson
Linda Ackerman Anderson
Durango, Colorado
Spring 2010

ACKNOWLEDGMENTS

We deeply appreciate the wonderful people who supported us while writing these new editions of *Beyond Change Management* and *The Change Leader's Roadmap*.

We received abundant help from our trusty readers—friends, and colleagues all—including insightful input from Anne Polino, Carol Tisson, Jan Christian Rasmussen, and Steen Ruby. Their insight, feedback, and encouragement were invaluable to us.

Our staff was untiring in their assistance and encouragement. We sincerely appreciate Erin Patla and Lindsay Patterson for their dedication and patience.

We appreciate our clients whose investment and commitment to partner with us produced the many insights and outcomes you read about in these books. Their willingness to work in conscious ways helped to formulate and demonstrate what we are most passionate about—leading transformation consciously. Many are true pioneers, and we feel honored to share in their journey.

We also appreciate one another for partnering in this co-creative process, modeling to the other what we deeply know is true, even when we individually may have forgotten. Our voices are stronger, our work is deeper, our lives are richer, and our spirits brighter from the experience.

Beyond Change Management

INTRODUCTION

There is nothing more difficult to take in hand, more perilous to conduct, or more uncertain in its success, than to take the lead in the introduction of a new order of things.

—Niccolo Machiavelli, *The Prince* (1532)

We can remember when change consultants were few and far between. About the only people thinking about and promoting planned change back then were a handful of organization development practitioners, and they seldom captured the attention of senior leaders.

Now in the twenty-first century, change and how to lead it successfully has become a critical topic on the minds of organizational leaders. And for good reasons: Change is happening everywhere; its speed and complexity are increasing; and the future success of our organizations depends on how successful leaders are at leading that change. In today's marketplace, change is a *requirement* for continued success, and competent change leadership is a most coveted executive skill.

Organizations' track records at change are not very good. The vast majority of today's change efforts are failing to produce their intended business results. These struggling efforts are producing huge cost to budgets, time, people, customers, and faith in leadership. Organizations are spending tens of millions of dollars on change efforts such as information technology installations, supply chain and reengineering, yet not obtaining their intended return on investment. Furthermore, the very methods used in these failed efforts are causing tremendous resistance and burnout in people, loss of employee morale, and turmoil in the cultures of organizations. Put simply, organizational leaders are falling short in their efforts to lead change successfully.

Over the past twenty years, technology and other marketplace drivers have radically altered the very nature of change. Whereas change was once a contained transactional event (and easier to manage), it is now more open-ended, radical, complex, personal, and continuous. "Transformation" is the new type of change that has emerged, and it is by far the most prevalent and complex type occurring in organizations today. In general, leaders do not understand transformational change or how to lead it, which is causing virtually all of the change-related problems they are now facing.

These struggles have given rise to the field of change management. For the most part, change management practitioners have attempted to provide solutions to two major problems—how to plan better for implementation and how to overcome employee resistance. However, these two necessary components of change have not produced adequate positive results, especially for transformational change. Why? Because attention to implementation and resistance is only the tip of the iceberg of what is required in transformation. It is now time to move beyond change management into conscious change leadership; time to develop the advanced change strategies that support this new type of change; time to move from managing resistance and implementation to co-creating a positive future through successful, well-run transformational change efforts.

Leaders in need of change assistance have always been a window of professional opportunity for organization development (OD) and change management consultants. However, for the most part, these practitioners have not been as effective at providing the necessary support and guidance to organizational leaders as is necessary for transformational change. Put bluntly, most change consultants need to expand their awareness, skills, and approaches to leading transformational change as well.

What is the source of the problem? Is the issue about the changing nature of change? Is it about leadership? Or is it about organization development and change management consulting practices? *Our premise is that it is about all three: change, leadership, and today's consulting approaches.*

Transformational change involves a number of very essential and unique dynamics that demand a new leadership perspective, skill, and style. Most leaders, however, are viewing transformation through old mindsets with limited critical awareness and are applying traditional management approaches that just do not work. Because leading transformational change is so radically different from managing or leading a stable organization, leaders cannot simply lay their old way of thinking, behaving, and operating on this new world and expect success.

Leading transformation calls for a deeper understanding of change and a new set of leadership skills and strategies. Leaders must broaden their understanding and insight about what transformational change requires, let go of or build off of their old approaches, and guide the process of transformation differently. In particular, they must transform their beliefs about people, organizations, and change itself; they must view transformation through a new set of mental lenses to see the actual dynamics of transformation; and they must alter their leadership style and behavior to accommodate the unique requirements of transformation.

This means that leaders themselves must transform to lead transformation successfully in their organizations. Only then will the new skills of conscious change leadership become available to them. Only then will they be able to see, understand, and apply the strategies and approaches that make transformation work. And only then will they want to.

This is not to say that leaders are bad, wrong, unskilled, or somehow flawed. In fact, quite the contrary. Over the past two decades, leaders have done a phenomenal job of increasing the productivity of their organizations. However, because today's change is so often transformational (making it much more complex), the requirements for today's leaders, out of necessity, are expanding. The challenge is that today's marketplace is not asking for just leadership. It is demanding *change leadership*—even more, *conscious change leadership*—a new breed of leader for a new breed of change.

The term *conscious* signifies a required shift in both leaders' and consultants' *consciousness* regarding how they view change, themselves, and their roles as change leaders. Let's explore the terms.

Webster's dictionary defines *conscious* as "to know, awareness of an inward state or outward fact; perceiving, noticing with a degree of controlled thought or observation; capable of thought, will, design and perception; acting with critical awareness."

Webster defines *consciousness* as "awareness, especially of something within oneself, and also the state of being conscious of an external object, state, or fact; the state of being characterized by sensation, emotion, volition, and thought; the upper level of mental life as contrasted with unconscious processes; mindfulness."

Change leadership implies seeing the future and being able to lead people to co-create it. *Conscious change leadership* infers that leaders and consultants become more "conscious" and aware of the deeper and more subtle dynamics of transformation, especially regarding people and process dynamics. Conscious change leaders see what others miss because they operate with expanded awareness and understanding. They perceive human dynamics more fully and the nuances of designing and implementing change processes that build commitment in stakeholders, transform culture, and achieve results beyond what others would deem possible. Conscious change leaders apply this increased awareness to expertly lead people through the process of change to co-create a future that will enable their organizations to win in the ever increasingly competitive marketplace.

A MULTI-DIMENSIONAL, PROCESS APPROACH

Mastery of any skill requires that you develop all aspects of the task. You cannot specialize in one area and neglect the others. There is always at least one set of two "polarities" that you must master to excel at anything. For example, to be a masterful communicator, you must develop both speaking and listening skills. Masterful golfers must be able to hit both the long ball and the short ball well. Masterful parents must know how to discipline as well as how to nurture their children. Being exceptionally good at one or the other polarity is not enough. You need both the "yin" and the "yang."

Mastery, then, requires a focus on all areas of an endeavor and the pursuit of excellence in each. The more you improve your skill in one area, the more it calls forth your developmental needs in the others. Whatever you neglect becomes your weak link.

Mastery suggests that leaders and consultants must become conscious of and competent in *all* of the different dimensions of transformation, even those that they are not yet aware of or are comfortable addressing—areas that are outside their box of understanding.

For thirty years, we have been promoting the idea that leading transformation *masterfully* requires leaders and consultants to design and implement change processes that attend to both internal and external dynamics at the individual, relationship, team, and organizational levels. We have called this a "multi-dimensional, process approach" to transformation to denote all these different but interdependent areas of required attention. Now, with the rapidly growing global movement

Figure I.1.   The Conscious Change Leader Accountability Model

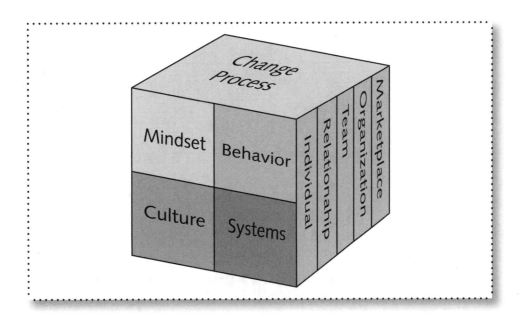

catalyzed around Ken Wilber's groundbreaking work at the Integral Institute, we can also describe our approach as "integral" as defined by Wilber. Regardless of what we call it, the principle of mastery lies at the heart of it; you must attend to all the dynamics at play to succeed. Most change efforts fail because the leaders neglect critical dimensions.

Figure I.1 graphically portrays what we call the Conscious Change Leader Accountability Model. Change leaders are accountable for each of these areas because attending to them is required to succeed at transforming their organizations. Again, what you neglect becomes your weak link and cause of failure. Before we address the individual dimensions, let's discuss the way the model is organized. We borrow from Wilber's core work that he calls All Quadrants, All Levels (AQAL).[1] Notice that the face of the model is a matrix built on an x axis (internal and external) and a y axis (individual and collective), making four "quadrants." (Figure I.2, as a segment of the overall model, further clarifies this.) The two quadrants on the left describe aspects of internal reality, while the two quadrants on the right describe external reality. The upper two quadrants address the individual, and the lower two address the collective.

Figure I.2. The Four Quadrants of Conscious Change Leader Accountability

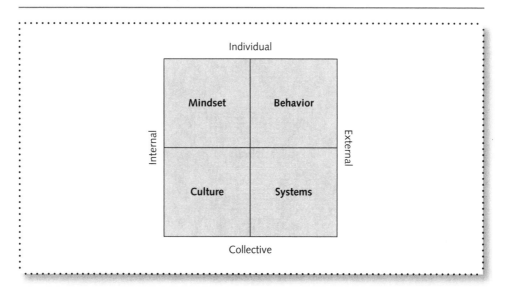

Conscious change leaders must attend to all four quadrants: (1) mindset (internal, individual); (2) culture (internal, collective); (3) behavior (external, individual); and (4) systems (external, collective).

The **mindset** quadrant includes values, beliefs, thoughts, emotions, ways of being, levels of commitment, and so on. **Behavior** includes work styles, skills and actions, and behaviors. **Culture** includes norms, collective ways of being, working and relating, climate, and esprit de corps. **Systems** includes structures, systems, business processes, and technology.

Each of these quadrants must be addressed at all levels. Organization transformation is not simply about organizational systems or culture. It demands attention to individuals, how people relate, how teams function, and the marketplace itself. All will have an influence on your attempt to transform your organization.

We benefit greatly from Wilber's brilliant and clarifying AQAL model to depict this graphically, and we acknowledge his contribution to our improved way of communicating the full scope of required conscious change leader attention. Most importantly, the model makes it clear that conscious change leaders must always attend to internal and external dynamics within both individuals and the collective.

We complete our Conscious Change Leader Accountability Model by capping it all off with "change process." Change processes occur within all the quadrants at all levels. Of critical importance, a successful organization transformation requires a change strategy and process plan that organizes and integrates all of these change processes and the activities within them into a unified enterprisewide process that moves the organization (all its quadrants and levels) from where it is today to where it wants to be—transformed to something new that produces significantly improved results in its marketplace. In our consulting practice, we accomplish this very challenging and essential outcome using The Change Leader's Roadmap methodology, which you can read about in the companion volume to this book under the same title. The book you are now reading outlines our multi-dimensional process approach to transforming organizations. We will describe it in detail, make a case for it, rationalize why it is necessary, and hopefully demonstrate the improved results and return on investment (ROI) it will bring to your change efforts. We will visit the Conscious Change Leader Accountability Model periodically throughout the book, each time making further distinctions about what transformation requires and how the quadrants and levels—and the processes within them—can be successfully addressed to deliver the results you are after in your change efforts.

Keep in mind that some of these "dimensions" are common, familiar, and understood by leaders and their consultants. Others are not. Those that are familiar to most leaders and traditional management consultants pertain to *external* reality, as in organizational structures, systems, and business processes. Those that are most familiar to change management specialists and OD consultants pertain to *internal* reality, such as perception, feelings, interpersonal relationships, norms, and culture. Mastery, of course, requires that leaders and consultants develop their awareness and skill in *both* arenas—internal and external—as applied to all levels and their change processes.

For us, the backbone of our consulting and training practices and experience over the past three decades has been human consciousness as it relates to breakthrough performance and outcomes in individuals, teams, and organizations, and the transformational change process. Our consulting careers have been dedicated to understanding the multidimensional nature of change, including how to change organizations as well as people. We have always attempted to integrate both the "hard" external and "soft" internal aspects of change, believing deeply that this integration was not only required but also represented the next evolution (beyond change management) that change leadership and consulting practices needed to embrace.

Building a multidimensional, process approach to transforming people and organizations to achieve extraordinary results has been our sole field of study. By nature, we are "action theorists." We read, study, and research, and then rely heavily on our intuition to crystallize and integrate new learnings. We then build models and processes that we test heavily in the field with our clients. With their assistance, we next refine and evolve our thinking and practices. We attempt to be "pie-in-the-sky" visionaries, while remaining true and devoted pragmatists. We stretch ourselves continually; we like our feet on the ground while our heads are in the stars, and our writing reflects this. To achieve the extraordinary results we seek with our clients, we must take extraordinary measures and travel new territory—beyond the normal, beyond the traditional, beyond the current change management practices. We welcome you into this inquiry about what *really* is required to successfully transform ourselves and our organizations.

OUR AUDIENCE

Over the years, we have been fortunate to work extensively with both change leaders and change consultants. Sometimes, our clients are the senior executives of the organization; at other times, our clients are the internal change consultants supporting those leaders. Usually and ideally, our clients include both the senior leaders and their internal change consultants.

In this book, we will thoroughly explore transformation and will provide an overview of what we believe it takes to both *lead* transformation and *consult* to it successfully. Consequently, we write for *both* leaders and consultants.

Certainly, there is a school of thought that suggests that we ought to separate the leader and consultant audiences and write specifically for each. However, we feel strongly that treating leaders and consultants separately and delivering individual messages, tools, and techniques to them has been part of the reason for failure in transformation.

Yes, leaders and consultants have unique roles that require specialized skills, but transformation demands a common understanding and skill set. This does not mean that the two roles (leading and consulting) should merge into one. Leaders must continue to lead, and consultants must continue to consult. Yet to be effective in transformation, leaders must develop people and process skills previously reserved for or shunted to their consulting counterparts, and consultants must become more grounded in core business skills and strategies previously reserved for leaders. We intend this book to assist both along their respective developmental paths to becoming more competent "change leaders."

Some of our discussions will clearly be geared to one or the other audience. At times, we will offer specific insights and techniques for leaders, and at other times, we will present specific consulting approaches and tools. However, in all cases, the "secondary" audience will benefit greatly from the discussion and from fully exploring the information and insights offered.

Given our bias and intent, we use the labels "leader" and "change leader" to refer to both leaders and consultants. When we refer solely to one or the other, we will make that clear.

We write with leaders of all levels in mind, with the key focus on leaders who have responsibility and decision authority for designing, influencing, or implementing their organization's transformational change plans. This obviously includes CEOs and other senior executives but can also include mid-managers, supervisors, and employees who play vital roles on change project teams.

The change consultants who will receive the most value from this book are those responsible for educating, advising, and coaching line leaders to develop and implement large-scale transformational change strategy. Such consultants definitely include *process consultants,* such as organization development (OD) and organization effectiveness (OE) practitioners, change management specialists, process improvement facilitators, and LEAN and Six Sigma consultants. It also includes all *content consultants,* especially those with expertise in information technology, supply chain, creating e-commerce businesses within existing organizations, business process reengineering, knowledge management systems, business strategy, organizational redesign and restructuring, activity based costing, manufacturing technology and systems, and human resources.

We believe that this book will have broad appeal to anyone interested in or impacted by transformation. Consequently, we also write for educators and students of change. Educators can include college and graduate school professors, vice presidents of human resources, management development trainers, college and public school administrators, executive coaches, and public speakers. Students of change can literally be anyone, whether enrolled in school, working in the public or private sectors, or even lay people seeking to further understand one core dynamic of the twenty-first century—transformation!

And last, we write this book for all the targets of change, those people who are directly impacted by the quantity and quality of change that is rolling through all of our lives. For these people, who may not be able to influence directly *how* their organization's transformation is occurring, we offer this material as support, knowing that anyone equipped with a better understanding of the dynamics of transformation will be better able to cope with it and thrive through its implementation.

A LARGER BODY OF WORK

The structure of the book is designed as part of a larger body of work that includes a companion book, *The Change Leader's Roadmap: How to Navigate Your Organization's Transformation,* a Web-based application of The Change Leader's Roadmap methodology (CLR), and a complete set of change tools, published by Being First, Inc., our training and consulting firm (www.beingfirst.com).

Either book can stand alone; you do not need to read the other in order to get value from them. However, the two books were written simultaneously and thus provide a complete overview of conscious change leadership: both concepts and the tools and methods. If you can, we suggest you read this book first, followed by *The Change Leader's Roadmap.*

This book describes the *conceptual overview* of conscious change leadership and what it requires to lead transformation successfully, whereas *The Change Leader's Roadmap* provides a thorough description of the actual Change Process Methodology that puts these concepts into *practice.* In other words, this book provides the theoretical foundation, and *The Change Leader's Roadmap* provides pragmatic guidance and tools. We have written both because of our devotion to blending concept and technique. (One without the other always falls short.) Given this bias, we offer tools and worksheets where appropriate throughout this book as well. And *The Change Leader's Roadmap* connects its pragmatic guidance directly back to the theoretical basis offered here. The Web-based CLR application and the change tools published by Being First are more comprehensive and detailed than what is offered in either book. You can learn more about both at www.changeleadersroadmap.com.

We provide premium content in various places throughout the book. Premium content is additional information that supports the topic being discussed, and is identifi ed by an icon in the margin. You can access the Premium Content at www.pfeiffer.com/go/anderson. A list of all of the premium content is provided at the beginning of the book.

College and graduate school professors can access for use in their courses an Instructor Guide for both this book and The Change Leader's Roadmap at www .wiley.com/college/anderson. Corporate trainers can access the Instructor Guide for use in their executive and management development programs by sending an email request to instructorguides@beingfirst.com.

Our desire in writing these two books and in publishing the change tools is to provide all the support we can for your application of this conscious, multidimensional, process-oriented approach to leading and consulting to organization transformation.

STRUCTURE OF THIS BOOK

Throughout the book, we continually deepen a conversation about what conscious change leadership entails and why we must move beyond change management. We will use our Conscious Change Leader Accountability Model as a reference point throughout the book, referring to it periodically to guide and highlight critical aspects of our discussion.

There are four sections to this book. Section One, A Call for Conscious Change Leaders, contains five chapters. In Chapter One, "Achieving Breakthrough Results from Change," we outline the costs of failed change, the common mistakes that cause it, and the great opportunity for extraordinary results that competent change leaders who attend to three critical focus areas can deliver.

In Chapter Two, The Drivers of Change, we outline what is driving change and how we must respond to those drivers to succeed. We reveal how transformation includes more drivers than other types of change, making it more complex and challenging. We also track the history of change over the past fifty years and demonstrate how that history corresponds with an increase in the drivers we face. This sheds light on what is catalyzing change in today's organizations, specifically, what is catalyzing transformational change.

In Chapter Three, Three Types of Organization Change, we define transformation and contrast it with the two other types of change that leaders face. We reveal why transformation is more complex and the additional areas that change leaders must attend to in order to get the results they seek.

In Chapter Four, Two Leadership Approaches to Transformation, we describe two very different approaches that leaders and consultants bring to transformation and the impact each has on their potential success. In this discussion, we clarify why transformation requires leaders and consultants to become more conscious in their approach. We provide the details of what that means and how it can catalyze breakthrough results from change.

In Chapter Five, Building Organizational Change Capability, we describe why change must become a strategic discipline in organizations to meet the challenges of the twenty-first century. We outline five strategies for building superior change capability in your organization.

In Section Two, People Dynamics, we focus directly on the essential human dynamics of change. Specifically, in Chapter Six, Human Dynamics: From Resistance to Commitment, we address the inner dynamics of people, their core needs, and the causes of resistance to change. We describe emotional transitions and provide guidance on how to assist people through them to generate solid levels of commitment.

In Chapter Seven, The Role and Impact of Mindset, we define mindset and demonstrate how it influences what change leaders perceive in their transformations, the behaviors they model, and the results they are able to produce. We also discuss why self-management and personal transformation are required competencies in both leaders and consultants.

In Chapter Eight, The Role and Impact of Culture, we define culture and explore different types of culture and their impacts on organizational outcomes. We provide an overview of our approach to transforming culture and establish a model for clarifying what needs addressing in culture change efforts.

In Section Three, Process Dynamics, we explore a greatly expanded view of the process dynamics inherent in transformation. In Chapter Nine, "Conscious Process Thinking," we demonstrate that leaders' traditional "project thinking" mentality limits transformation and show how systems thinking is a move in the right direction, albeit one leaders have not taken far enough. We introduce conscious process thinking and demonstrate why it is essential to successful change leadership.

In Chapter Ten, Change Process Models, we outline change process models, contrast them to change frameworks, and describe why change frameworks do not suffice for guiding transformation. We also introduce The Change Leader's Roadmap, our own process model built on three decades of action research. We describe why a successful change process model must be both "fullstream" and a "thinking discipline," and why linear prescriptions for action are not applicable to the realities of transformation.

In Section Four, Answering the Call to Conscious Change Leadership, we conclude our journey. In Chapter 11, Answering the Call, we provide an overview of our discussion and put it all together. We discuss the choice to become a *conscious* change leader and the commitment and accountability that accompany that choice. And we ask you, "Do you choose to answer the call to conscious change leadership?"

In writing this book, we aspire to communicate what is possible in leading transformation consciously. We dream a dream here, a dream that has transformation actually deliver breakthrough-level business results, culture change and superior change capability—all at the same time. We dream of transformation that has positive impacts beyond profitability and shareholder value. We dream of transformation that improves people's lives, deepens their ability to get what they want, and strengthens their relationships, trust, and joy in working together for common goals and aspirations. We dream of transformation that positively contributes to organizations, communities, societies, and nations. We dream of transformation that is so user friendly that it bolsters people's resolve and capacity for even more positive change in themselves and the world. And we dream of the possibility of collectively working together to create a world of greater social justice and environmental sustainability.

Nothing would give us greater satisfaction than to know that this book has added to the possibilities of these dreams. We hope it serves you well.

ENDNOTE

1. Wilber, K. *A Theory of Everything*. Shambala, 2000, p. 70.

A Call for Conscious Change Leaders

Achieving Breakthrough Results from Change

Good is the enemy of great.

—Jim Collins

Imagine your organization being wildly successful at change. We don't mean marginally successful; we mean so successful that your achievements are truly extraordinary, and not just in your current change initiatives, but in the vast majority of them going forward.

We adamantly believe that you, your team, and your organization can become so masterful at change that breakthrough results become consistently achievable. It won't be easy, and it won't be immediate, but it will be worth every ounce of effort. To get to great, we have to get beyond good, beyond managing change to truly leading it to extraordinary outcomes.

Our purpose in writing this book, and its companion, *The Change Leader's Roadmap*, is to highlight how to radically increase the outcomes you get from change. We are not interested in the "normal" way change goes, how to make it a bit more effective, or how to reduce employee resistance so things go a bit smoother. We are after breakthrough results from change—not the average but the extraordinary.

Breakthrough results (Figure 1.1) are outcomes that far exceed what would occur if your organization continued to do change in the same way it always has. Breakthrough results, by definition, are a level of achievement beyond what most people would even conceive as possible. They represent a radical, positive departure

Figure 1.1. Breakthrough Results

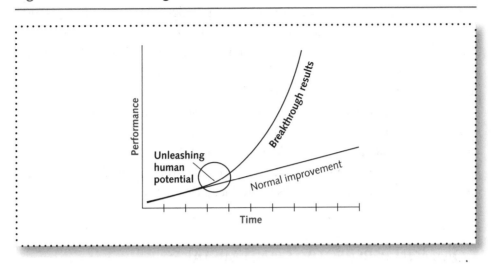

from your normal rate of improvement—a "break through" the usual or predictable to an unheralded potential that has not yet been tapped or actualized.

Breakthrough results come in many forms. You can achieve far greater business results through change: greater profitability, increased market share, faster cycle times, improved customer satisfaction, and enhanced product innovation. You can also produce powerful, positive impacts on people through change: greater empowerment, increased collaboration across functional and hierarchical boundaries, improved morale, and increased engagement and commitment of stakeholders. Breakthroughs can occur in your culture and its ability to catalyze great performance in your people: enhanced commitment to service, more innovation and learning, more openness and authenticity, more alignment, and dedication to enterprise success.

Breakthrough results occur primarily from unleashing the human potential in your organization. You achieve this by designing better change processes that free up people to contribute more of their abilities and passion.

Generally, people do not think in terms of achieving breakthrough results, during change or any other time. They unconsciously accept middle-of-the-pack approaches and outcomes. Of course, if you ask, they will say that they are going for great, not average results. But their decisions, behaviors, and actions reveal something different.

High achievers are few and far between, in any activity. Few athletes become superstars, just as few organizations reach the pinnacle of their industries.

The middle of the bell curve, the "territory of the average," is the norm in just about everything. People expect average results during change, just as they unconsciously pursue average results in other areas of their work and life.

More is possible—far more, for you and your organization right now. But first you have to determine the level of results you are after. Certainly, what you learn in this book will help you reduce resistance and run your change efforts more smoothly. It will help you overcome common problems and assist you to deliver greater return on investment (ROI) on your change efforts. This is all good, but is good, good enough for you? We want you to think really, really big. Let's go for breakthrough. Let's go for great. Let's go for the truly extraordinary. And let's develop the change leadership skills to produce such results.

COMMON PERSPECTIVES AND MISTAKES IN LEADING CHANGE

I cannot say whether things will get better if we change; what I can say is they must change if they are to get better.

—Georg C. Lichtenberg

Change is the nature of life. Nothing ever remains the same. Growth and decay are as fundamental to our existence as our needs for water and air.

While change goes in one of two directions—either toward what we do want or toward what we do not want—most people think of change as bad, as a negative experience we endure as best we can. Leaders often talk of "getting change over with," minimizing its disruption, and overcoming people's resistance to it. Employees speak about how uncomfortable it is, how it is a disturbance, and if it would just go away, then they could get back to their work. Stress tests measure the amount of change in our lives because change produces extra stress for most of us.

But change is not always bad, nor does it always lead to negative outcomes. In fact, change is the vehicle to everything better, the essence of improvement, innovation, growth, expansion, and evolution. But if change is the path to breakthrough and greatness, why does it have such a bad rap? Why do people resist it?

Part of the issue is internal. Sometimes we simply unconsciously assume that the change we face will lead to bad outcomes, to some future we will not like. Many of us live in a myth that things will remain the same, that there is a normalcy that change disrupts and that we want to maintain. Some of us have a difficult time adapting. We do not like the extra effort required to figure out how to thrive in the changed circumstance. Other times we feel victimized by change, that it is happening to us and that we are powerless to influence it. The bottom line is that most of us are just not very change ready or change capable. We want and expect things to remain the same.

Another part of the issue is poor change leadership, which gives change a bad name in the minds of employees. Most leaders design and execute lousy change processes, and when the process of change is bad, the experience of change is bad, which exacerbates stakeholders' negative reactions. They do not like it and resist the change process, even when they can accept, tolerate, or commit to the outcomes it *could* produce. And change fails when stakeholders resist.

A commonly quoted statistic over the past two decades is that 70 percent of all change efforts fail to deliver their intended outcomes. The most recent large study substantiating this finding is IBM's study[1] of 1500 change management executives across fifteen countries. They found that 60 percent of change efforts fail to deliver their objectives. These are alarming numbers. Is the failure rate because people inherently resist change, the intended outcomes and direction are wrong, or because of poor change leadership? Our research is very clear about this. While it is a bit of all three, the real culprit is poor change leadership.

With greater understanding of human dynamics, we can learn to lead change in ways that alter people's negative perspectives. And achieving breakthroughs requires us to shift those perspectives. We—and those we lead—must see change as the harbinger of a more positive future. Change must become our friend, our ally, something in which we are both confident and competent. When seen this way, new possibilities occur, new heights become reachable, greater outcomes feasible. But if we cannot lead change well, it can beat us up rather severely. For this reason, change leadership is a most coveted skill and a strategic advantage.

We have been researching what works and does not work in change for over thirty years. (See premium content: Ten Most Common Mistakes in Leading Transformation; www.pfeiffer.com/go/anderson.) We have been engaged in change projects in virtually every for profit industry; city, state and federal government agencies; the military; and large global nonprofits. Exhibit 1.1 highlights our findings of the common mistakes leaders are making in leading transformation that impair the change process, cause resistance and minimize ROI. One interesting note is that these same mistakes are being made regardless of the type of industry

Exhibit 1.1. Common Mistakes in Leading Transformation

▸ **Relevance and Meaning:** Not overtly linking the change effort to the market and business strategy to create clarity in the minds of stakeholders.

▸ **Change Governance:** Not providing clear change leadership roles, structure, and decision making, and how the change effort will interface with operations.

▸ **Strategic Discipline for Change:** Not providing a strategic discipline for how to lead change across the organization—no enterprise change agenda, no common change methodology, and inadequate infrastructure to execute change successfully.

▸ **Misdiagnosing Scope:** Misdiagnosing the scope of the change either in magnitude, or by initiating only technological or organizational initiatives, and neglecting the cultural, mindset, and behavioral requirements.

▸ **Initiative Alignment and Integration:** Running the change through multiple separate or competing initiatives rather than aligning all initiatives as one unified effort and ensuring the integration of plans, resources, and pace.

▸ **Capacity:** Not creating adequate capacity for the change—setting unrealistic, crisis-producing timelines and then laying the change on top of people's already excessive workloads.

▸ **Culture:** Not adequately addressing the organization's culture as a major force directly influencing the success of change.

▸ **Leadership Modeling:** Leaders not being willing to change their mindsets, behavior, or style to overtly model the changes they are asking of the organization.

▸ **Human Dynamics:** Not adequately or proactively attending to the emotional side of change; not designing actions to minimize negative emotional reactions; not attending to them in constructive ways once they occur.

▸ **Engagement and Communications:** Not adequately engaging and communicating to stakeholders, especially early in the change process; relying too heavily on one-way top-down communication; engaging stakeholders only after design is complete.

or sector. For profits, nonprofits, and governments all make the same mistakes. We are convinced this is because people are people, and how leaders approach change is similar across the board and is based on common worldviews, styles, and methods. How many of these mistakes do you recognize your organization making?

These mistakes are all products of how your organization is designed to handle its changes. Failed change is costly, and these mistakes cost organizations millions of dollars and vital employee commitment. For example, implementing Electronic Health Records (EHR) in a medium-sized hospital system can cost 20–50 million dollars just in hard capital costs. Customer Relationship Management (CRM) and Enterprise Resource Planning (ERP) implementations systems can be even pricier, some topping $100 million. Add in the costs of leaders' and employees' time and the cost of taking their attention away from running operations or serving customers, and the cost of failure grows significantly. Now add in the cost of morale and productivity dropping as people's motivation, time, and attention are diverted to failed efforts. The true cost of failed change is beyond any sensible limit. Organizations simply cannot afford change that does not deliver its ROI, especially in difficult economic times.

What is the cost of failed change in your organization?

If leaders should put their attention on getting really good at anything, it should be leading change. No other leadership skill would bring a higher ROI. Stellar change capability can be applied to every improvement, growth opportunity, innovation, merger or acquisition, technology implementation, restructuring, process improvement, systems change, or cultural transformation the leader ever does—not just this year, but for the rest of their careers.

Imagine the financial and cultural benefit of superior change leadership skill in your organization: change efforts that consistently deliver their ROI on time and on budget; stakeholders who are committed to the outcomes and contribute fully to achieving them; projects that run efficiently with clear roles, decision making, and accountability; and capacity that is well managed to maintain operational success while change occurs. Imagine the value to your organization if you could avoid the cost of failed change and instead consistently deliver maximum ROI from change, year after year. Innovation, growth, and expansion become far greater possibilities, as does winning in the increasingly competitive battles in the marketplace.

Superior change leadership capability is an essential skill in our twenty-first century world. From our perspective, every organization should have building change capability as a key strategic objective, because when achieved, it is a real strategic advantage. Substantial increases in your personal success and your organization's success at leading change are possible. Just how much improvement you can achieve is up to you.

Levels of Success

In our client engagements, we have an upfront conversation that informs the entire relationship and scope of work. In that conversation, we ask a simple question, "How do you define success in this effort?" Our client's answer is important to us because we know that if the change leaders are collectively aware and aligned to a common definition of success, then every aspect of the intervention can be designed to support those outcomes. Plus, this is a key conversation where we can begin to introduce the idea of pursuing real breakthrough.

Figure 1.2 depicts five different criteria for defining successful transformation. We call them Levels of Success: (1) when you have **designed** your new state, (2) when you have **implemented** that new state solution, (3) when you have achieved your desired **business outcomes** from the implementation because engaged employees are using and refining the new state design, (4) when your **culture** has transformed as necessary to sustain and increase these results over time, or (5) when your organization (leaders and employees both) has increased its **change capability** so future changes go even more smoothly and produce even greater results.

These criteria depict five very different levels of success that transformation can produce. The five levels have a "nested" relationship. The higher levels include and require achievement of the lower levels.

The higher the level of success you pursue, the greater the ROI you will achieve from your change effort. But keep in mind, as the level of success you pursue increases, so will the required attention to people and process dynamics. Because of this, success at Levels Four and Five requires far more complex and well thought out change strategies and process plans than do Levels One, Two, and Three.

Figure 1.2. **Levels of Success**

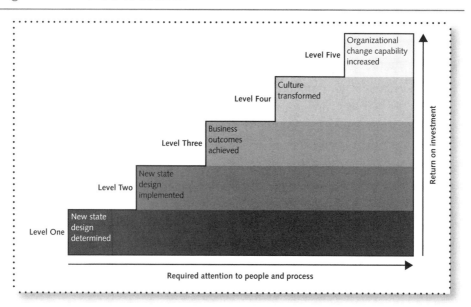

When asked, most leaders say they want Level Four or Five Success. They want business results as well as culture change and increased change capability. But we find that few leaders truly understand what it takes to achieve those outcomes. When we arrive on the scene, their initial change strategies are built to deliver only Levels One and Two. They have the scope of work planned to design the future state and get it implemented, but they have insufficient attention to people and process dynamics to ensure that they will even get the business outcomes they are after, let alone culture change and increased change capability. Remember, 60–70 percent of all change efforts fail to produce their desired business outcomes.

Achieving business outcomes requires committed stakeholders, which usually requires a change process that has high stakeholder engagement *from the start*. Most leaders design their future state in isolation and then attempt to roll it out to already resistant stakeholders who feel victimized by the change because they were not represented adequately in its early phases. The leaders get the future state designed and implemented, but stakeholders do not completely buy into it. So the new state never gets fully embedded in operations and owned by end users. The results produced are mediocre and far from the breakthrough levels that were possible.

You must build your change strategy and process plan to match the level of success you pursue. A significant value we offer clients upfront is the "get real" conversation about what it really takes to achieve Levels Three, Four, and Five, especially at breakthrough levels. We do not want clients aspiring to outcomes their change strategy and process plan will not deliver, just as we do not want them to settle for average results when they can easily expand their scope and achieve breakthrough results. Our firm's promise to clients is that they will achieve Level Five results—extraordinary business results, culture change and increased change capability—*simultaneously* by applying what we call the Being First Approach. This approach is not for every organization. It takes real commitment and resources to achieve Level Five Success.

You might be thinking that achieving already-specified business results is adequate for your change effort and that you are not after breakthrough, culture change, or change capability. You simply need your change efforts to run more smoothly, without major people or process issues, so they deliver their expected "normal" results. Here is the good news: Increasing your success at transformation—a little or a lot—requires similar types of improvements and new change leadership approaches. For breakthrough results, you just need to take these new methods farther. For culture change, you likely need to expand the scope of work to include the entire enterprise, more leadership modeling, systems alignment to the desired culture, and greater attention to internal human dynamics. For capability building, you add training and development, coaching, and learning clinics to your already planned consulting support, all based on advancing your actual change efforts. We do not want to make this sound easy. It is anything but easy, but it is doable and affordable with committed and competent change leadership and a well-designed strategy.

This book and its companion, *The Change Leader's Roadmap,* describe the thinking and orientation behind the Being First Approach. In them, we will show you how to avoid the common mistakes your competitors are making and will reveal what they are not seeing that is causing those mistakes. We will inform you about exactly what you need to pay attention to and how to ensure both efficient and well-designed change processes as well as committed stakeholders. We will pull back the surface level discussions and explore more deeply the root causes of successful transformation. Together, we will lay the foundation for not just Level Three Success, but Levels Four and Five as well. Let's start now with the basic model of what successful change leaders must attend to in order to achieve extraordinary results.

Three Critical Focus Areas of Change Leadership

Successful transformation and breakthrough results require competent attention to three critical focus areas: (1) content, (2) people, and (3) process (see Figure 1.3). *Content* refers to *what* about the organization needs to change, such as strategy, structure, systems, processes, technology, products, services, work practices, and so on. Content refers to the tangible aspects of the organization undergoing change, which are quite observable and reside in the external world we can all see. *People* refers to the human dynamics of change, including behaviors, skills, emotions, mindset, culture, motivation, communications, engagement, relationships, and politics. People includes the less tangible, "soft" dynamics of the inner thoughts and feelings of the human beings who are designing, implementing, supporting, or being impacted by the change. *Process* refers to *how* the content and people changes will be planned for, designed, and implemented. In other words, process denotes the decisions and actions that will produce both the content and people outcomes. In our use of the word *process* here, we are not talking about business processes, but rather, the change process.

Referring to our Conscious Change Leader Accountability Model (Figure I.1 in the Introduction), note that *content* is the systems quadrant, and *people* refers

Figure 1.3. Three Critical Focus Areas of Change Leadership

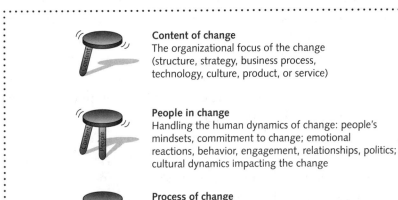

Content of change
The organizational focus of the change
(structure, strategy, business process,
technology, culture, product, or service)

People in change
Handling the human dynamics of change: people's
mindsets, commitment to change; emotional
reactions, behavior, engagement, relationships, politics;
cultural dynamics impacting the change

Process of change
The way in which change is planned, designed,
and implemented; adjusting to how it unfolds;
its A–Z roadmap, governance, integration
strategy, and course corrections

to the mindset, behavior, and culture quadrants. And as stated earlier, change will need to occur in all quadrants and be unified into one overall change process.

Most leaders are very good at designing the content solutions for their change. When they need assistance, they can and often do engage expert content consulting firms to help design their new structure, system, business process, or technology. These subject matter experts, partnered with internal talent, usually get the content right.

Breakthrough results in organizations *can* occur because of great content, but only if the organizational changes are implemented successfully and effectively used by committed employees. Content changes set up the potential for improvement, but they do not guarantee it. The potential benefits of well-designed content only get realized when the change process is efficient, does not impact operations negatively, and is driven by passionate stakeholders who "own" the new content and are committed to applying and improving it over time. Reengineering business processes or implementing a CRM system may look very attractive on paper, but only if implemented well and adopted successfully in the organization. Clearly, you have to get the content right, but that is the easy part. The greatest possibility and challenge for breakthrough in your organization right now reside in the areas of *people* and *process*.

Consistently across industries, government agencies, and large nonprofit organizations, we see leaders under-attend to people and process. They get consumed in the problem of how to fix the mechanical aspects of their organization and forget that a car does not drive itself. You can give the engine a tune-up or even replace it with a more powerful model, but you still need a skilled and committed driver to reap the benefits. Similarly, a more effective structure or streamlined business process or better technology *can* deliver greater outcomes, but only if you have committed and passionate people to unleash that potential.

People and process dynamics are highly interdependent. The design and implementation of your change process impacts people greatly. For example, a restructuring effort will run into problems if its change process looks like this: You convene a small team to design the new structure behind closed doors; you communicate little to stakeholders and then tell them the new design in a one-way memo only after the design is complete; you then make staff compete for limited jobs, without an opportunity to really understand why the new structure was needed in the first place; you provide no teambuilding to include new members and little assistance to out-placed individuals.

Does this sound familiar? Thousands of restructuring efforts have been run this way, often driven by content consulting firms who get the structure right (content) but have little understanding of people and process dynamics. No wonder people resist such changes. When people are subjected to poorly designed change processes, they naturally resist, even if the content changes fit the needs of the organization. Tightly controlled, top-down efforts that are forced on the organization with little attention to capacity, communication, or engagement, consistently cause negative reactions in people, limiting the possible outcomes that sound content solutions could have produced. And that, in short, is why 60–70 percent of all change efforts fail to deliver their intended ROI.

When change is designed well, and promotes positive human dynamics, breakthrough can occur.

All three areas—content, people, and process—must be *integrated* into one unified change strategy that moves your organization from where it is today to where it chooses to be in the future. Organizations that take a piecemeal approach and separate their organizational and technical changes (content) from their human and cultural changes (people) and run many separate unintegrated change processes fail miserably.

But separating *content* change and *people* change is common practice. Generally speaking, the content advocates, such as those promoting reengineering,

Exhibit 1.2. What Level of Success Are You Seeking?

WORKSHEET

The results you are after in your change effort will frame everything else. Use this work-sheet to specify your desired outcomes from your change effort. Also use it to stimulate a conversation with the other change leaders in your project to get alignment. Then use what you learn in this book and *The Change Leader's Roadmap* to assess whether your project is set up to deliver those results. If not, course-correct as needed.

1. What Level of Success are you after?

   _____ Level One: New state design determined

   _____ Level Two: New state design implemented

   _____ Level Three: Business outcomes achieved

   _____ Level Four: Culture transformed

   _____ Level Five: Organizational change capability increased

2. Specify your desired outcomes. Use SMART criteria. Be sure to make them: Specific, Measurable, Achievable, Realistic, Timebound.

   Business Results:

   Cultural Results:

   Change Capability Results:

3. Identify who you need to discuss this with:

   _____ Sponsor of the change:

   _____ Executives:

   _____ Change project leader:

   _____ Change project team:

restructuring, information technology applications, and business strategy, do not understand human and cultural change. In the same way, most people proponents, such as human resource professionals, organization development practitioners, team builders, personal growth trainers, and executive coaches, do not understand pure organizational and technical changes. Consequently, transformation is usually

Exhibit 1.3. What Common Mistakes Is Your Organization Making?

WORKSHEET

Use this worksheet to identify the common mistakes your organization is making. Rate each mistake high, medium, or low. If you can, ask your executive team or change project team to assess your organization's common mistakes. One simple yet powerful way is to list them all on a flip chart, and then give each person five votes that they can place on any one or multiple choices, using all but no more than five votes. Tally the votes, and then discuss the outcome. Ask participants to share the impacts of the top three mistakes on the people and organization, and then generate strategies to improve.

Mistake	Rating (H, M, L)
1. **Relevance and Meaning:** Not overtly linking the change effort to the market and business strategy to create clarity in the minds of stakeholders.	
2. **Change Governance:** Not providing clear change leadership roles, structure, and decision making, or how the change will smoothly interface with operations.	
3. **Strategic Discipline for Change:** Not providing a strategic discipline for how to lead change across the organization—no enterprise change agenda, no common change methodology, and inadequate infrastructure to execute change successfully.	
4. **Misdiagnosing Scope:** Misdiagnosing the scope of the change either in magnitude or by initiating only technological or organizational initiatives, and neglecting the cultural, mindset, and behavioral requirements.	
5. **Initiative Alignment and Integration:** Running the change through multiple separate or competing initiatives *rather* than aligning all initiatives as one unified effort and ensuring the integration of plans, resources, and pace.	
6. **Capacity:** Not creating adequate capacity for the change—setting unrealistic, crisis-producing timelines and then laying the change on top of people's already excessive workloads.	
7. **Culture:** Not adequately addressing the organization's culture as a major force directly influencing the success of change.	
8. **Leadership Modeling:** Leaders not being willing to change their mindsets, behavior, or style to overtly model the changes they are asking of the organization.	
9. **Human Dynamics:** Not adequately or proactively attending to the emotional side of change; not designing actions to minimize negative emotional reactions; not attending to them in constructive ways once they occur.	
10. **Engagement and Communications:** Not adequately engaging and communicating to stakeholders, especially early in the change process; relying too heavily on one-way top-down communication; engaging stakeholders only after design is complete.	

designed and run as separate, nonintegrated initiatives. This just does not work. Focusing only on content, or fantasizing that organization transformation is only about people, or attending to both content and people yet in an insufficient or non-integrated way, are all equally effective paths to failure.

How can you integrate these often conflicting elements? By *consciously* designing your change process to deliver that integration! Process is the integrating factor—the dimension that brings all the activities of change together. Transformation requires an integrated process approach that attends equally to content and people. And when you get that balance right, breakthrough occurs. You realize the full benefits of your content, and your improvement from change goes through the roof.

Implications for Change Leaders

The sphere of influence of change managers is often only in the area of *people*. They do not have influence over the *content* or the change *process*. Change managers are usually not included in decisions about *how* (process) the content solution of a change is designed. The process for designing the new structure, systems, process, or technology gets determined by the content experts. The problem with this common approach is that resistance can get catalyzed by how the solution is designed as much, if not more, than from what the solution is. Stakeholders may or may not like that your new structure integrates two functions or increases the size of managers' departments, but if you design the new structure without their input or participation, they are more likely to resist no matter what the content. Content experts usually do not have the people expertise to design change processes that build commitment. Consequently, they focus on what the new state should be and not on how that solution should be designed or who needs to be involved in the design process to ensure stakeholder commitment.

Change leadership takes a different approach. While change leaders do not design the content, they engage with the content experts to influence the design process to ensure that it builds commitment in stakeholders by gathering their input, keeping them informed, and in many cases sharing decision power. In other words, change leaders have a greater sphere of influence over the design of the change process, including *how* content gets designed and implemented. In fact, the design of the change process is one of their primary responsibilities, which we will discuss thoroughly in Section Three. In short, change leaders attend to and integrate all three areas of content, people, and process to ensure the best results occur in each.

SUMMARY

Change can either be positive or negative, depending on our perceptions of it, the outcomes it is expected to produce, or the way in which it is run and led. Most change fails. Leaders across industry are making common mistakes. The price of failed change can be devastating. Organizations must develop change capability to increase their success rates.

With superior change capability, breakthrough results become possible. To achieve extraordinary results from change and succeed at transformation, change leaders must attend to three critical areas: content, people, and process. Most leaders have greater competency in business content and less in the areas of people and process. This reveals their key areas of needed improvement.

In the next chapter, we will explore the history and evolution of change management toward change leadership, and discover what is driving change. This will begin our exploration into the nature of how change is changing and causing an expansion in what leaders attend to and what they are responsible for. It will also move us along in our exploration of why we must move beyond change management to change leadership, as well as deepen our understanding of what change leadership entails.

ENDNOTE

1. IBM Global Study: Majority of Organizational Change Projects Fail, October 14, 2008.

The Drivers of Change

If you don't like change, you're going to like irrelevance even less.

—General Eric Shinseki, Chief of Staff, U.S. Army

Organization change does not happen out of the blue. It is catalyzed by a number of forces that trigger first awareness and then action. These signals for change usually originate in our organization's environment or marketplace. Such signals can include bold moves by competitors, new technology, or shifts in government regulations. Failures in the performance of our own organization can also signal the need for change. Whatever their source, these events require the organization to respond and change.

Understanding what drives change is critical because the "drivers" establish the overall context within which any organizational change occurs. They create the impetus and motivation for change, and establish a change effort's relevance and meaning. They form its purpose for both those leading the change and those who are targets of the change. Making what is driving change clearly understood by everyone involved is a key to minimizing resistance. When the intelligent people we have hired into our organizations understand the bigger picture of what is driving change, they are always more likely to commit to it.

We must correctly perceive the signals for change to accurately scope the change needed and the outcomes it needs to produce. Signals for change can occur without us noticing. Or we may acknowledge a signal for change and act on it without fully understanding its implications, or worse, without appreciating what change in our organization the signal is requiring. How do we best explore these signals and accurately interpret their meaning? How can we be certain that we are asking our organizations to change in the ways that are really needed?

Because of the increasingly dynamic nature of the marketplace, many leaders have become very attuned to reading the trends in their changing environments and markets and, from this, creating new business strategies (content) to respond appropriately to them. They are making great strides in changing how their organizations are structured and run to fulfill these new business strategies. However, many of us are not yet seeing all of the drivers catalyzing change in our organizations, and therefore, are not carrying the required changes far enough. We often do not see the full scope of "people" change that is required to get the business outcomes we need, let alone real breakthrough results.

Understanding the entire breadth of today's drivers for change can help remedy this problem.

THE DRIVERS OF CHANGE

The Drivers of Change Model (Figure 2.1) clarifies what drives the need for change, especially transformational change. The model describes seven drivers, four that leaders are traditionally familiar with and three that are relatively new areas of serious focus for many.

The model illustrates that the need for change is catalyzed by dynamic shifts in the environment, which establish new requirements for success in our organization's marketplace. These new customer requirements catalyze a need for new business imperatives (strategies), which then require changes in our organization to execute them. These may include changes to structure, systems, business processes, or technology (content). If these organizational changes are significant enough, then the culture of our organization must also change to shift the way our people operate to fully realize the benefits from the organizational changes and effectively execute the new business strategies. Culture change then drives the need for change in both our leaders' and staff's behaviors and ways of thinking. The model shows that what drives change moves from what is *external* and impersonal (environment, marketplace, organizations) to what is *internal* and personal (culture and mindset).

The Drivers of Change Model portrays a sequence to these change triggers, with one trigger calling forth change in the next, and the next, and so on. While a demand-and-response relationship exists between these various catalysts, there is

Figure 2.1.   The Drivers of Change Model

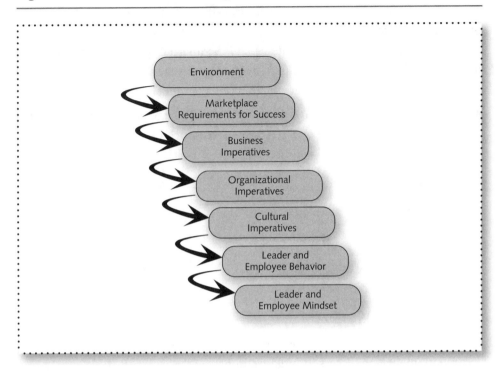

not necessarily a time delay from one driver to the next. Based on the scope of the changes required in an "upstream" driver, it calls forth changes in downstream drivers, but the execution of the overall set of changes that must occur should be designed and implemented together, that is, all quadrants and all levels together as one integrated change process. In other words, this is a theoretical model to help identify what is driving change and the scope of the changes being called for; it is not an implementation model. (We will discuss implementation models in Section Three.) The linear sequence shown in Figure 2.1, however, is helpful to understand the complexity, cause, and scope of change that leaders face today, and to evaluate if you are attending to all your required drivers.

The external drivers—environment, marketplace, business, and organization—are clearly more familiar to leaders, while the more internal and personal ones—culture, behavior, and mindset—are new to most, yet equally essential. Many of the current struggles with transformation are a result of leaders not attending to the people components or not attending to them in ways that make a real impact. Throughout the book, we will provide guidelines for how to address the more person-focused drivers of change while *simultaneously* meeting the needs of the external drivers. Of course, it is equally true that attending only to the internal drivers and neglecting the external ones will also cause transformation to fail. The point is that both the external (content) *and* the internal (people) drivers must be included in the scope of change. Let's define the terms in the Drivers of Change Model and then further investigate the message the model delivers.

▶ **Environment:** The dynamics that occur in the larger context within which organizations and people operate. These forces include the following:

- ○ Social
- ○ Business and economic
- ○ Political
- ○ Governmental
- ○ Technological
- ○ Demographic
- ○ Legal
- ○ Natural environment

Major shifts in any one or more of these areas can catalyze new marketplace requirements for success for organizations.

▶ **Marketplace Requirements for Success:** The aggregate set of customer requirements that determines what it takes for a business to succeed in its marketplace and meet its customers' needs. This includes not only actual product or service needs but also requirements such as speed of delivery, customization capability, level of quality, need for innovation, level of customer service, and so on. Changes in marketplace requirements are the result of changes in environmental forces. For instance, as the environment becomes infused with new technology that makes speed and innovation commonplace, customers demand higher quality customized products and services and expect them faster. To succeed in the marketplace, you must meet these new requirements for success, and your organization must go through the changes required to do so.

▶ **Business Imperatives:** What the company must do *strategically* to be successful, given its new marketplace (customer) requirements. New business imperatives can include the systematic rethinking and change to the company's mission, strategy, goals, business model, products, services, pricing, or branding. Essentially, business imperatives pertain to the organization's strategy for succeeding in its market. As environmental forces catalyze new marketplace requirements for success, leaders must respond with a new business strategy.

▶ **Organizational Imperatives:** What must change in the organization's structure, systems, processes, technology, resources, skill base, or staffing to implement and achieve its strategic business imperatives.

▶ **Cultural Imperatives:** The norms, or collective way of being, working, and relating in the company, that must change to support and drive the organization's new design, operations, and strategy. For instance, a culture of teamwork may be required to support reengineering business processes (organizational imperatives) to drive the strategy (business imperative) of faster cycle time and increased customer responsiveness.

▶ **Leader and Employee Behavior:** How behavior must change in both leaders and staff to express the organization's desired culture. Behavior speaks to more than just overt actions: It describes the style, tone, or character that permeates what people do. It speaks to how people's way of being must change to establish a new culture. Therefore, leader and employee behavior denotes the ways in which leaders and employees must behave differently to re-create the organization's culture to implement and sustain the new organizational design.

▶ **Leader and Employee Mindset:** How leaders' and staff's worldviews, assumptions, beliefs, or mental models must change for people to enact the desired behavior and culture. Mindset is the underlying force that causes people to behave and act as they do. Becoming aware that each of us has a mindset—and that it directly impacts our behavior, decisions, actions, and results—is often the critical first step in building a person's and an organization's ability to transform. Marilyn Ferguson, in *The Aquarian Conspiracy* (1987), states, "If you continue to think as you have always thought, you will continue to get what you have always gotten." Transforming mindset is a prerequisite to sustained change in behavior and culture. A shift of mindset is often required for organizational leaders to even recognize changes in the environmental forces and marketplace requirements, thereby being able to determine the best new strategic business direction, structure, or operation for the organization. A change in employee mindset is often required for them to understand the rationale for the changes being asked of them. And almost always, if the organization is going through significant transformation of its strategy, organizational design, and culture, then leaders and employees must transform their mindsets to operate in it successfully.

A brief review of the current implementation of Electronic Health Records (EHR) in health care is a great illustration of the Drivers of Change Model in action. We use this example because change in the health care industry is so widely discussed and impacts virtually everyone. Plus, many health care executives and politicians see EHR as a technology implementation, but it is much more. The Drivers of Change Model quickly demonstrates this and reveals how EHR requires an expanded change leadership perspective to deliver its intended results.

EXECUTIVE BRIEFING

Here is an overview of electronic medical records provided by our colleague, John Haughom, MD, Corporate Senior Vice President of Clinical Quality and Patient Safety at PeaceHealth, a premier health care system in the Northwest area of the United States. John's briefing will provide you context for our application of the Drivers of Change Model to an EHR implementation.

On February 17, 2009, a law was established in the U.S. as part of the economic stimulus bill to facilitate and encourage the implementation of electronic health records, promote the use of advanced forms of decision support, and foster the growth of health information exchange. David Blumenthal, MD, appointed by President Obama to head the Office of the National Coordinator for Health Information Technology, states, "We have the tools to begin a major transformation in American health care made possible through the creation of a secure, interoperable nationwide health information system . . . it provides the best opportunity for each patient to receive optimal care."

The U.S. Federal Government envisions all Americans having individual electronic health records by 2015. It has allocated $30 billion dollars to jumpstart adoption of health information technology by physicians and hospitals. EHR will enable a comprehensive management of medical information and its secure exchange between health consumers and providers. In order to receive a share of government funding, meaningful use of the technology must be shown by meeting specific criteria. Installing the technology is not enough. Using it to increase patient safety and improve quality is a requirement. The goal of EHR is to improve the quality and reliability of patient care and reduce costs by preventing medical errors, increasing efficiency of both care delivery and administration, expanding access to affordable care, and improving the U.S. population's overall health.

Now let's apply the drivers to see how they reveal the full scope of change required to implement EHR successfully. Imagine that you are at an executive change leadership retreat, assessing the drivers as a member of the executive team of a health care organization with ten hospitals across four states. You have a facilitator operating a computer that is projecting the data you collectively generate on a screen in the front of the room. At the end of the day, here is what your team likely produced.

Environmental Forces

▶ Cost of health care out of control

▶ 40 million U.S. citizens without health insurance

▶ Aging baby boomers stressing the current health care system

▶ Quality of U.S. health care lower than other rich nations but more expensive

▶ Information technology now available

▶ High hospital mortality rates due to human errors made very public

▶ Malpractice lawsuits and insurance premiums out of control

▶ Competitive pressures as hospital systems are merging

▶ Medicare payments going down

▶ U.S. government mandate to implement EHR by 2015 with meaningful use requirements met or be financially penalized

Marketplace Requirements for Success

▶ Higher quality of care

▶ Fewer preventable health care errors

(continued)

> More people with access to quality care

> Lower cost of health care services

> Patients with more access to their own health records

> More disease prevention, less intervention

> Increased ability to easily share a patient's health records across disciplines

BUSINESS IMPERATIVES

> Implement EHR and achieve meaningful use.

> Standardize and consolidate care delivery processes and systems across the entire system.

> Maximize use of evidence-based, best care delivery practices and protocols.

> Cut care delivery and administrative costs.

ORGANIZATIONAL IMPERATIVES

> Upgrade IT infrastructure.

> Implement EHR.

> Standardize care delivery processes across all hospitals and clinics.

> Highly functioning, multi-disciplinary care delivery teams deliver coordinated care across the continuum of care delivery.

CULTURAL IMPERATIVES

> Establish teamwork as preferred method of care delivery.

> Build relationship orientation and cross-boundary support (across disciplines; doctor/nurse; care delivery/lab/pharmacy).

> Create transparency about what is working and not working (over hiding of issues).

> Deliver patient-centered care.

> Support patient's families with information.

> Provide accurate and timely information.

> Communicate openly.

> Establish trust-based collaboration among clinicians.

LEADERS AND EMPLOYEE BEHAVIOR

▶ Doctors and nurses share information across functions and lines of specialties.

▶ Care providers raise issues of safety without fear of recourse.

▶ We input medical information accurately and in a timely manner; today not tomorrow.

▶ Bedside manners are improved to balance increased attention to technology.

▶ Clinicians listen more to each other and patients.

▶ Clinicians make time to share information with patients and their families.

▶ Clinicians allocate time for care delivery team collaboration.

LEADER AND EMPLOYEE MINDSET

▶ Everyone is responsible for the quality of the patient's care and the support of their family.

▶ I see our care delivery as an integrated system in which I am a vital team player.

▶ I value and readily adopt standard evidence-based treatment protocols over my own.

▶ We work as a team and rely on each other.

▶ We are all doing our best, and mistakes will be surfaced and addressed without blame and shame.

▶ I do what is best for patients and their families, even if it is an inconvenience to me.

▶ I choose standardized practices because they enable us to do the best collective good.

▶ I put extra attention on record keeping because it enables for greater collective results.

▶ I keep my other team members needs in mind at all times.

▶ My highest goal is quality of care benchmarks, not pay or stature.

▶ Listening enables me to deliver better care.

(*continued*)

Notice how the seven drivers reveal the full scope of change required to implement EHR successfully. Imagine if your organization neglected the culture, behavior, and mindset change required. You would get the technology implemented (Level Two Success), but you would not achieve the ultimate desired results you are after of improved patient outcomes and reduced costs. To get those outcomes, you *must* transform culture, behavior, and mindset, as well as organizational systems, processes, and technology (all quadrants, all levels). Doctors, nurses, lab technicians, pharmacists, and administrators must all operate differently. They must perceive care delivery as an integrated system in which they are vital team players and technology is an enabler of improved patient outcomes and lower costs. Their way of being, working, and relating must shift to achieve the potential the technology of EHR provides. This is true of most of today's information technology implementations across industries.

When the scope of change in the environment and marketplace is minimal, content (external) change usually suffices. When change is required only to business and organizational imperatives (content) and not to culture, behavior, or mindset (people), the type of change is developmental or transitional. (The different types of change will be described in detail in the next chapter.) However, when the magnitude of environmental or marketplace change is large, then it triggers the need for *radical* content change, which drives the need for change in culture and people to execute it successfully. This type of change, which then includes all the drivers, is transformational. By definition, transformational change requires that leaders attend to content (external, impersonal) as well as people (internal, personal).

USING THE DRIVERS OF CHANGE MODEL

The Drivers of Change Model is useful on many fronts: (1) helps us understand the scope of change required and expands our view beyond simply the external dimensions; (2) helps define the type of change our organization must undergo; (3) defines the case, or reason, for the changes required; and (4) provides a framework for communicating the desired outcomes, scope, and case for change to our stakeholders.

Building a business case for change has become a fairly common practice over the past fifteen years. The business case establishes the marketplace rationale for change and specifies what ROI the change is meant to deliver.

Most business cases attend to environmental and marketplace drivers, business and organizational imperatives. This is adequate for changes that are purely external. However, if your change is transformational, your case for change must also address the internal drivers of how and why culture, behavior, and mindset must also change.

The Drivers of Change Model is an extremely useful framework for building your case for change for transformation because it helps leaders and staff see and understand the full scope of what is required and why. It demonstrates why your desired outcomes include both business results and cultural outcomes. It provides the logic of why you need to attend to culture, behavior, and mindset. This broader understanding can mobilize your entire organization on a common path of transformation because it elegantly outlines the relevance of the change and makes it meaningful for those who must make it happen.

Use Exhibit 2.1 to assess the drivers at play in your organization and the scope of change required for you to succeed. You can fill it out yourself to develop your own thinking, use it to stimulate dialogue among your peers or executives to get them aligned, or use it to facilitate a very large number of people to build consensus about your drivers.

We have had a number of opportunities where we facilitated leaders to identify what they believe are the drivers of change in their own small group session, and then convened a large number of staff (100–300) to input to the assessment as well. Most often, the two groups come up with the same data. Leaders are always surprised and pleasantly relieved by this. When staff identifies the drivers themselves, they do not need to then be "sold" on why change is needed. They become instantly committed to the change because they have logically thought through what is causing it, why it is necessary, and its required scope. This is far more effective than writing a memo or report and letting them read it. Such top-down, one-way communications often trigger resistance.

You can use many of the large group meeting technologies available today to support your planning of such meetings.[1] The key is using the Drivers of Change Model to organize the conversation in these meetings and the conclusions it generates.

Exhibit 2.1. What Is Driving Your Organization's Change?

WORKSHEET

▶ **Environmental Forces:** What environmental forces exist that are driving change in your organization?

▶ **Marketplace Requirements for Success:** What new standards or requirements for success do the marketplace and your customers demand?

▶ **Business Imperatives:** What new business strategies must you deploy to meet those marketplace and customer requirements?

▶ **Organizational Imperatives:** How must you change your structure, systems, processes, roles, or technology to successfully implement the new business strategies?

▶ **Cultural Imperatives:** How must you change your culture to get the most out of these new organizational elements?

▶ **Leader and Employee Behavior:** How must your leaders and staff shift their behavior to make these cultural changes?

   ▶ Leaders:

   ▶ Employees:

▶ **Leader and Employee Mindset:** How must your leaders and staff shift their mindsets to make these behavioral changes?

   ▶ Leaders:

   ▶ Employees:

THE EVOLUTION OF CHANGE AND THE REQUIRED EXPANSION OF LEADERSHIP AWARENESS AND ATTENTION

Over the past forty years, the nature of organization change has evolved tremendously, expanding the areas of organizational life to which we must attend. The Drivers of Change Model both predicts and describes the direction of this evolution and the subsequent increase in change leadership awareness and methods required. Understanding this history and its direction provides perspective on why we must evolve our methods beyond change management to keep pace with the current type of change we face.

The History of Organization Change

Before the 1970s, leaders as a whole paid relatively little attention to their external environment, including their customers, competitors, or the marketplace in general. If they had market share, that was all that mattered. Then, during the 1970s, technology, innovation, and deregulation (environmental forces) began to shake up many industries, including automobile, steel, manufacturing, communications, banking, and retail. These environmental forces began to alter the marketplace requirements for success in these industries. As leaders struggled to differentiate their organizations' strategic advantages and product and service offerings, strategy development (business imperatives) became the leadership rave. Led by a few large consulting firms, many of the Fortune 500 sought to better comprehend their business imperatives and subsequently evolved their business strategies. As a result, an increase in new business strategies, products, and services occurred during this time.

In the late 1970s, the scope of change increased, causing leaders' focus to turn to the organization and how to improve it (organizational imperatives). The new business strategies required changes in the organization to be implemented successfully. Productivity improvement, restructuring, downsizing, diversification, work redesign, and quality swept the country. This focus on organizational improvement intensified in the mid-1980s with the quality movement, then again in the early 1990s with the reengineering craze, and continues today with attention to information technology, Enterprise Resource Planning (ERP), Customer Relationship Management (CRM), LEAN, fast cycle time, the search for how to master global connectivity via the Web, and other content changes.

Up to the mid 1990s, most of these change efforts focused on external drivers. These content changes were, for the most part, *relatively* comfortable for most leaders. Why? Because most of today's leaders come from engineering, financial, military, or legal backgrounds. For them, altering the strategy, structure, systems, processes, and technology of the great organizational "machine" is familiar territory. It is tangible, observable, and measurable. And, most importantly, it carries the illusion of control.

Truth be told, many of these "content" changes *could* be tightly managed. Leaders could command and control many of them to their desired outcomes. This was possible for three reasons. First, most of the changes occurred within silos of influence. Cross-boundary collaboration was not required. Consequently, sharing power and decision making were not critical. Leaders could push their own agendas in the functional or geographic areas where they had the power to do so. Second, leaders could often design and implement changes as separate initiatives, requiring little integration and no special attention to the change process. They could manage change implementation like they managed other projects in their organizations. And third, these changes usually did not require any significant or profound personal change on the part of the leaders or the people impacted by the change. A bit more communication and training in the new systems were usually enough to handle the "people" aspects of these "content" changes. Including extra communication or training in their project plans was easy to manage.

The "change is manageable" bubble began to burst in the mid-1980s, and by the 1990s it became glaringly obvious that truly managing change was becoming less and less possible. The technological revolution, primarily fueled by information and communication technology, had increased the speed and scope of change so much that the process of change became significantly more complex. Isolated and distinct change initiatives no longer sufficed as organizational change became more enterprise-wide in scope. Leading change now demanded the integration of numerous cross-functional initiatives, and leaders' traditional project management techniques did not provide adequately for complex process integration or the increasingly nonlinear change processes that were occurring. New, more evolved approaches were required to handle the more complex change processes.

Also, the tangible domain of changing organizational strategy, structure, systems, processes, skills, and technology suddenly required a significant focus on the less tangible domain of culture and people (cultural imperatives). This new requirement for attention to people was captured in an article in *The Wall Street Journal* on November 26, 1996. It stated, "Gurus of the $4.7 billion reengineering industry like [Michael] Hammer forgot about people. 'I wasn't smart enough about that,' Hammer commented. 'I was reflecting my engineering background and was insufficiently appreciative of the human dimension. I've learned that's critical.'" Suddenly, change was significantly less manageable because of the volatile and dynamic nature of the "people component" and required more attention to people and process than leaders were equipped to give.

The change management field had begun in the early 1980s through the work of thought leaders such as Linda Ackerman and Daryl Conner. For the most part, change management practitioners were expected to provide solutions to two major problems—how to plan better for the complexities of implementation and how to overcome employee resistance. Key change management methods included communications and training, as well as tools for implementation planning, all of which were meant to reduce the stress and resistance in people and make change run more smoothly.

These methods were very helpful, but they were used sporadically until the mid-1990s when change management began to be seen as absolutely necessary. Overnight, the major "content" change consulting firms began change management practices. We remember these days well because many of them tried (unsuccessfully) to buy our consulting firm as they were all looking for acquisitions to immediately put them at the cutting edge of change management.

The early mass-marketed change management approaches that ensued only scratched the surface of the attention to people and process needed. The approaches offered were mostly insufficient, as the content consulting firms did not really understand the internal dynamics of people and culture, nor how to design change processes that integrated basic human needs. Most of these early approaches made the mistake of applying change "management" techniques to people and process dynamics that were inherently unmanageable, but we'll provide more on that later.

A major chasm occurred in the late 1990s that the emerging field of conscious change leadership is attempting to bridge. By the time change management went "mainstream," the complexities of change were requiring more robust support. In other words, the nature and type of change evolved so radically in the 1990s that by the time change management went mainstream, more robust approaches were required.

Starting in the late 1980s and early 1990s, the marketplace forces were requiring such significant content change that an organization's people and culture also needed to change to implement and sustain the content changes successfully. Culture change was no longer a "nice to do" aspect; it was now beginning to be recognized as a "must do," as noted in Michael Hammer's comment.

When change in the business and organizational imperatives are relatively small, leaders can ignore culture because the existing culture simply absorbs the incremental changes. But when the change to the strategy, structure, systems, processes, or technology is significant, as they were becoming in the 1990s, a new way of being, working, and relating is required to operate the new organization. Leaders are required to change cultural norms in order for these "radical" content changes to take hold. With this requirement of attending to culture, organizational change officially entered the realm of transformation, where change management methods are insufficient.

Not surprisingly, in the early 1980s the Organization Transformation (OT) movement was born through the efforts of a small number of "leading edge" consultants. OT focused heavily on cultural and personal change because these consultants were seeing that the nature of some of the more radical content changes they were dealing with required this attention. Some factions of the organization development (OD) profession embraced and explored this new field enthusiastically. Operational line leaders, however, did not take this movement seriously as they were just getting started with change management. A major source of the failure of many of the business process reengineering efforts and IT implementations of the time was a lack of leader and consultant skill in the internal domains of people and the complexities of the change process. Change management simply did not provide the needed support. Let's continue to explore the historical chronology, using the remaining Drivers of Change, to discover what more is needed beyond change management.

To change culture, or the collective norms of how people behave, individuals must change their behavior (leader and employee behavior). If the individual behavior changes that are required are minimal and simply entail skill improvement or minor adjustment to work practices, then basic skill training or slight behavior modification is all that is required. Deep personal reflection and self-development is not required. However, when behavior and style change are significant, as in most of today's transformations, then people's mindsets must also change (leader and employee mindsets). If people do not alter the worldview or beliefs that drive their current behavior, then they will not sustain major behavioral change.

Let us underscore that change in behavior and mindset is required by *both* leaders and employees. Ideally, leaders and employees must change their behavior and mindset *simultaneously* because key aspects of culture are largely the product of interactive behavior patterns between them and the underlying mindsets that drive those behaviors. For culture to change, these patterns must break, which requires change on both sides of the equation. For example, the cultural shift from entitlement to empowerment requires leaders to step out of their command-and-control style while employees step into greater self-reliance and responsibility. A shift on only one side of the equation creates conflict; a shift on both sides creates sustainable change that can lead to greater collective results.

By the mid 1990s, the scope and required focus of organization change had fully evolved and entered the unpredictable and uncertain world of the inner dimensions of human beings. It is no wonder that empowerment, self-management,

We worked with a large bank in California and ran smack into this leadership issue. This was during the time that the "change is manageable" bubble was just beginning to burst, and most leaders were unaware of the deep personal change being required both for themselves and for employees.

The bank was installing a new computer system throughout its many branches that would revolutionize tellers' jobs by putting substantial customer information at their fingertips. Equipped with this information, tellers would then be expected by management to introduce and sell appropriate insurance and investment products to their customers while the customers were standing at the tellers' windows making deposits or withdrawals. The technology installation was part of a comprehensive strategy to expand the bank's service offerings to retain customers and build market share, which the bank was quickly losing to large investment brokerages.

Senior management asked us to audit their existing change strategy and to predict how we thought it would proceed. After interviews with senior executives, we realized that the leaders clearly understood that their marketplace had new requirements for success and that they had developed a solid business strategy based on new business imperatives. They had effectively translated that strategy into new organizational imperatives, primarily the installation of new computer technology. However, that was as far as they had gone. They conceived the change as a simple technology installation. So they focused on the content and under-attended predictable human dynamics they could not see.

The senior leaders had no idea that their new marketplace requirements and business and organizational imperatives were so significant that they were driving the need for a fundamental transformation of their culture, as well as their leaders' and employees' skills, behaviors, and mindsets. Their change strategy neglected any attention to culture, behavior, and mindset beyond training the tellers in how to use the new computer system. To the leaders, that was enough. They planned to shut all of their numerous branches down on a Friday, work through the weekend installing the system and training employees, and reopen the bank on Monday morning without skipping a beat. They were in for a painful surprise.

(continued)

We issued a loud warning that their plan was going to backfire and cause tremendous upheaval because their strategy neglected any attention to changing their culture or their leaders' and employees' behavior and mindset, all of which was essential to realize the full benefits of the new technology. We suggested that, in the best-case scenario, their change effort would alienate employees and customers; in the worst case, it would cause both to leave in droves.

Here were the key issues as we saw them. Notice how the Drivers of Change "predict" these issues.

1. Each branch was a fiefdom, run top-down by largely autocratic branch managers who made all significant customer decisions. The new technology significantly altered the tellers' role. We suggested that this would create a power struggle between the branch managers and the tellers. The fact that the tellers would now have the information and power to make significant customer decisions would undermine the branch managers' historic authority, and the branch managers would be likely to withhold their support, which the tellers would so desperately need, especially during the initial stages of implementation. We suggested a fundamental transformation of culture from command and control to collaboration, coaching, and support was needed to support the new desired behaviors in both branch managers and tellers.

2. Many of the tellers had worked for the bank for ten or more years and were hired because of their style and skill at doing accurate and predictable work, that is, helping customers to make deposits and withdrawals. The tellers had no sales training. Most, if not all, were not salespeople by nature or behavioral style, and their communication skills were not highly sophisticated. They took jobs at the bank because they were attracted to the safe and predictable work of making customer transactions.

    We suggested that employees would learn the new system (they were all "good soldiers") but not be willing to use it because to do so would be too threatening to them. Not possessing the mindset, behavior, or skills of a salesperson, they would simply not engage their customers in the new sales-oriented conversation that their leaders expected. And, if they did attempt such conversations, their lack of skill might backfire, creating resentment or embarrassment for customers and reducing customer satisfaction.

3. Management planned to change the tellers' compensation system to drive the required new behavior. A significant portion of their compensation was to be based on hitting sales targets. We suggested that installing this new compensation system at startup, before the tellers had time to develop new behaviors and skills, would alienate the tellers and that their emotional resentment would further amplify the weakness in their sales skills. We also suggested that the new compensation system would increase the conflict between the tellers and their angry branch managers because the branch managers would pressure or punish the tellers for not hitting their "sales" numbers.

The unfortunate conclusion to this story was that the leaders rejected our concerns and proceeded with their original plan. Given their mindset and lack of desire to address any potential problems, they simply did not want to hear what we had to say about the need to attend to culture, behavior, and mindset as a part of their overall change strategy. The outcome of their change was as we predicted. Over the next eighteen months, the bank lost both market share and many of its top employees, including both tellers and branch managers.

---

emotional intelligence, personal mastery, and learning have become topics of interest over the past twenty years. In the twenty-first century, however, these must become more than simply points of interest, experiments, or topics of casual conversation; leaders and consultants must seriously engage in them to produce tangible transformation. *In today's business environment, significant transformation cannot happen without the simultaneous transformation of a critical mass of leaders' and employees' mindsets and behavior and the organization's culture.*

This concept of attending overtly to mindset, behavior, and culture as part of transformation is not yet widely embraced, nor addressed by change management. However, change leadership attends to required personal and cultural change as integral aspects of an organization's transformation. Change leadership includes change management approaches—communication, training, and implementation planning—and goes beyond to embrace more completely the human dynamics (mindset, behavior, and culture) and the complex process dynamics that we will discuss in Section Three. Change leadership transcends, yet includes change management.

SUMMARY

The scope of required change in our organizations has increased dramatically over the past forty years, moving from the external domains to the internal, from the organization and technical to the human and cultural, from content to the deeper dimensions of people. Prior to the 1990s, leaders could limit the scope of their change efforts to business strategy and the redesign of their organizations and be successful. But that's no longer the case—not today and not tomorrow.

As the demands of the environment and marketplace have increased, content changes have become more complex and so have the change processes to implement them. Successful implementation now requires attention to all seven drivers of change, including culture, behavior, and mindset. Reliance on change management for adequate attention to people and project management to design complex change processes is not sufficient in today's world of transformation.

The next evolution of change is already here, requiring us to move beyond change management into the new world of change leadership, which attends to all seven drivers of change. Change management primarily focuses on employee behavior, but change leadership, in its pursuit of breakthrough business results (content), addresses the inner dynamics of organizational culture and individual mindset as well. Change leaders also possess advanced change process design skills to fully integrate this deeper attention to human dynamics into their content implementations. Change leaders develop these advanced people and process skills in the context of a more complete understanding of transformation and its unique dynamics and requirements, which we will take up in the next chapter as we outline the three types of change.

ENDNOTE

1. Holman, P., Devane, T., and Cady, S. *The Change Handbook: The Definitive Resource on Today's Best Methods for Engaging Whole Systems* (2nd Edition). San Francisco, CA: Berrett-Koehler Publishers, Inc., 2007.

Three Types of
Organizational Change

I don't want to use the word reorganization. Reorganization to me is shuffling boxes, moving boxes around. Transformation means that you're really fundamentally changing the way the organization thinks, the way it responds, the way it leads. It's a lot more than just playing with boxes.

—Lou Gerstner

The Inuit people are widely believed to have twenty different words to describe "snow," all referring to the same cold, white stuff. When you are as familiar with something as the Inuit people are with the different types of snow, you recognize subtle differences and distinctions that the rest of us do not see. These distinctions enable the Inuit people to deal appropriately with the challenges of massive amounts of snow. They have clothes and snowshoes designed for wet snow and clothes and snowshoes designed for dry snow. So it is with change; leaders must know the type of change they face before they can know how to effectively lead it.

Before the 1980s, the term "change" described everything that needed to be different in organizations. However, as change proliferated, and we had more experience with it in our consulting, we began to notice differences in the changes our clients faced. Linda Ackerman Anderson (1986), in an article in the *Organization Development Practitioner*, defined the three most prevalent types of change occurring in organizations as *developmental change*, *transitional change*, and *transformational change*. As we described in the previous chapter, it had become painfully apparent that consultants and executives alike needed to understand and differentiate the types of change they were attempting to manage in their organizations. One size did not fit all. As with snow, knowing the type of change you are dealing with is paramount to building an effective strategy to deal with it, as each type of change requires a different approach.

In this chapter, we describe in detail the three types of change occurring in organizations, discussing similarities and differences, especially as they relate to the critical focus areas of content, people, and process. Additionally, we include some of the implications that each type of change has for change leadership and for change strategy. Figure 3.1 graphically shows the three types of change. Table 3.1 compares them across a range of relevant factors.

DEVELOPMENTAL CHANGE

Developmental change represents the *improvement* of an existing skill, method, performance standard, or condition that for some reason does not measure up to current or future needs. Metaphorically, developmental changes are improvements "within the box" of what is already known or practiced. Such improvements are often logical adjustments to current operations. They are motivated by the goal to do "better than" or do "more of" what is currently done. The key focus is to strengthen or correct what already exists in the organization, thus ensuring improved performance, continuity, and greater satisfaction. The process of development keeps people motivated, growing, and stretching through the challenge of attaining new performance levels.

Developmental change is the simplest of the three types of change. The new state *content* is a prescribed enhancement of the old state, rather than a radical or experimental solution requiring profound change. The impact on *people* is relatively mild, usually calling for developing new knowledge or skills. From a *process* perspective, traditional project management approaches suffice, as the significant work flow variables can be known in advance and managed against time and budget, and there is little need for a more strategic guidance system to the change process.

Developmental change applies to individuals, groups, or the whole organization and is the primary type of change inherent in all of the following improvement processes:

▶ Training (both technical and personal), such as communications, interpersonal relations, and supervisory skills

Figure 3.1. Three Types of Organization Change

Developmental Change

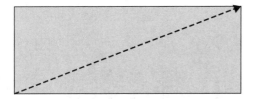

Improvement of what is; new state is a prescribed enhancement of the old state.

Transitional Change

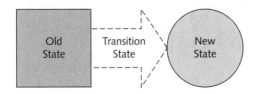

Design and implementation of a desired new state that solves an old state problem; requires management of the transition process to dismantle the old state while putting in place the new state; managed timetable.

Transformational Change

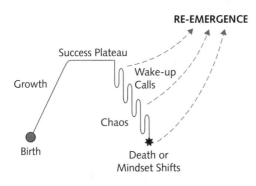

Market requirements force fundamental changes in strategy, operations, and worldview: (1) New state is unknown—it emerges from visioning, trial and error discovery, and learnings. (2) New state requires fundamental shift in mindset, organizing principles, behavior, and/or culture, as well as organizational changes, all designed to support new business directions. Critical mass of organization must operate from new mindset and behavior for transformation to succeed and new business model or direction to be sustained.

Table 3.1. Matrix of the Three Types of Organization Change

Type	Degree of Pain Felt	Primary Motivation	Degree of Threat to Survival	Gap Between Environmental Needs & Operations	Clarity of Outcome	Impact on Mindset	Focus of Change	Orientation	Level of Personal Development Required	How Change Occurs
Developmental Change	1	Improvement	1	1	4 It is prescribed against a standard	1 Little if any	Improvement of skills, knowledge, practice, and performance	To do better in a certain area: project-oriented	1	Through training, skill development, communications, process improvement
Transitional Change	2	Fix a problem	2	2	4 It is designed against a criteria	1 Little if any	Redesign of strategy, structures, systems, processes, technology or work practices (not culture)	Project-oriented; largely focused on structure, technology, and work practices	2	Controlled process, support structures, timeline
Transformational Change	3–4	Survival: change or die; or Thrival: breakthrough needed to pursue new opportunities	1–4	3–4	1 It is not initially known; it emerges or is created through trial and error and continuous course correction	2–4 Forced to shift: old mindset and/or business paradigm must change	Overhaul of strategy, structure, systems processes, technology, work, culture, behavior, and mindset	Process-oriented requires shift in mindset, behavior, and culture	3–4	Conscious process design and facilitation; high involvement; emergent process

Rating Scale: 1 is low, 4 is high

- Some applications of process or quality improvement
- Some interventions for increasing cycle time
- Team building
- Problem solving
- Improving communication
- Conflict resolution
- Increasing sales or production
- Meeting management
- Role negotiation
- Survey feedback efforts
- Job enrichment
- Expanding existing market outreach

Developmental change is usually a response to relatively small shifts in the environment or marketplace requirements for success—or simply the result of a continuous need to improve current operations, as in continual process improvement. The degree of pain triggering developmental change is usually low, at least in comparison to the other types of change. This does not mean that developmental change is not important or challenging; it is. However, the risks associated with developmental change, and the number of unpredictable and volatile variables tied to it, are considerably fewer than with the other two types of change.

In developmental change, the gap between what the environment or marketplace calls for and what currently exists is comparatively low. Consequently, the degree of threat to the organization is also low. This makes creating and communicating a clear case for developmental change a far simpler matter than with the other two types of change.

Leaders can best initiate developmental change by sharing information about why the performance bar has to be raised and by setting stretch goals. When leaders challenge people to excel and provide them the resources and support to do so, this usually produces the necessary motivation for successful developmental change.

There are two primary assumptions in developmental change. First, people are capable of improving, and second, they will improve if provided the appropriate reasons, resources, motivation, and training.

The most commonly used developmental change strategy is training—in new skills, better communication, or new techniques or processes for accomplishing the higher goals. Leaders can use an assessment and problem-solving approach to identify, remove, or resolve what has blocked better performance. They can also use the existing goal-setting and reward systems to improve motivation and behavior. Making minor process improvements, where existing processes are simply made more efficient, is also a common developmental change strategy. Do not be fooled—radical process improvement can be very transformational, as we will discover shortly.

TRANSITIONAL CHANGE

As shown in Figure 3.1, transitional change is more complex. It is the required response to more significant shifts in environmental forces or marketplace requirements for success. Rather than simply improve *what is*, transitional change *replaces what is with something entirely different*.

Transitional change begins when leaders recognize that a problem exists or that an opportunity is not being pursued—and that something in the existing operation needs to change or be created to better serve current and/or future demands. After executives, change leaders, or employee teams have assessed the needs and opportunities at hand, they design a more desirable future state to satisfy their distinct requirements. As can be seen from Figure 3.1, to achieve this new state, the organization must dismantle and emotionally let go of the old way of operating and move through a transition while the new state is being put into place.

EXAMPLES OF TRANSITIONAL CHANGE

▶ Reorganizations
▶ Simple mergers or consolidations
▶ Divestitures
▶ Installation and integration of computers or new technology that do not require major changes in culture, behavior or mindset
▶ Creation of new products, services, systems, processes, policies, or procedures that replace old ones

Beckhard and Harris (1987) first named and defined transitional change in their Three States of Change Model, which differentiated "old state," "new state," and "transition state." They articulated that transitional change requires the dismantling of the old state *content* and the creation of a clearly designed new state, usually achieved over a set period of time, called the transition state. The transition state is unique and distinct from how the old state used to function or how the new state will function once in place. Beckhard and Harris were the first to suggest that changes of this nature could be and needed to be *managed*. These two pioneers in the field of change management provided some critical strategies that continue to be useful today for transitional change.

The *process* of transitional change can be managed against a tight budget and timeline. Transitional changes usually have a specific start date and end date, as well as a known concrete outcome designed according to a set of preconceived design requirements. Traditional approaches to project management are usually quite effective for overseeing transitional change, especially when the people impacted by the change are fully aware of what is going on and are committed to making it happen. Because the future state (content) can be defined in detail before implementation, the change process can be well articulated and usually does not trigger significant people issues. Project-management approaches work best when there are few people issues because significant human variables usually make a project less "manageable." Transitional change processes are fairly predictable and "linear," with minimal need for course corrections due to either emergent process dynamics or significant human dynamics. So, like in developmental change, there is little need for a more strategic guidance system to navigate the change process.

People dynamics in transitional change efforts are more complex than in developmental change. Along with needing to gain new knowledge and develop new skills, people often must change or develop new behaviors as well. This, along with the fact that they must operate in a new state, which is, by definition, less familiar than an improvement of the old state, makes transitional changes more of a challenge for people. However, there is not a need for deep personal change (mindset) in either developmental or transitional change.

It must be noted that William Bridges' well known and very effective work on transitions (1980, 1991, 2004) is different from the transitional change to which we refer. Bridges' work focuses on understanding how people go through change psychologically and emotionally and on how to help people get through their personal process in effective and caring ways (in other words, make the emotional "transition"). Bridges' work is essential to appreciate and apply in all types of change in organizations, including transitional change from an old state to a new state. All organizational change, regardless of the type, impacts people. The variable that affects what change strategies are necessary is the degree and depth of the impact. We will discuss this in detail in Chapter Six.

Building a transitional change strategy and well-planned change process assists with the human requirements because people can then see very overtly the scope of activity that will be occurring. If leaders experience difficult human and cultural impacts in transitional change, it is usually the result of one of the following human dynamics:

▶ People possessing inadequate skills for functioning in the new state

▶ People being "left in the dark" and feeling uncertain about what is coming next

▶ People's lack of understanding of the case for change or the benefits of the new state

▶ People's reluctance to stop doing what they have always done in the past

▶ Homeostasis or inertia—people's natural resistance to learning new skills or behaviors

▶ People's emotional pain or grief at the loss of the past

▶ Poor planning and implementation of the change, which creates confusion and resentment

▶ Unclear expectations about what will be required to succeed in the new state

▶ Fear about not being successful or capable in the new state

▶ Inadequate support to succeed in the new state

Good change management practices can help alleviate many of these people issues. In fact, change management is a very effective support for transitional change. The most significant problems occur when executives view their organization's transitional changes as purely technical or structural and do not provide adequate change management support, especially when people are stressed with heavy workloads. Neglecting stakeholder impacts, or inadequately planning or communicating the change process, produces greater human trauma than this type of change necessarily dictates.

Strategies for Managing Transitional Change

With the right transitional change strategies, the critical impacts of the change—organizational and human—can be dealt with effectively. Such strategies include a well-communicated case for change, a clear change plan, high employee involvement in designing and implementing that plan, local control of implementation, effective workload and capacity management, a sound training plan, and adequate support and integration time to ensure that employees succeed in the new state.

A critical aspect of both a transitional and transformational change strategy is to clarify the key differences between the old state and the desired state and determine the implications of those gaps. We call this process *impact analysis*. An impact analysis assesses both organizational and human impacts and provides essential information for building a good change plan and reducing human trauma. The impact analysis reveals: (1) what aspects of the old state serve the new state and can be carried forward; (2) what aspects will need to be dismantled or dropped; and (3) what will need to be created from scratch to fill the needs of the new state. Conducting an impact analysis during the early stages of the transition state will indicate how much change is actually required and determine how long the transition will likely take. From this knowledge, leaders can develop a logical plan of action and appropriate timetable to guide the implementation of the new state, handling both the content and people impacts.

Complex transitional changes are best run through two parallel and separate governance structures—one that keeps the operation running effectively and one that oversees the change, including the design of the new state, the impact analysis, and the implementation planning. Roles in an effective change governance structure are an executive-level change leadership team, a sponsor and change process leader (who is responsible for the overall change strategy), and a change project team to execute the change plan. Using such a parallel change structure enables the change to occur with minimal disruption to operations, clear decision making, and the best use of resources. For more about change governance structures, refer to the companion book, *The Change Leaders Roadmap*, and the online methodology at www.changeleadersroadmap.com.

TRANSFORMATIONAL CHANGE

Transformational change (shown earlier in Figure 3.1 and outlined in Table 3.1) is the least understood and most complex type of change facing organizations today. When led well, it can lead to extraordinary breakthrough results. When led poorly, it can lead to breakdown throughout the organization. Transformation is one of the most challenging yet potentially rewarding undertakings for leaders.

Simply said, *Transformation is a radical shift of strategy, structure, systems, processes, or technology, so significant that it requires a shift of culture, behavior, and mindset to implement successfully and sustain over time.* The new state that results from the transformation, from a *content* perspective, is largely uncertain at the beginning of the change process. Both this outcome of change and the process to get there are often emergent; you discover things along the way that you could never have known without first initiating the journey. Clarity emerges as a product of the change effort itself. This makes the *change process* very nonlinear, with numerous needs for course corrections and adjustments. While including a radical change in content, transformation also requires a shift in human awareness, mindset, and culture (*people*) that significantly alters the way the organization and its people see the marketplace, their customers, their work, and themselves. Transformation significantly impacts all areas of content, people, and the change process. You can determine whether your change is transformational by answering these three basic questions:

1. Does the change require your organization's strategy, structure, systems, operations, products, services, or technology to change radically to meet the needs of customers and the marketplace?
2. Does your organization need to begin its change process before the destination is fully known and defined?
3. Is the scope of the change so significant that it requires the organization's culture and people's behaviors and mindsets to shift fundamentally in order to implement the changes successfully and succeed in the new state?

If the answer is "yes" to any two of these questions, then you are likely undergoing transformation. If the answer is "yes" to all three, then you are definitely facing transformation.

As we saw in the Drivers of Change Model, organization change stems from changes in the environment or marketplace, coupled with the organization's inability to perform adequately using its existing strategy, organizational design, culture, behavior, and mindset. The pain of the mismatch between the organization (including its human capability) and the needs of its environment creates a wake-up call for the organization. Ultimately, if we do not hear or heed the wake-up call, and our organization does not change to meet the new demands, it will struggle. To thrive, we must hear the wake-up call, understand its implications, and initiate a transformation process that attends to all the drivers required by the change.

In developmental change, simply improving current operations is adequate. In transitional change, replacing current operations with new, clearly defined practices suffices. But in transformational change, the environmental and market-place changes are so significant that a profound breakthrough in our worldview is required, often to even *discover* the new state with which we must replace current operations. If we make that discovery early, the pain of the required transformation is far less than if we discover it late. We may discover in our forties that we need to quit smoking or make a radical lifestyle change to remain healthy. If we neglect the wake-up calls, when we are seventy, they will be louder and more critical. The same is true in organization transformation.

In developmental and transitional change, we can manage the change process with some semblance of order and control. We know where we are going and can plan with great certainty how to get there. In transformation, the change process has a life of its own and, at best, we can influence and facilitate it. If we attempt to control it, we stifle creativity, learning, and progress. The "order" of the future state emerges out of the "chaos" of the transformational effort itself. Transformation, in fact, is the emergence of a new order out of existing chaos. Chaos, as used here, refers to the increasingly unstable dynamics of our organization as its current form becomes obsolete and is no longer as functional as it once was. The resulting new state content is the product of both this chaos and the discovery process that ensues, where a critical mass of stakeholders commit to co-create a better future.

The Transformation Process

The story of the phoenix rising from the ashes is a great metaphor for the transformation process. At the risk of oversimplification, the generic transformational process begins with ever-increasing disruption to the system, moves to the point of death of the old way of being, and then, as with the phoenix, proceeds toward an inspired rebirth (refer to Figure 3.1). Applied to the organization, the generic process goes something like this: An organization is initially born out of a new idea that serves the needs of its environment and marketplace. In serving these needs, it grows and matures until it reaches a level of success. The organization works hard to maintain its success and, over time, functions on a plateau of sustained performance. Keeping the status quo becomes a habit, if not a goal in this phase. This is the period in which vibrant, entrepreneurial, and innovative organizations often turn bureaucratic and staid as they try to hold on to their current success.

In the 1980s, Apple Computer was a great example of this. Once successful, Apple's creative, entrepreneurial, fly-by-the-seat-of-your-pants culture gave way to bureaucratic controls leaders thought were necessary to run the organization more effectively and maintain its market position. As necessary as this was, it squelched people's creativity, innovation suffered, and Apple's stock price plummeted. But there is more to the Apple story, as you surely know. Apple rose from the ashes to claim a market leadership position over the past five years by revitalizing its cutting edge spirit of product development innovation. It re-embraced its original mindset and culture as well as established more effective systems and processes. Its story has been truly transformational.

Over time, most organizations on the success plateau begin to experience difficulties in any number of areas: hovering stock price, stagnation in product development, equipment failure and obsolescence, productivity drops, loss of control over costs and information, dips in employee morale, threats from competition, inadequate resources and skills, loss of market share, or relentless customer demands for innovation. These difficulties are all examples of the wake-up calls signaling the need for change that we mentioned in the previous chapter. Too often, leaders' attachment to the old ways that brought them success, coupled with their fear of the unknown, causes them to deny, explain away, or overlook these wake-up calls. Or, the organization's systems and culture are simply so entrenched that they are reluctant to attempt the radical transformation required. Consequently, the wake-calls get louder, more painful, and more costly.

As these difficulties increase, the organization moves into a period of struggle between internally and externally driven chaos. Finally, leaders wake up and attempt various "fix-it" initiatives to maintain some semblance of order and control. Some leaders respond by trying harder at what brought them initial success, but this only perpetuates the pain and further deepens the hole they are in because these strategies no longer suffice. Other leaders approach the problems from a developmental perspective, throwing training at the organization or trying to squeeze more performance out of their existing operations. Or they apply a Band-Aid' such as cost-cutting efforts with no tie to any real strategic intent. With insufficient responses to the wake-up calls, the disturbance level increases, and the organization's performance drops until finally something snaps. The organization is either forced out of business or it hears the essential wake-up call to shift its worldview (for example, Apple).

The true transformational moment occurs when the organization's leaders finally hear the wake-up calls, catalyzing a breakthrough in their awareness and beliefs. This "aha moment" where they see and understand what is required to move forward, denotes the initial and required shift in the leaders' mindsets. This shift sets the internal conditions in motion for the leaders to see new options for responding to their external circumstances. They begin to formulate new intentions about what is possible and necessary for the organization and its people to thrive. And they begin to see the transformational actions required to turn these intentions into real results.

Wake-up calls can often best be heard not in the executive suite, but on the shop floor. Intel is a great example of this. Their exit from their core memory business to microprocessors began when people on the factory floor began reprioritizing what they were building based on customer demands and ROI. This occurred long before the executives realized that their core memory business was dying. Intel's customers were pronouncing a wake-up call, but the executives were too far away from the initially not-so-loud voice. Those lower in the organization heard it, responded, and ultimately the executives shifted their mindsets and started making heavy investments in what would become Intel's breakthrough business for decades to come. Keep in mind that Intel's "can-do, get it done" culture enabled this. A more staid command-and-control culture would have stifled the employee initiative.

Ultimately, a breakthrough in leader mindset and awareness is a key catalyst to possible breakthrough results because the leaders control where the company invests its resources. This breakthrough in leader mindset is the source of the emergence of the phoenix in organizations that are struggling. Even if the insight starts on the shop floor, it often has to penetrate the executive suite to get traction. When it does, the transforming organization rises out of the ashes of its old beliefs, behavior, and form to take on a new direction that, in its new world, raises its performance capability to a much greater level of effectiveness. Armed with new insight, leaders begin to see the possibility of an entirely new direction that better serves their marketplace. All efforts to design a new state are driven by this shift in mindset.

But what happens when leaders do not hear the wake-up call and make the required shifts in their own mindsets? The only choice then is to get new leaders. Problems can arise, though, if the new leaders arrive with new ideas about business strategy or how to make operations more efficient but not new mindsets that drive real breakthrough. In these cases, improvements happen, but they are not substantial. However, sometimes a company is fortunate, as Apple was when the board re-instated Steve Jobs in 1997 as CEO. Because he rekindled the creativity, innovative, and entrepreneurial mindset that made Apple successful from the beginning, real transformation occurred. In a period of just a couple years, the company's expansion beyond computers into music, entertainment, and communications (iPod, iPhone, iTunes, AppleTV) were all products of the company's transformed collective mindset and culture, initially sourced and enabled by Jobs.

When the wake-up call is heard and mindsets begin to shift, both leaders and the rest of the organization[1] come to recognize that their world is not as it once was and that now they must be and do something radically different, no matter how successful they have been. The leaders' shift in mindset enables them to transform

MINDSET SHIFTS CATALYZE TRANSFORMATION

Examples of how shifts in mindset drive transformation can be seen in the following:

1. A mindset shift is causing transformation in many companies who are "going green," either by applying their core competencies to solving environmental problems or by making their operations more ecologically sustainable (for example, reducing their carbon footprint).

2. The political view that banks should not become "too large to fail" is a fundamental mindset shift from the old view that regulating growth is bad for business.

3. The mindset shift to build smaller, energy-efficient homes is very different from the worldview at the turn of the century when owning a large home announced that you were successful.

4. An emerging mindset shift in America is that health care is a birthright and that all citizens should have insurance coverage.

5. A mindset shift in American auto manufacturers is redirecting their operations to build smaller, better quality, and more fuel-efficient vehicles.

Fairly loud wake-up calls are announcing the need for a shift in worldview in each of these examples. But transformation will not occur in companies in the related industries until the wake-up calls are heard and mindsets shift accordingly. When this occurs, radical change will ensue. Not only will business practices change but so will people's ways of working and relating to one another and their customers. The shifts will happen in "all quadrants and all levels" if they are to take hold and deliver sustainable transformation.

how they think, behave, and lead. Not only do they realize that they must create something entirely new in the organization, but they begin to see that they must approach the transformation in a completely new way. They also begin to acknowledge what is required of them personally to shepherd the process of moving forward. In short, they realize that their old ways won't work for their new challenge, and fundamentally *they must change personally*.

Transformation Requires Learning and Correcting Course

The journey of transformation is anything but a straight line. The process requires significant turns in the road because of the simple fact that it is full of uncertainty. This is for three reasons. First, because the future state (content) is being discovered while the organization is undergoing change, the transformation process is literally the pursuit of an emerging target. As the target shifts, so must the process required to get there. Second, proceeding without a definitive and well-defined destination requires heading into the unknown, which makes most people uncomfortable. As resistance goes up, commitment and performance levels become uncertain, and the need to deal with emergent human dynamics becomes critical. No matter how much you plan, unpredictable human reactions will occur and require adjustments to your change plan. Third, because of all this, there is no way of knowing in advance the pace or actual scope of work that will be required, which will undoubtedly grow as you proceed.

Figure 3.2 graphically portrays the journey of transformation. The vision of the transformation, which provides the general compass heading, determines the gap that must be closed between the organization's current state and its desired future. Notice how the classic change or transition plan is drawn as a straight line, as if it can be rolled out without deviation (as in a traditional project management plan). Of course, this is often true in developmental and transitional changes, but the transformational change process (the actual journey) represents a vastly different path, making innumerable turns as the transformation unfolds.

How do you manage such an unpredictable and emergent process? Well, you don't in the traditional sense of the word! At best you facilitate it. First, give up any expectation of actually controlling the change process. Second, actively pursue information and feedback that help you discover how you need to alter your desired outcome or course of action. And third, optimize your ability to learn from the feedback you gather and turn that learning into appropriate, rapid course

Figure 3.2. The Journey of Transformation

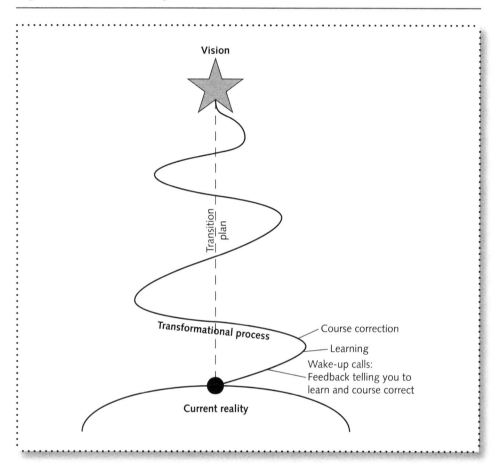

corrections. Learning and course correcting are so essential for transformational success that from a process perspective, they could be its motto.

Most of us tend to see deviation from our change plan as a tremendous problem. In transformation, deviation is never the problem. The issue is always how quickly we can spot a need to course-correct, then learn from the situation, and expediently change course. The better and faster our organization is at learning and course correcting—as individuals, teams, and a whole system—the smaller the adjustments need to be. This requires building specific skills and practices.

Developing comfort and expertise at learning and course correcting requires a significant change of mindset for most leaders and employees, which must be supported by appropriate shifts in cultural norms. In many organizations, the messengers of needed course corrections get shut down. "Kill the messenger of bad news" is an all too common norm, which stands directly in the way of succeeding in transformation. To increase your organization's transformational change capability, you must build a culture where people are not blamed for making or surfacing "mistakes" but are held accountable for learning from them and fixing them. This cultural shift is often best done as part of the actual content transformation you are undergoing.

Learning and course correcting also requires putting in place the systems and processes that enable it. This requires either establishing new systems or modifying existing ones. Many typical operational systems exist in organizations that limit the ability to learn and course-correct rapidly during change. Examples include the following: (1) too many layers of approval required in the chain of command; (2) reactive instead of proactive monitoring systems, or monitoring the wrong data; (3) barriers to sharing information across functional, process, or geographic boundaries; (4) too little access by change leaders to executives after the project has been launched; (5) no formal process for "stopping the train" and quickly calling decision makers together to evaluate emerging data that suggests a course change; and (6) tying compensation or recognition to change projects getting implemented by a certain date rather than to the outcomes they produce. Building an organizational competency in learning and course correcting will require you to thoroughly audit and change some of your existing practices and norms. Again, this is often best accomplished as part of the current transformation.

Project management methodologies are very useful in transformation to manage the details of the change process but only as a "rolling plan" with a 90–150 day window, the willingness to alter the plan as needed, and when used in conjunction with a more strategic change process guidance system. We explain how The Change Leader's Roadmap provides this strategic guidance to the change process in Section Three, with greater detail provided in the book of the same title. Because of the certainty that course corrections will be required and the significant human dynamics at play in transformation, a change process methodology that accounts for these challenges is of utmost importance.

Human Dynamics in Transformation

A key differentiator between transitional and transformational change is the degree of impact on people and the required attention to human and cultural dynamics. In transformational change, human and cultural issues are key drivers. In transitional change, they are often present but are not dominant. For instance, in technology installations that are transitional in nature, such as simple software upgrades, the only behavioral changes required are learning the new system or minor modifications in work flow. The new technology does not change people's roles, responsibilities, or decision-making authority. It merely improves how they do their current jobs, without altering them in major ways. Therefore, the emotional transition that people must go through is not extreme, like it often is in transformational change. In technology changes that are transformational, such as in significant information technology installations, the new technology requires people's behavior, jobs, and perspectives on their roles and customers to change, making the human impact and the change strategy required to deal with it much more complex. Recall the bank Case-In-Point at the end of the previous chapter. The executives conceived that intervention as a transitional change because they could not see its human impacts, and this, of course, is what caused its failure.

Dealing with the chaos and "emergent nature" of transformation creates some interesting and challenging human dynamics. Because the process of figuring out and creating the new state is not highly controllable, organization members must be able to operate effectively within a heightened state of uncertainty and confusion. This presents the ultimate challenge: How can your people function effectively when they feel out of control and confused? Can they—executives, mid-managers, supervisors, and front-line employees alike—unite across boundaries and differences and stay connected as a cohesive "team" to meet this challenge? Or will the uncertainty exacerbate their self-doubt, distrust, turf wars, and conflict?

We tend to be most confident when we know the direction of the change and the path forward is clear. The more ambiguous the circumstances, the more fearful we become. Failure in transformation often results from our personal insecurities and work relationships weakened by the stress of marching into the unknown. When there is no definite answer about how to get where the organization needs to go, fear and blame can run rampant.

Change leaders cannot stamp out or negate these predictable human reactions to the unknown, nor can they manage around or through them. They can—and must—create processes to support people to deal effectively with the unknown and, by doing so, assist these people to evolve as the organization determines its future. For this reason, organizational transformation strategies must include personal transformation strategies. The organization and the people in it must transform together.

And that includes leaders. They are often going through the same emotional turmoil that other stakeholders are experiencing. But leaders carry the added burden of needing to effectively manage themselves as they lead others. They have to be able to process their own fears and concerns to find a level of internal centeredness, confidence, and calm so they can effectively lead. This challenge cannot be taken lightly, and addressing it is a vital aspect of any comprehensive transformational change strategy.

Leaders must attend to people as much as they attend to content and process. Attending to human dynamics includes addressing mindset, behavior, and skills, and the ways of being, working, and relating between individuals, among teams, and within the entire culture. This attention is more than the typical change management approaches of increasing communications, training, and stakeholder engagement to overcome resistance. Instead, change leadership requires assisting people to evolve how they think, feel, and collectively work so they can co-create their positive future. We will discuss this in detail in Section Two: Human Dynamics.

Formulating the strategies and methods to transform mindset and culture are critical aspects of change leadership. Numerous high-leverage people strategies must be incorporated into the overall change strategy, often including the following:

- High stakeholder engagement, especially early in the change process
- Leadership development, self-development, and personal growth training
- Listening sessions that model openness and authenticity
- Healing the past
- Communication strategies and plans that promote two-way dialogue
- Team development that instills self-reflexive behaviors and open discussions
- Interpersonal communication skill development, including self-disclosure, truth-telling, and active listening
- Visioning and understanding the case for change
- Conflict resolution and cross-functional relationship building
- Turning resistance into commitment by helping people resolve core human needs
- Repairing broken relationships and reestablishing trust

Change management attends to some of these strategies; change leadership integrates them all into a comprehensive change strategy and process plan.

Maintaining a Sense of Stability in the Chaos

Amid the uncertainty in transformation, the organization's "spirit"—its core purpose or unique reason for being—usually remains the same. The basic way the organization provides value to society endures. Its fundamental vision for contributing to its customers and marketplace remains intact. In fact, during the height of the chaos of the organization's resurrection, the people of the organization must reflect on these critical questions: "What is our core purpose?" "What do we stand for? "What is our vision for serving the new marketplace needs?" To provide focus during the chaos, people need to remember why the organization is in business and what it stands for—its values.

Organizations that lose touch with their core purpose, vision, and values have no inspiration to fuel their process of transformation. Without the stability and firm foundation of knowing "who we are," fear and panic can take over, causing leaders to "throw spaghetti at the wall" and try all sorts of new ventures, hoping that something will stick. A great example of this occurred in the 1980s when companies pursued broad diversification through acquisitions, followed in the 1990s by massive divestitures. The dot-com bubble of the early 2000s was fueled in part by this same dynamic. When organizations lose touch with themselves and forget what core business they are in, they become rudderless ships in the night, diffusing their energies until they finally either sink or are taken over by an organization that has greater clarity.

Core purpose, along with shared vision and shared values, become the stable ground on which the people in the organization can align and move as a united whole from the past, through the uncertainty, into its tangible future. Purpose, vision, and values guide the organization forward before tangible goals and outcomes can be identified. They align all parts of the organization and ensure that everyone remains emotionally connected and able to operate in the face of the challenges that could otherwise tear the organization apart. Clarity of who the organization is from an inner perspective ultimately generates clarity about who it will become from an external perspective.

Change leaders have a clear responsibility to build into their change strategies ways to keep stakeholders from succumbing to the "comfort" of old solutions, beliefs, and behaviors, and instead, get reconnected to the organization's core purpose, vision, and values so the organization can test new content options without getting lost.

Detroit Edison (DTE Energy) experienced significant spiritual renewal when it reconnected to its core purpose, vision, and values early in its transformation. Not knowing the exact form that industry deregulation would take, or exactly when it would happen, and not knowing what new niche it should pursue to be successful in a competitive environment, the electric utility struggled mightily to re-create itself for the future. With no clear or inspiring direction, the organization was losing its footing and, in many ways, was adrift.

In response, the CEO, John Lobbia, and then president and now CEO, Tony Earley, together sponsored a two-day visioning offsite meeting for the top 300 leaders in which the emotional uncertainty turned to excitement and passionate action. The group revisited the company's history and founding mission. They recalled their major successes and failures and relived their vibrant past. Together they challenged, debated, and ultimately re-ignited their ninety-year-old purpose in their own collective words. It reads: "We energize the progress of society—we make dreams real—we are always here!"

In a staid electric utility culture, energizing the progress of society and making dreams real was quite inspirational. Remembering their vital role in their customers' lives boosted their confidence about their future. It expressed their rekindled vitality. As one leader put it, "Of course we will succeed and figure out a viable form for our contribution to society; by providing the energy to fuel dreams, we play a vital role in our community and the world." During chaos and uncertainty, such spiritual renewal is often exactly what is needed to mobilize unified action, out of which clarity of form can manifest.

Personal Introspection in Transformation

Successful transformation requires a deeper dialogue among the people in the organization than is typical. It demands greater introspection into the very fabric of who the people of the organization are, what they stand for, and how they contribute to the larger environment they serve. Transformation calls for not only a new worldview but also a different way of being, working, and relating to meet the needs of the future state. If an organization neglects this deeper personal and cultural work in the early stages of its transformation, then chaos can consume the organization, and the phoenix will never rise. This is true for everyone in the organization but especially for those leading and shaping the initial stages of the transformational process.

Clearly, transformation requires significant personal strength on the part of leaders to trust the wake-up calls for change and the personal and collective discovery process required for inventing a new way of being and operating in the organization. To do the personal work, leaders must possess significant internal fortitude. It takes internal discipline to lead the organization into the unknown and still remain confident. Leaders can experience profound angst when they hear the wake-up calls for radical change and then must confront their long-held beliefs about how to succeed. Quite often, leaders feel an enormous burden during the prolonged uncertainty of the transformational change process.

It is not uncommon to hear executives who have stayed in the saddle during this turbulent period reflect on how much soul searching they did during the process. Feeling vulnerable, which is not frequently expressed in leadership circles, is common. Vulnerability goes hand-in-hand with leaders accepting that they do not have all of the answers and cannot control the process or outcome for which they feel so responsible. They must, in fact, have a significant degree of faith, trust, and commitment to proceed despite their concerns. When executives have climbed to the top of their success ladder through knowing what to do when and always being in control, facing the uncertainty of transformation is one of the toughest personal challenges of their professional lives. Often the toughest issue they face is the fact that perhaps their own beliefs, mindsets, or styles are the barriers to their organization's success. All of this internal reality has to be addressed openly and directly.

This is such an important concern that our company, Being First, Inc., includes a four-day executive retreat at the beginning of transformational consulting interventions. In this retreat, we provide new insights and tools for executives to deepen their personal process of self, relationship, and team development. This work expands their awareness and shifts their mindset about human dynamics and what is required in the people and process domains to achieve breakthrough results. It catalyzes the personal changes they must make to lead the transformation successfully. It reveals to them what is required to transform culture to unleash the full human potential in their organization. It also delivers the self-management skills that enable them to remain centered and focused amid any of their own emotional turmoil. The retreat provides a foundation for leading breakthrough results. It starts the process of leaders attending to all quadrants and all levels, including and especially, their own mindsets and beliefs.

You might think that executives would resist this type of work, but to the contrary, it opens a door they have always wanted to open, but just did not know how. And the outcome is often life and career shaping. We believe strongly that this depth of personal work, which goes far beyond what occurs in change management, is the key to achieving breakthrough results from transformation. In our experience, the quality and quantity of transformational outcomes is in direct proportion to the degree to which leaders embrace their own personal introspection and change. (See premium content: Leadership Breakthrough: Topic Options and Methods www.pfeiffer.com/go/anderson.)

DETERMINING THE TYPE OF CHANGE TAKING PLACE

Every major change effort can be classified as primarily one of the three types of change. You do not choose your type, you *discover* your type. In other words, the type of your change effort is determined by the dynamics of your marketplace and the nature of change it demands from your organization. This may seem obvious, but we constantly hear both leaders and consultants calling their change transformational, when it is in fact transitional. They do this because they do not understand the types, and transformational change is the new thing, more sexy and exciting. Be sure to type your change accurately because the type of change determines the change strategy required to succeed.

Figure 3.3. Relationship of the Types of Change

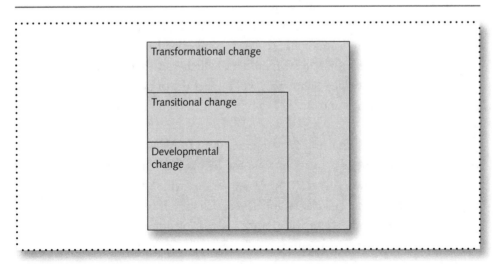

Often, one or both of the other types of change will also be present within the overall change but are not as influential or paramount. The relationship between the three types is nested frame, as shown in Figure 3.3. Transitional changes often have developmental changes occurring within them, and within a larger transformation, you will usually find both developmental and transitional initiatives.

Exhibit 3.1 offers a questionnaire to help you determine which type of change you are leading. Remember that none of the types of change is more valuable or better than the others. Each serves a different need.

TRANSFORMATION AND THE CONSCIOUS CHANGE LEADER ACCOUNTABILITY MODEL

Now that we have made these distinctions about transformation, let's apply the Conscious Change Leader Accountability Model to further our understanding. We will highlight key dynamics about the quadrants and levels to reveal important insights into leading transformation successfully.

To begin, change leaders must understand that for any given organization, all quadrants and levels are present and are interdependent. Events or dynamics in one dimension will impact the other dimensions. For example, if market economics has a downturn, it can negatively impact the organization, which will impact various functions and teams within it. A team may lose its budget and be merged with another team, which will impact team morale and work practices. The team merger will shift working relationships, and displaced individuals may feel left out and uncertain, triggering anger and resistant behavior. Their frustration may upset other team members, which can then impact the performance of the newly formed team. This will impact the organization's performance in its market. Influence and impact moves in all directions across the quadrants and levels.

Now here is an interesting question: In our example, what influenced peoples' resistance? Was it the lost relationships, the breakup of the team, or the market downturn? The answer is that all were influences, which highlights the interdependent nature of the quadrants and levels. Change leaders must perceive this interdependence, or they run the significant risk of not effectively designing or course correcting their change processes because they cannot accurately assess the

Exhibit 3.1. Determining the Types of Change

Instructions: Determine the primary type of change you are leading by answering these "litmus test" questions. If you answer "yes" to two or more questions for one type of change, then that is the primary type of change you are facing. Remember to think of the overall change that is likely occurring, not the subinitiatives within it. In many cases, all three types of change will be occurring, but only one is primary. The primary type is almost always the most complex. Be sure to build your change strategy to serve the most common type.

Developmental Change

1. Does your change effort primarily require an improvement of your existing way of operating, rather than a radical change to it?

2. Will skill or knowledge training, performance improvement strategies, and communications suffice to carry out this change?

3. Does your current culture and mindset support the needs of this change?

Transitional Change

1. Does your change effort require you to dismantle your existing way of operating and replace it with something known but different?

2. At the beginning of your change effort, were you or will you be able to design a definitive picture of the new state?

3. Is it realistic to expect this change to occur over a predetermined timetable?

Transformational Change

1. Does your organization need to begin its change process before the destination is fully known and defined?

2. Is the scope of this change so significant that it requires the organization's culture and people's behavior and mindsets to shift significantly to implement the changes successfully and achieve the new state?

3. Does the change require the organization's structure, operations, products, services, or technology to change radically to meet the needs of customers and the marketplace?

Conclusions

1. Which of the three types of change is the primary type required?

2. Which of the other two types of change will also be needed to support this primary type? In what ways?

dynamics influencing them. We need to know the forces at play and where they are coming from before we can mitigate those forces.

Change leaders must also realize that isolated events, dynamics, and changes in any one quadrant or level will be "resisted" by the current state inertia of the others. This is why piecemeal approaches to transformation simply do not work, and why an integrated—and integral—approach is required.

Yet most change is done in piecemeal fashion. For example, changes to organizational structures or systems are usually made in isolation from the culture changes they require. Changes to performance management systems are often not overtly linked to the changes in work redesign within the line organizations that have prompted the new HR systems. Leadership and management training is often not made relevant to business imperatives or organizational changes they are meant to support. Team development is often not integrated with the culture change and systems implementations that impact the teams. Run in isolated fashion, each change, while important in its own right, struggles to produce its intended benefit because it is held back by the "old state" dynamics present in the other related quadrants and levels.

Change leaders must also understand that while influence moves in all directions, the "larger" levels tend to dominate the smaller. Organizational cultures and systems tend to heavily influence team cultures and systems; a team's norms and how it operates usually reflects the larger organization of which it is a part. It then heavily influences individual team member mindset and behavior; people tend to adopt the "group think" of the team. This does not mean that the larger levels *dictate* what is below; rather, they exert significant influence on them.

Anomalies in individual mindset and behavior and team subcultures can exist within an organization, but the organization's overall culture and systems will always be a force to contend with. Subcultures can exist for a number of reasons. A strong leader can sometimes protect his or her subgroup from the influence of the larger organization. This is especially possible when the subgroup performs extremely well. Or, some other cultural force can dominate the individual or subgroup's way of being and exert more influence than the organization does. Take for example a company such as Harley-Davidson. Many of its factory workers ride Harleys, and they were and are a part of the Harley social culture that got firmly rooted in the rebellious, independent thinking style of the 1960s and early 1970s. They build these motorcycles because they love them. Excellence is in their blood and they put their hearts and souls into them because the bikes represent a way of being and lifestyle that is important to them to sustain. As long as this personal and larger social meaning is in place, these factory workers will build the highest quality bikes they know how, no matter what happens within the larger corporate culture.

Certainly, individuals *can* influence their relationships, team, or organization because the individual is always a part of those larger collectives, and their actions have impact. This is a structural basis of political democracies, which are theoretically built on the idea that each citizen should have a vote, an equal opportunity to influence (up the levels to) the larger whole. But the degree of individual influence tends to dissipate as the levels increase in size. This is not an absolute rule but rather a tendency. The bigger the level, the more powerful, influential, and capable the individual needs to be to cause significant change in the organization, but it does happen, even on a grand scale. Think of Gandhi, Martin Luther King, and others.

Making overt the influence of the larger levels on the smaller is critical because much change is sourced within individual business units, regions, functions, line organizations, teams, and departments. Many of these changes struggle against the powerful limiting force of the larger organization's current culture and systems. Leaders at all levels must understand these forces and address them in their change efforts.

This issue is exacerbated because leaders often operate with a silo mentality. They orient down into their own organizations rather than up and across to the needs of the larger enterprise. From our perspective, less than 25 percent of executive teams are actually high-performing teams that focus effectively as a team on the strategic needs of the business. Most are not teams at all, but simply groups of individuals that keep each other informed about their own organization's activities and needs.

In general, executive teams must lift their heads and put continuous focus on the market and how the organization's systems and culture must continually evolve to serve it. Accepting this enterprise responsibility, leaders can then align the changes occurring within business units, functions, teams, and individuals to drive those larger organizational outcomes. In this fashion, the influence of the larger organizational systems and culture becomes enablers of effective "smaller level" changes. And symbiotically, the smaller changes, now effectively supported, generate a tipping point for the organization, where the gravitational inertia to remain the same is overcome, and the organization's transformation readily proceeds.

These organizational and human dynamics point us to one key conclusion: Transformation requires change leader attention to all quadrants and all levels as depicted in our Conscious Change Leader Accountability Model (see Figure I.1 in the Introduction). From a quadrant perspective, transformation clearly includes radical change to organizational *systems*, structures, business processes, and technology (content). The organization's *culture* must change as well to enable the content changes to be effectively implemented, adopted, and sustained by the people of the organization. Both leader's and employees' *mindsets* and *behaviors* must change and new skills must be developed to embrace the new way of being, working, and relating required by the new culture. Without these "people" changes, the "content" changes never deliver their ROI because they never get fully implemented or mastered. The four quadrants of systems, culture, behavior, and mindset must all be addressed.

This must occur, not just within *individuals* and the larger *organization* but also within *relationships* and *teams* throughout the organization. The new mindsets and behaviors must come to life in how people work together, for that is a central means for how the new systems become fully functional and the larger cultural transformation takes root. New organizational systems often require cross-boundary collaboration among people, teams, departments, regions, and business units, demanding that all redesign workflow, reporting structures, and their collaborative use of technology and information. New relationship and team norms and behavior about support, information and resource sharing, and decision making become essential. In transformation, you must attend to all levels.

Designing a *change* process that organizes and integrates the changes in all quadrants and levels into a unified process that moves the organization forward is critical. That, of course, is the role of The Change Leader's Roadmap, which we'll discuss in Chapter Nine. To this end, change leaders can call on many different types of professional support: OD and OE consultants, change management professionals, team builders and facilitators, organization design specialists, quality consultants, information technology experts, change strategists, executive coaches, training specialists, and of course, content experts in each of the areas of change. Change leaders do not have to be competent in all these areas, but they do need to be familiar with them enough to know where in their organization to get the expertise they need when they need it. A change leader's primary accountability is to ensure that the overall change process brings this expertise together to address all quadrants and levels effectively.

SUMMARY

We have described three very different types of change operating in organizations, each of which requires different change strategies. Developmental and transitional changes are the most familiar and are easier to lead than transformation. Developmental change is the improvement of something that currently exists, while transitional change is the replacement of what is with something entirely new, yet clearly known. Both developmental and transitional change possess common characteristics: (1) Their outcomes can be quantified and known in advance of implementation; (2) significant culture, behavior, or mindset change is not required; and (3) the change process, its resource requirements, and the timetable, for the most part, can be managed with some semblance of control.

The third type of change, transformation, requires a completely different set of change leadership skills. Transformation is the newest and most complex type of organization change, and the one that is often required to achieve breakthrough results. Transformation possesses very different dynamics: (1) The future state cannot be completely known in advance; (2) significant transformations of the organization's culture and of people's behavior and mindsets are required; and (3) the change process itself cannot be tightly managed or controlled because the future is unknown and the human dynamics are too unpredictable, making the change process nonlinear. Constant discovery, learning, and course correcting are required.

Transformation requires leaders to expand their worldview and increase their awareness and skill to include all the drivers of change, both external and internal. It requires a different mindset and style. And it demands that both leaders and employees undergo personal change as part of the organization's transformation. It requires full attention to transforming organizational systems and culture, and mindset and behavior in individuals, relationships, and teams.

Over the years, we have seen two very different approaches to transformation from our clients. These approaches produce very different results. In the next chapter, we will describe these approaches, further clarifying what successful change leadership demands.

ENDNOTE

1. We don't mean to imply that "the breakthrough to new awareness, beliefs, and intentions" must begin, or always begins, with the top leaders. Quite often, employees come to this realization long before the leaders do. Our point, however, is that *usually* enterprise-wide transformation does not get traction *until* the top leaders hear the wake-up call. Until that time, most leaders—intentionally or not—stifle employee-driven transformation. However, it is not uncommon to see the wake-up call for transformation emerging out of employee feedback to leaders about changing customer needs or from employee's that develop new work practices that generate substantial performance improvements. Employees are closer to the customer and the work and can play a vital role in initiating transformation, if only leaders will listen. A key strategy for insightful leaders is to create a formal structure and process to proactively seek out employee input.

Two Leadership Approaches to Transformation

May you develop mental concentration . . . for whoever is mentally concentrated, sees things according to reality.

—The Buddha

In the previous chapter, we defined the three different types of change occurring in organizations, explored the challenges they present, and clarified several strategies and outcomes for each. We suggested that transformation and the pursuit of breakthrough results requires full attention to both the external content and the internal dynamics of people and culture, specifically stating that change leaders must help transform organizational, team, and relational systems and culture, as well as individual mindset and behavior to succeed.

In this chapter, we address how the state of awareness that leaders bring to transformation influences their approach and success at leading it. We define two very different approaches and explore each in depth, including the leadership behaviors and outcomes they each tend to generate. We highlight how only one of these approaches really works to lead transformation and give you an opportunity to reflect on your own approach going forward.

This chapter begins an inquiry into the critical inner dynamics of successful change leadership, which we will continue throughout Section Two, where we address human dynamics. We believe that what we discuss in this chapter—and your mastery of it—will be the greatest determinant of your success as a change leader. This topic of approach to transformation should be front and center in any conversation about organizational change and human performance, but it seldom is. It requires a high level of awareness and personal development to see the distinctions we will attempt to articulate, and even greater awareness and development to apply them. That is not a reason to overlook this topic but rather a compelling reason to study it deeply and practice it diligently.

TWO APPROACHES TO TRANSFORMATION

By *approach* to transformation, we mean the *state of awareness or level of consciousness* that leaders personally bring to transformation. This level of awareness impacts every aspect of a leader's change leadership capability, experience, and outcome. Nothing is left untouched. Their level of awareness influences the change strategies they develop, change plans they design to execute those strategies, decisions they make, leadership style, interpersonal and organizational communication patterns, relationships with stakeholders, what they model to others, emotional reactions and personal ability to change, and ultimately, their outcomes. Fundamentally, *a leader's approach determines what the leader is aware of and what the leader does not see.* And this shapes everything else.

> *Every man takes the limits of his own field of vision for the limits of the world.*
> —Arthur Schopenhauer

In the simplest of terms, leaders approach transformation with either expanded awareness or limited awareness. We call the expanded awareness mode the "conscious" approach and the limited awareness mode the "autopilot" (or unconscious) approach. We use these terms because they accurately denote two critical functions of the mind that we will describe shortly.

When we take a conscious approach, our greater awareness provides more perspective and insight about what transformation demands and better strategic options to address its unique people and process dynamics. Expanded awareness is like getting the benefit of both a wide-angle lens and a high-powered microscope at the same time. Through the wider view, we can see more broadly the dynamics at play in transformation, such as how change in one area of the organization impacts operations in another, how leadership style contributes to employee resistance and commitment, or how competition across the supply chain limits enterprise success. Through the microscope, we can see the deeper and more subtle human dynamics that would otherwise go unnoticed, such as how people's emotions influence their commitment, how culture stifles the use of a new technology, or how our own internal state impacts how we design and run our change efforts. Expanded awareness provides both greater breadth and greater depth to our view.

When we take an autopilot approach, we respond automatically and unconsciously to the dynamics of transformation based on our conditioned habits, existing knowledge, and dominant leadership style. Our lens is filtered by the biases and assumptions of our own mental conditioning, causing us to often not see critical people and process dynamics. We can only apply our old management techniques because our limited awareness offers us no other possibilities: "If it worked for us before, it will work for us again."

We do not want to imply that the autopilot approach is bad or that when we are in it we are poor leaders. Even though not optimal, the autopilot approach has sufficed for leading organizations and developmental and transitional change for a long time; it just is not adequate for leading transformation or delivering breakthrough results. When we are on autopilot, we are doing the best we can; we just have limited awareness. We do not know what we do not know and cannot see what is outside the angle or power of our lens. But to succeed in transformation, we must increase our scope of awareness.

Autopilot has been the most prevalent approach historically, while the conscious approach is becoming increasingly evident in today's organizations. As leaders acquire more experience with transformation, they are discovering more of what transformation entails and requires. Although there is much inertia to overcome, we believe that the conscious approach will dominate change leadership behavior in the twenty-first century. It has to. As change has become more complex, evolving from developmental to transitional to transformational, operating with expanded awareness to see the subtle human and process dynamics at play has become a requirement of success. This level of leadership awareness is the primary enabler of transforming today's organizations, successfully running tomorrow's, and achieving breakthrough results. We cannot overemphasize this point. The transformational success formula is simple: *On average, your results from change will be in direct proportion to the level of awareness you bring to the effort.*

To further understand these two approaches, we need to first define *conscious* and *unconscious*. Later in the chapter, we will outline the value of each approach and the different behaviors that change leaders taking them display.

Conscious Versus Unconscious

We define the term *conscious* as possessing conscious awareness; being mindful; witnessing your experience; reflecting; and being alert, clear-minded, and observant. Being conscious is being *aware that you are aware and being aware of what fills your awareness.*

Perhaps the most direct way of describing what we mean by "conscious" is to describe what it is not. In our application, we *could* easily use the word "unconscious" as the opposite of conscious. However, this would be misleading without an explanation of terms. Our use of unconscious would *not* mean "without awareness," as in someone who has been knocked unconscious or who is asleep. Instead, in our definition, unconscious would mean *without conscious awareness,* as with people who are awake and alert but not witnessing their experience; not *consciously* aware of themselves, their behavior, their impact, the motivation for their choices, or the full extent of what is going on around them.

A common example of this use of the term "unconscious" is a phenomenon that happens to many of us as we drive down the freeway, especially if we drive the same route regularly. You have likely had the experience of driving down the highway and when the sign announcing your desired off-ramp catches your attention, you realize that you have been driving on autopilot, without any conscious awareness of your surroundings. You have been lost in your own thoughts and not consciously present to what was occurring on the road. Your eyes have been open. You have been taking in information, yet processing it "unconsciously." Then, when you pop back into conscious awareness, you are startled by the fact that you have been driving for so long without any memory of the scenery or the cars around you. You realize that you must have slowed and sped up with traffic, even changed lanes, but your behavior occurred without *conscious* intent. You are surprised because you did not "witness" any of your experience.

Conscious awareness (the witness) and unconscious awareness (the autopilot) are literally two different states of consciousness. In both, we are aware, taking in information from our environment. In the witness state, we are *consciously* aware of information as our senses collect it. On autopilot, however, the information enters our system and we respond automatically and unconsciously, without witnessing the information or our response.

This oscillation in and out of conscious awareness goes on continuously, even for people who are highly aware. Our awareness level can oscillate every day, every hour, every minute. The key to the conscious approach is expanding the amount of time that you are mindful and the frequency of "waking up" so you can use that expanded awareness to evaluate and choose effective change leadership behaviors and strategies.

The Value and Cost of Autopilot

Autopilot is our default state of awareness and is a very useful human function. It has its place, especially in routine tasks. It can save us energy, increase our efficiency, and deliver rote activities successfully even when we are not paying attention. After we learn a routine like brushing our teeth or serving a tennis ball, autopilot is a nice feature to have. It is great not to have to think about our technique and still get the results we are after. However, in complex activities such as leading transformation, or even basic tasks done in a highly dynamic environment such as driving home in freeway traffic, autopilot can lead to disaster. A far more reliable way to succeed in those situations is being awake to what is occurring around—and within us—so we can consciously evaluate and choose our behaviors and actions.

We only truly choose our behaviors and actions when we are consciously aware, and choosing is the source of our personal power. When we give up choice, we diminish our impact, contribution, and options. Although autopilot can be useful at times, the more novel, unknown, or challenging the situation, the more important it is to be consciously aware so we can evaluate and choose our response rather than react automatically and unconsciously.

As a change leader, operating on autopilot at the wrong times, and not being consciously aware that we are doing so, can lead to many undesirable outcomes, such as the following:

- Developing change strategies that do not fit the type of change occurring
- Being rigid and inflexible; not being able to course-correct our change process as needed
- Misdiagnosing the root cause of breakdowns in the change process
- Arguing for an invalid position
- Not seeing the best solution in a situation
- Not engaging the right people in change in critical ways
- Missing opportunities
- Misinterpreting events or a person's comments
- Reacting in negative ways and not modeling desired behaviors
- Denying the need for learning when it really exists
- Not seeing how to constructively use feedback

Developing Conscious Awareness

Like all capabilities, we can develop greater conscious awareness and mindfulness over time. We just have to exercise the right "muscles" (see the sidebar titled "Tools to Develop Conscious Awareness" later in this chapter).

Developing mindfulness is a process. The key is diligently observing our inner state. This mere turning inward and observing our state of consciousness becomes a moment in which we have enlisted our conscious awareness. In that moment, autopilot is no longer engaged. The more we do this, the more we will find ourselves operating from conscious awareness with greater mindfulness.

Over time, this makes it easier for us to get out of autopilot when we wake up and choose to do so. Think of all those times when you know you should think, behave, or speak differently, but you just cannot get yourself to do so. Like when you listen to yourself say something you know you will regret but cannot keep your lips from speaking it. As you pop into conscious awareness repeatedly over time, your autopilot will have less of a stronghold on your awareness and behavior, and you will have more ability to choose your desired behavior or action.

It is important to note that we do not *become* conscious; we already are conscious. We simply become *more* consciously aware more of the time as we notice and shift out of autopilot functioning. Think of it this way. Within us is pure, unconditioned awareness. It already exists, and there is nothing for us to do to develop it. It is just a matter of accessing it. Our highest internal state is to operate from this source within our innermost being. In sports, we call it being in the "flow" or "zone," and it leads to optimal performance. Psychologists refer to it as our higher or transpersonal self. Meditation teachers call it the Witness, Observer, True Self, or Soul. Peter Senge and his colleagues call it Presence.[1] To us the name does not matter. What matters is that we acknowledge there is a source within us that is a higher state than our normal autopilot functioning, that it delivers greater results, and that we *pursue* operating from that state as much as possible.

As we operate with conscious awareness more often, we access higher levels of consciousness within ourselves. Over time, this develops our level of awareness and we find ourselves operating from a higher state on a more regular basis. This essentially generates for us a higher stage of cognitive development, and is the foundation for achieving breakthrough results.

The Four Sights

The general direction of this inner development is toward perceiving situations with both greater breadth and depth. We begin to perceive reality more broadly across time and space and more deeply into inner human dynamics, both in ourselves and in others. Rather than being limited by the myopic view autopilot allows, we perceive with a more comprehensive and integral perspective. We describe this as developing the "four sights," or four critical ways of perceiving that drive change leadership success:

▸ **Seeing Systems:** Perceiving the interdependencies among organizational functions, events, or circumstances; seeing connections across boundaries; seeing relational impacts across the supply chain; *seeing across space.*

▸ **Seeing Process:** Being aware of how events and circumstances influence each other over time; perceiving how the present is a natural outgrowth of the past, and how to influence it to create a desired future; seeing the relationships between inputs and outputs; seeing future impacts of today's activities; seeing the process nature of reality, and how development is occurring or can occur in any situation; *seeing across time.*

▶ **Seeing Internal/External:** Perceiving the inner dynamics of external circumstances, and vice versa; seeing how mindset and culture influences actions and results; seeing the outer impacts of thoughts and emotions, how resistance and commitment impacts outcomes; *seeing how internal and external reality reflect each other.*

▶ **Seeing Consciously:** Witnessing objectively what is occurring; being mindful and present to the moment; perceiving without the bias of autopilot or mental conditioning; *seeing mindfully.*

This general direction of personal growth, where you perceive with both greater breadth and greater depth, is outlined and corroborated in numerous disciplines: emotional development, interpersonal development, moral development, cognitive development, psychological development, and spiritual development.[2] All areas of development follow this path toward greater span and depth, including change leadership.

We will discuss seeing systems and seeing process again in Chapter Nine, and seeing internal/external and consciously in Chapters Six and Seven. The important point for our inquiry here is to realize that conscious awareness is the path to all human development, and turning your attention inward to observe your state of consciousness to develop greater mindfulness will naturally lead to growth and development—as a person and as a change leader. Nothing is more critical to your success.

Conscious Awareness, Learning, and Performance

All learning and development is based on realizing (becoming consciously aware) that we do not know how to do something, then expanding our awareness of the task at hand, and mastering the mechanics. The Competency Model (see Figure 4.1) depicts the universal path of learning. Let's explore this model to see how conscious awareness is key to all learning and development.

As learners, we all pass through four stages on our way to becoming proficient in a new task or skill. At the beginning, we are "unconsciously incompetent": We

TOOLS TO DEVELOP CONSCIOUS AWARENESS

Many tools and techniques exist to help us develop our conscious awareness. Meditation is the best, but you may not understand it if you are new to it. But give it a chance. It is not weird at all. In its simplest form, meditation is putting our attention on an object (something we can see, hear, touch, taste, feel, or imagine) and then bringing our awareness back to the object when it wanders. Meditation is not thinking about the object or thinking about anything for that matter. In fact, it is the cessation of thinking and is, rather, simply being . . . aware. What could be simpler?

An elegant and powerful form of meditation is simply watching your breath. We use this technique in two ways: (1) "offline" for ten minutes or longer when we can be alone and simply sit and be still, and (2) "online" throughout our day as a trigger to come to conscious awareness and center ourselves.

The power of meditating and consciously breathing—both offline and online—is that it (1) strengthens your inner witness and ability to be consciously aware; (2) shortens the time you spend in autopilot and makes it easier to pop out of it when it is useful to do so; (3) builds your ability to observe your thinking and let go of negative or distracting thoughts; (4) dramatically increases concentration; (5) improves self-management of emotions; (6) reduces stress; (7) develops confidence; (8) increases your ability to stay centered and alert during stressful situations; and (9) increases your access to intuition and pure, unadulterated awareness.

Tools that increase conscious awareness include the following:

- Meditation
- Focusing techniques
- Conscious breathing techniques
- Body awareness exercises
- Appreciation and gratefulness exercises
- Prayer

do not know what we do not know, or even that we do not know. We are either unaware of our incompetence or in denial and not able to psychologically accept that we are not yet skilled.

No learning takes place until we awaken our conscious awareness and become "consciously incompetent"; we now realize that we do not possess the knowledge

Figure 4.1. Competency Model[3]

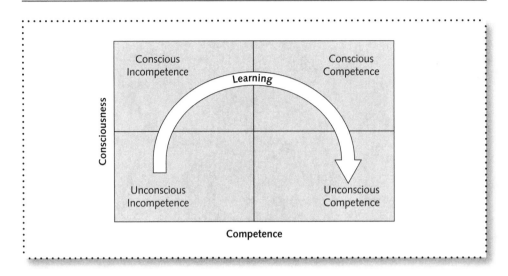

and skill we need. This new awareness and personal insight opens the possibility of learning. Without it, our learning is limited.

If we have a high psychological need to be perceived as right and competent, we can become very uncomfortable at this point, especially if we are not emotionally secure in our lack of skill. Rather than pursue the necessary learning, our ego can take over, deny our need to learn, and put on a façade of competence. Our internal doubt, left unchecked, can generate denial that causes us to remain unconscious of what we do not know. We remain "unconsciously incompetent," held back by our own personal denial and delusion of being sufficiently capable. Stuck in autopilot, we end up making the same mistakes repeatedly. If the task is playing tennis, we keep hitting the ball into the net. If the task is leading transformation, we keep misapplying our habitual developmental and transitional strategies, not understanding why they do not work.

When we are more confident learners, we accept our incompetence and choose to pursue learning the new skill. We then begin practicing the new methods, and over time, become "consciously competent," able to perform the new task as long as we are thinking about it, or, said differently, as long as we are awake and "consciously aware of what we are doing." To the degree we slip into autopilot, we "forget" our new techniques and apply our old, habitual approaches and perform poorly. The key in this stage is for us to remain consciously aware and attentive to the learning so we can completely develop and engrain the new skill.

As we practice and apply the new skill over time, it becomes second nature, and we become able to perform it successfully without thinking about it. We are now "unconsciously competent," able to perform the task without conscious awareness. We are now proficient in the new skill.

The model in Figure 4.1 stops at this stage, but higher levels of learning and performance exist beyond proficient, and awareness continues to play a critical role in them as well. We can progress to becoming an expert or master. Repetition and practice are keys, of course, but real mastery comes from developing our internal state of consciousness to access that higher internal state mentioned earlier that elite performers call being in the "flow"[4] or "zone." This is a heightened state of consciousness in which our new skill can flow out of us naturally and impeccably. It is a pure state of awareness in which thoughts and feelings do not distract our one-pointed concentration. Clearly, elite sports performers such as Michael Jordan, Roger Federer, or Peyton Manning possess superior skills and work ethics. But what sets them apart from their competitors is their mental ability to perform more consistently in the "zone." While repetition and practice will continually develop their skill, they will perform their best only when they are in the zone of pure concentration and heightened awareness.

We will discuss this elevated level of awareness and performance in more detail in Chapter Seven. The point here is simply to establish that conscious awareness is critical to developing a proficient level of skill in any task, including change leadership. And that mastery and breakthrough performance comes from both practice and a heightened level of awareness, far beyond autopilot. Awareness and consciousness are key to both learning and performing optimally.

The Choice to Be a Conscious Change Leader

Now that we have a common understanding of the functioning of conscious awareness and autopilot, we can discuss what we mean by taking a conscious approach versus an autopilot approach to leading transformation.

Remember, we all have both of these mental capabilities and we fluctuate continually between them, sometimes operating with conscious awareness and other times operating on autopilot. Taking a conscious approach to leading transformation does not mean, then, *always* operating with conscious awareness. Similarly, taking an autopilot approach does not mean *always* operating on autopilot. What is the difference then between these two *very* different types of leaders—the conscious change leader and the autopilot change leader?

Conscious change leaders are just that because they *choose* to be, and they make a significant personal commitment to how they operate as human beings and leaders. Conscious change leaders turn inward, introspect, and put their *attention* on their inner awareness and mindset, and their *intention* on proactively developing their innermost being. In our language, they "put their being first." They seek greater self-awareness and understanding because they know that their level of awareness and mindset influence everything about their lives and leadership. They seek to develop their own level of consciousness so they can operate at the highest levels possible, and therefore, contribute fully. They understand that "to be first, they must put their being first."

Conscious change leaders choose this path because they have enough self-awareness to see the difference in themselves when they are operating consciously versus on autopilot. They see their mindset in action, the impact of their conditioned perceptions and behaviors on their outcomes. They are familiar with the fluctuations in their own inner states and realize that they can influence their inner reality and consequently have greater positive impact in the world. They directly experience the benefits that greater conscious awareness affords. They see that operating consciously opens up an entirely new possibility for outcomes that goes far beyond the limitations of their conditioning and autopilot functioning.

A key differentiator, then, between conscious and autopilot change leaders is that conscious leaders attend to both inner reality and external reality in their leadership, whereas autopilot leaders focus nearly exclusively on external dynamics. Their attention is primarily on content, the design solution, implementation plans, reporting mechanisms, and metrics. Conscious change leaders see the critical nature of all three critical focus areas—content, people, and process—and address the inner human dynamics that are critical to all three, starting with their own. They do not attend to external dynamics less; they simply attend to internal dynamics more, including their own mindset and their organization's culture. They consciously attend to all quadrants and all levels.

This does not make conscious change leaders perfect, but it does put them on a path of greater effectiveness and development that over time radically accelerates their change leadership competency vis-à-vis their autopilot counterparts. It makes their ways of thinking and behaving more conducive to success.

Wake-Up Calls to Conscious Change Leadership

Over our careers, we have witnessed numerous leaders wake up to become conscious change leaders. Not all experience a moment of choice where they choose the conscious approach. Instead, this way of being, working, and relating emerges within them as their internal awareness grows over time. For many, they hear and respond to four levels of wake-up calls that catalyze within them this new, more effective way of being. Each of these wake-up calls triggers greater insight and skill development in both the internal and external dynamics of transformation and in all areas of related content, people, and process (see Figure 4.2).

The levels show increasing magnitudes of conscious awareness and the typical sequence in which conscious change leadership awareness develops. The figure shows these levels as a hierarchy of nested frames, the first included within the second, which is included within the third, and so on.

The first level of wake-up call is the easiest for leaders to hear. It is the recognition that the status quo in the organization no longer works and that a change is required. The second level of wake-up call is the realization that the change is

Figure 4.2. Wake-Up Calls to Conscious Change Leadership

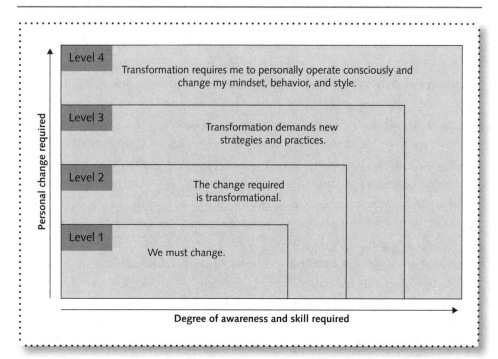

transformational. This level requires that leaders understand that the process of transformation is uniquely different from that of developmental or transitional change, and that deeper attention to people and the change process is required. This wake-up call requires leaders to increase what they *know*. Using what you are learning in this book, you can help provide this education.

The third level of wake-up call, certainly more of a stretch, is the realization that transformation requires new strategies and practices beyond their traditional leadership and change management approaches. In other words, leaders must change what they *do*. This wake-up call begins the leadership breakthrough that is necessary for successful transformation.

The fourth level of wake-up call, the most far-reaching and eye-opening, is the realization that transformation requires leaders to change *personally*, that they must change how they are *being*: expand their awareness, become more introspective and conscious, shift their mindsets, and transform their behaviors and change leadership style. This is the level of wake-up call that turns the focus of leaders' attention into themselves, into observing their own awareness and mindset in action. This increases not only their self-awareness but also their understanding of human dynamics in general. In other words, their own inner dynamics become their action research laboratory about human functioning and performance.

This Level Four wake-up call carries for leaders the insight that within their own consciousness lie the source of their current limitations and failures as well as future breakthroughs and successes. These leaders realize that without putting themselves overtly into their organization's change process, the full potential of the transformation cannot manifest. They now choose to transform themselves to become a model of the desired change. Upon accepting the Level Four wake-up call, leaders have begun to take a conscious approach to change leadership and transformation, and true breakthrough results become possible. They are now conscious change leaders because they *choose to be*.

Notice how these wake-up calls parallel the greater span and depth of awareness that the history and evolution of change highlighted in our discussion of the drivers of change in Chapter Two. We have gone from implementing change in functional silos without needing to attend to deeper human dynamics to now having to implement transformation systemwide, with constant attention across boundaries of hierarchy, function, regions, time, and supply chain (greater span), while also having to address core human dynamics of mindset and culture (greater depth). While the exterior dimension of content has become more complex, the

John Lobbia, the ex-CEO of Detroit Edison, quickly moved through the first three levels of wake-up calls to the fourth, perhaps faster than any CEO we had worked with previously. When we met John, he was very clear that his organization had to change (Level One) to meet the challenges of possible deregulation in the electric utility industry. A brilliant man, John's gut instinct was that the change required was transformational (Level Two); he knew that his organization needed to begin its change long before he or anyone else could be certain about its future state. He also realized that the change needed was so significant that the organization's culture and the behavior and mindsets of its leaders and employees would need to transform to sustain the mammoth content changes required. Initially, John did not realize that his and his leaders' old approaches, strategies, and mindsets would not suffice for this transformation. However, with a bit of coaching, he quickly saw the obvious (Level Three). To share his insights with his top leaders, he and the then company president, Tony Earley, agreed to sponsor an executive retreat called *Leading Breakthrough Results: Walking the Talk of Change.*

Perhaps the most endearing moment of working with John and his executive team came during this retreat when it truly hit John that his organization's transformation required him to change personally (Level Four). As John stated to his team so pointedly, "I have been so focused on us surviving deregulation that I haven't attended to how we could thrive in a deregulated environment. I've been operating in a mindset that with competition there won't be enough success to go around in the future, and, therefore, we need to protect what we now have. But I see that this defensive orientation is only in my mindset. The fact is that we have more than enough talent, resources, and commitment to create a very successful future. Let's pursue growth, not stability."

John's "breakthrough" of insight that his own mindset was limiting his organization catalyzed tremendous growth for his company. In John's words, "Soon after that session, we adopted a growth goal of building new businesses that would generate $100 million in net income in five years. We surpassed our goal, earning $108 million. Quite a success."

John's insight that his mindset was limiting his perspective for the organization triggered significant personal introspection. By "witnessing" the impact of his internal reality on his decisions and actions as CEO, John became very committed to bringing the inner human dimension of transformation into Detroit Edison's change effort. Mammoth transformation ensued at Detroit Edison, with John initiating the way through his own dedicated efforts to become more consciously aware, change his leadership style, and model the transformation he was asking of his organization. He was a model of a leader choosing the difficult but rewarding path of taking a conscious approach.

interior dimension of people has moved deeper toward the fundamental. Now, with transformation, a leader's ability to succeed is in direct proportion to his or her level of awareness. Seeing systems, seeing process, seeing internal and external reality, and seeing consciously have become core requirements of seeing solutions to the challenges and complexities we now face in the twenty-first century world of transformational change.

THE AUTOPILOT APPROACH

The autopilot approach to leading transformation is by far the most common, not because leaders adopt it intentionally, but rather *unknowingly*. In fact, most simply do not think about it. Autopilot is our default way of operating. So unless we intend differently, that is how we function. External events happen, and we react to them in habitual ways, automatically, without conscious awareness.

Leaders operating on autopilot habitually make many of the common mistakes outlined in Chapter One. Because they are not consciously aware of the more subtle people and process dynamics of transformation, they cannot formulate critical change leadership strategies. Inevitably, these unintentional oversights restrict their success and are usually the source of their failures.

When autopilot leaders hear the Level One wake-up call and acknowledge the need to change, they often respond with developmental or transitional change strategies because they are familiar with them and do not yet appreciate the differences among the three types of change or the strategies they each require. They will typically attempt classic problem-solving, change-management, and project-management techniques, including employee skill training and improving communications, each of which has value, but is not sufficient for leading transformation. Autopilot leaders are not very open to hearing wake-up calls for change, especially Levels Three and Four. Most people tend to avoid what makes them uncomfortable, and change can make autopilot leaders very uncomfortable, especially personal change.

Autopilot leaders often have a strong denial mechanism. They can unknowingly fall into the trap of unconsciously resisting or explaining away the signals for change, without even being aware that they are doing so. It is usually the marketplace's heightened threat to their organization's survival that becomes the Level One wake-up call that the leaders finally hear. The signal, by this time, is often cataclysmic and harsh. Because the signals have been ignored for so long, the situation is graver than it would have been with an earlier response. The organization is finally forced to face its transformational reality. Instantly, these leaders can feel out of control, resentful, and burdened by the formidable challenge of change they now face. They feel pressure to proceed and immediately want to get through the disruption as quickly as possible. They will change because they have to, not because they want to. Their primary motivation is to take away the pain and regain their comfort and sense of control, as opposed to seeing the situation as an opportunity to create a better future.

Leaders operating on autopilot attend mostly to the surface symptoms they face, inadequately addressing the underlying root causes. Their superficial efforts may create temporary relief but, ironically, can also increase the pressure and likelihood for a transformational breakdown because they address neither the systemic causes of the upheaval nor provide real change solutions.

In their attempts to gain control, these leaders often initiate any one of numerous "flavor of the month" change programs, hoping that something good will stick. Perhaps the worst case of this autopilot approach is found in the senior executive who returns from the latest management seminar or reads the most recent best-selling management book (even this one) and declares to the organization, "We are going to re-engineer!" (or implement a new EHR, CRM, or ERP information technology, do LEAN, install self-directed teams, or change the culture). In the best of these cases, the leaders search for safe, proven solutions or best practices that have worked for other organizations. For example, many autopilot leaders design their new organization as a reflection of some other organization's solution, hoping that it will work for them, too, but it seldom does. Such blatant reactive responses, not thought out nor customized to the unique needs of the organization, damage leadership credibility in the eyes of employees and catalyze tremendous—warranted—resistance.

Because of their urgent need for certainty, autopilot leaders are prime targets for expert-oriented (content) consulting firms who seek out situations where their solutions with previous clients can be installed as "the answer." With varying degrees of success, they may attempt to implement changes such as LEAN, Six Sigma, business process reengineering, information technology solutions, fast cycle time, autonomous work groups, and flat organizational structures.

Are these solutions guaranteed answers just because they worked elsewhere under different circumstances? Certainly not, although aspects of each solution can be of tremendous value. Autopilot leaders fall prey to attempting these content changes without *consciously* thinking about the fit with their organization's unique circumstances. They often tell the expert consultants, "Just go do it," because again, they want the pain to go away. However, a good solution applied to the wrong problem is still a mistake. A bit of healthy introspection would go a long way to limit the negative effects of such unconscious reactions.

Autopilot leaders often recognize the change required in the business' strategy or organizational design but not in the culture or leadership style—and certainly not in their own behavior or thinking. Although autopilot leaders may believe that personal or behavioral change is needed for the rest of the organization, they often refuse to acknowledge that they have to change themselves. They are already exceedingly uncomfortable because their need for control has been threatened, and exploring their own mindsets, styles, and behavior furthers that discomfort by making them more vulnerable. *The unwillingness of autopilot leaders to see that they need to transform themselves in order to transform their organizations is often the biggest stumbling block to their organization's successful transformation.*

Impact on Employee Morale

The morale of the employees who work for organizations run by autopilot leaders is often very low. We have witnessed numerous situations in which the employees see the need for transformation and want the company to transform, but their leaders either deny the need to change or cannot see the true scope of what needs to change or how to make the change happen. Employees on the front lines directly experience the disruption caused by their leaders' denial or inadequate change plans. Employees can often recognize—long before their leaders—that the leaders' strategies for transformation have little chance for success. Employees feel threatened because they believe that their future rests on the organization's ability to transform successfully, and they do not see success as a likely outcome. Often, the highest achievers are the most disenfranchised because success is more important to them, and they do not feel empowered to make it happen.

Autopilot leaders often have a command-and-control leadership style and do not see how this negatively impacts their employees and culture. Rather than empower and engage, their default need is to control people and the change process. This stifles creativity and builds resistance in stakeholders. Autopilot leaders seldom realize that they are generating this resistance through their change leadership approach and style.

Another reason for low employee morale is that their leaders often toss numerous uncoordinated and unintegrated change efforts at the organization with no context given for why they are needed or a way to integrate them into something that has impact. Employees feel like they are spinning their wheels. They see gaps and overlaps between these change initiatives and resent the poor planning and duplication of effort they require.

Perhaps the biggest reason for low morale is the capacity issues that autopilot leaders exacerbate when they add change-related work to employees' already full plates. Instead of consciously addressing what needs to be reprioritized, stopped, or modified to create capacity for change, these leaders unconsciously assume employees can "do it all." Daryl R. Conner describes this phenomenon well: "When change continues to be poured into a saturated sponge, the consequences are threefold: (a) morale deteriorates; (b) the initiatives that are attempted result in only short-term, superficial application of the intended goals; and (c) people stop listening to the leaders, who continue to announce changes that never fully materialize" (Conner, 1998, p. 15).

THE CONSCIOUS APPROACH

First and foremost, conscious change leaders pursue greater self-awareness. They may go to personal development seminars, read books on psychology, meditate, use stress reduction techniques, seek 360-degree feedback on the impact of their leadership style, and perform a host of other intentional activities to increase their awareness and management of their mindset and style.

Conscious change leaders are considerate of the internal states of others: what they think, how they feel, their values, desires, cares, and motivations. Similarly, they nurture their organization's culture and how to evolve it to unleash the full potential of their people. They consider how change strategies, levels of stakeholder engagement, methods and frequency of communication, training plans, content decisions, and everything else in a change effort will impact or be impacted by people's mindsets and the organization's culture. They give full attention to the inner dimensions, just as they do to the external dynamics.

Conscious change leaders are introspective. They reflect on things, and they develop the ability to hear their thinking in their own heads. Over time, they discover the patterns in their thinking and come to see and understand the deep-seated beliefs they hold about themselves, people, life, organizations, and change that govern their choices and outcomes. This enables them to witness the normally unconscious mechanism of forming assumptions in their minds and projecting them onto reality as if they were true. By witnessing this autopilot functioning, they are less apt to become trapped by false assumptions, which make them more capable of making better decisions and forming effective strategies.

Conscious change leaders realize that there are perspectives and truths beyond what their mindsets allow them to see. They have biases, beliefs, and assumptions about things, but they do not hold them as ultimate truths. They pause and take a deeper, alternative look, and they are open to other interpretations. They know their beliefs and assumptions may cause them to misinterpret things or miss vital information. Consequently, they ask a critical question, "Am I seeing things this way because that is how they are, or am I seeing things this way because that is how I interpret that they are." This opens possibilities for exploration and discovery that leaders operating on autopilot do not have. Autopilot leaders simply believe what their minds say is true or right, without questioning it.

Conscious change leaders often possess greater emotional intelligence. They are often more in touch with their feelings and have more understanding of what triggers them. This gives them insight into how others feel and builds empathy to consider people's feelings in how they lead. This, of course, makes them more effective with people and better able to design change strategies that minimize resistance in stakeholders. It also makes conscious change leaders far more competent in leading culture change.

Conscious change leaders are better at modeling desired behaviors. Developing their inner witness increases their ability to notice and stop their automatic habitual reactions to situations when they call for new transformational behaviors or strategies. Their greater self-awareness makes them more effective at altering their behavior as needed to model their organization's desired culture.

Conscious change leaders are better learners. They seek new methods and approaches, and they take feedback well. They are flexible and willing to course-correct and adjust both behaviors and strategies as needed. While the learning orientation of conscious leaders often leads them to breakthroughs, the denial mechanism of autopilot leaders often causes breakdowns. Conscious leaders seek to get it right; autopilot leaders think they are right.

Conscious change leaders are better at innovation. They are willing and able to think creatively and consciously design alternative strategies to respond to dynamic challenges of transformation. As new information emerges, they can see it for what it is, interpret it accurately, and create innovative solutions as needed. Conscious change leaders thrive in dynamic environments.

Our twenty-first century marketplace, with all its content complexities, speed of innovation, and economic challenges, is beckoning. The people and process challenges of transformation require our change leaders to increase their conscious awareness so they can see the solutions. To paraphrase Einstein's famous quote, we cannot solve today's problems with yesterday's worldviews. We must evolve ourselves and our level of awareness to see how best to evolve our world. And that is fundamentally why a conscious approach is so vital. (See Exhibit 4.1.)

SUPPORTING OTHERS TO CONSCIOUS CHANGE LEADERSHIP

The call to conscious change leadership is essentially a call to turn inward, introspect, and put your *attention* on your inner awareness and mindset. It is a choice to use the opportunity of leading transformation to continually grow and develop your innermost being, to put your "being first."

At this juncture, we assume and hope that you are making this choice to lead change consciously. If this is new to you, welcome to the world of conscious change leadership!

This choice places you on a personal development path that will generate tremendous insights and possibilities for achievement and fulfillment. It is very exciting, rewarding, and freeing in many ways. We know that you will want to share

Exhibit 4.1. Change Leadership Development Assessment

WORKSHEET

Where Are You in Your Change Leadership Development?

It is difficult to determine where we are in our personal development because the measurement is rather complex. All the different aspects of our development—emotional, cognitive, moral, interpersonal, spiritual, and so on—progress at different paces. Like most human beings, you are likely well developed in some areas and less developed in others.

From a change leadership perspective, however, there are four simple and practical measures to determine the personal foundation you have for change leadership capability. These include how you see systems, process, and internal and external dynamics, and how often you operate with conscious awareness.

SELF-ASSESSMENT

SEEING SYSTEMS

1. When confronted with a major challenge, do you automatically look for the solution inside the area in which the challenge is occurring, or do you consciously look for how the larger system or dynamics outside the immediate area are influencing the problem? To what degree do you automatically look to the larger system dynamics?

   Never   Seldom   Sometimes   Usually   Always

SEEING PROCESS

1. When planning major change events or interventions, do you automatically focus on the near-term needs, or do you consciously take into account how the past influences the present possibility, and how your desired future requires certain present action? To what degree do you think across time?

   Never   Seldom   Sometimes   Usually   Always

SEEING INTERNAL/EXTERNAL

1. When dealing with an external challenge or problem, to what degree do you consciously address how your mindset and others' mindsets and feelings and the organization's culture influence the situation and solution?

   Never   Seldom   Sometimes   Usually   Always

(continued)

it and assist others to expand their conscious awareness as well. But be careful in your initial exuberance about applying your insights about operating consciously to anyone other than yourself. People are sensitive about their inner worlds and will usually initially resist when others attempt to get in there with them. Be careful not to label, judge, or make others wrong if they are operating on autopilot. Do not try to change them or coerce them into operating differently; for now, simply lead from your new perspective and apply what you are learning in this book to yourself.

Our own modeling is the most powerful way to influence others. The more we own the impacts of our own behaviors, the more others take notice of theirs. As we overtly name our own assumptions and beliefs, others begin to see their own. We can best share the benefits of leading change consciously by modeling what that looks like to others.

In our own consulting practice, our bias is to provide personal development training that includes the "conscious approach" discussion presented in this chapter as part of all of our transformational change interventions. As you can imagine, the positive outcomes of this level of development set the foundation for truly breakthrough results for our clients.

But before you attempt this yourself, go get training in human dynamics and how to facilitate personal development. Rely on experts until you do this. Many are available but be sure they have facilitated this level of personal inner work in organizational settings. Personal growth conducted in an organization is very different from personal growth conducted in public seminars.

Welcome again to the world of conscious change leadership. We trust you will enjoy this journey, feel challenged by it, and appreciate the profound personal and professional rewards it will deliver.

SUMMARY

In this chapter, we introduced the conscious approach to leading transformation and contrasted it with the more common autopilot approach. We saw how two core mental functions, conscious awareness and autopilot, are the sources of these two approaches. We revealed how developing conscious awareness will increase a change leader's ability to "witness" what is occurring in transformation, especially key people and process dynamics. We discussed four levels of wake-up calls for conscious change leadership, suggesting that change leaders must hear the Level Four call to transform themselves, which initiates the choice to operate consciously. We also addressed the differences in the behaviors of autopilot and conscious change leaders, showing key benefits of leaders taking a conscious approach. We provided a simple assessment to identify the personal foundation you possess for successful change leadership and an opportunity for you to choose the approach to change leadership you will take going forward. We ended the chapter with a simple caution about how you engage others in this approach.

From the deeply internal perspective of this chapter, we now turn back to the external domain. In the next chapter, we will investigate how treating change as a strategic discipline in the organization leads to Level Five Success—increasing change capability.

ENDNOTES

1. Senge, P., Scharmer C., Jaworski, J., and Flowers, B. *Presence: An Exploration of Profound Change in People, Organizations and Society.* Broadway Business, 2005.
2. Wilber, K. *Integral Psychology: Consciousness, Spirit, Psychology, Therapy.* Boston, MA: Shambala, 2000.

3. Variations of this model have been widely used in organization development and human resource circles for years. Debate exists about the originator, but the most cited is Noel Birch of Gordon Training International in the 1970s.
4. Csikszentmihalyi, M. *Flow: The Psychology of Optimal Experience.* New York: Harper & Row, 1990.

Building Organizational Change Capability

Your success in life isn't based on your ability to simply change. It is based on your ability to change faster than your competition, customers and business.

—Mark Sanborn

By taking a more thoughtful and disciplined approach to change, conscious change leaders naturally begin to address how they can improve their organization's change capability. Their motivation is obvious: "If we can pro-actively increase our results in this change effort using these approaches, why don't we do so for all our changes for the years to come?" They begin to real-ize that strong change capability is vital to their organizations' near-term and long-term success, and they start to look for ways to build that capability. In this chapter, we will explore how approaching change as a strategic discipline is key to building your organization's change capability. This means not only building your leaders' and internal consultants' knowledge and skills but also the organizational systems and infrastructure that will enable change to be led more effectively and consistently.

CHANGE CAPABILITY: A KEY TWENTY-FIRST CENTURY COMPETITIVE ADVANTAGE

Organizations that excel at change have a competitive advantage. They capture market opportunities; significantly improve their operations; innovate, merge, downsize, rebrand, grow, restructure, acquire, and implement new products, services, and technologies; improve their supply chain; and perform numerous other critical activities better than their competitors who struggle with change.

Change capability establishes the core competency of improving just about every aspect of business performance. Conscious change leaders understand this and recognize the importance of building their organizations' change capabilities.

Change capability is the ability of an organization to plan, design, and implement all types of change efficiently with committed stakeholders, causing minimal negative impacts on people and operations, so that desired business and cultural results from change are consistently achieved and integrated seamlessly into operations to deliver maximum ROI.

Figure 5.1 shows how building change capability positively impacts your organization. In the diagram, A Work denotes your core business activities, that is, everything your organization does to provide value to customers. B Work is all of

Figure 5.1. The Impact of Change Capability

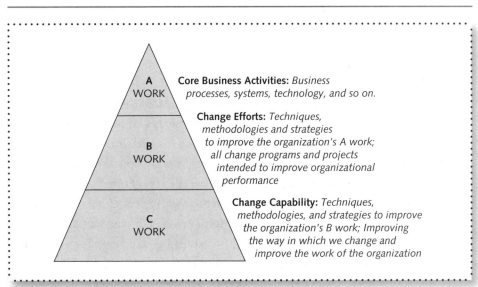

the change efforts you put into improving A Work, making you or your organization the best it can be. C Work is improving your ability to do B Work, in other words, improving your ability to improve, to change. C Work is consciously building change capability so you continually improve the results you get from change. Remember the statistic of the 60–70 percent failure rate from change? C Work stops the failure and delivers change results.

Building change capability requires commitment, resources, and time. It starts with increasing executive, management, and employee change knowledge and skills. Executives must learn how to sponsor change effectively. Change process leaders and change team members must develop solid competence in planning, designing, and implementing change. Managers must learn how to facilitate change in their operational areas, including how to engage employees to build commitment and ownership of the changes. Workers must learn how to adapt to change, make the changes relevant to them, and contribute to successful outcomes.

This requires a serious commitment to training and development, including real-time change project application that goes beyond the typical classroom. Action learning and ongoing feedback are critical. Communities of practice are vital for coaching, mentoring, and sharing best practices. All of this development will improve your track record in leading change, but a most important action is positioning change as a strategic discipline in your organization.

CHANGE: THE NEW STRATEGIC DISCIPLINE

Virtually all key functions in organizations—strategy, finance, marketing, sales, human resources, and information technology—are set up as strategic disciplines to ensure they function consistently at the highest levels possible. These disciplines, and the management protocols that go with them, are crucial to these business functions performing effectively. In today's organizations, change is as mission-critical as these other key functions and must be embraced as such. Otherwise, the approaches to building change capability will be superficial, temporary, and piecemeal, and not produce the sponsorship, resources, or operational excellence required.

We have identified five key strategies so far to creating change as a strategic discipline: (1) identifying and managing an enterprise change agenda; (2) having one common change *process* methodology; (3) establishing a change infrastructures; (4) building a strategic change center of excellence for all change practitioners; and (5) creating a strategic change office. We will describe each in order, although sequence is not implied here. You will quickly see that they fit together as an integrated approach, where the fifth strategy, the strategic change office, runs all of them. Read each description first for understanding, and then consider the possibility for creating each in your organization. You may find that your leaders have an appetite for one or more of the disciplines; build from there after value is demonstrated. Creating and mastering all of these strategies can easily be a three- to five-year undertaking. (See premium content: Building Change Capability: Leading Change as a Strategic Discipline; www.pfeiffer.com/go/anderson.)

As we explore each strategy, imagine your organization bringing to change a similar level of resources, organization, and strategic attention that it currently gives to finance, IT, and HR. What greater results would your organization be producing from change with this level of executive commitment, practice, and capability in place?

1. Enterprise Change Agenda

An enterprise change agenda names the most important change initiatives required to execute your organization's business strategy. Its purpose is to capture and integrate the major changes underway or planned in your organization, ensuring their strategic relevance to business success. It may or may not include less significant changes underway or planned, depending on your capacity to monitor them. Its intent is to focus on mission-critical changes for the enterprise as a whole and its primary businesses.

You may be familiar with project portfolio management—a method for collectively managing a group of current or proposed projects. While similar in concept, the enterprise change agenda is owned by the senior executives and designed to address the organization's strategic changes. Its focus remains high-level—appropriate to executive oversight. The specifics of project objectives, timelines, resource requirements, risks, and interdependencies are handled by a strategic change office (if you create one), project change leadership teams, and other mechanisms within your organization's change infrastructure, described later in this chapter. If you have a project portfolio office that serves the executives, the enterprise change agenda can be tailored as an extension of it.

Consciously establishing an enterprise change agenda counteracts the pervasive chaos, "project of the month," and costly capacity issues that leaders inadvertently create by initiating untold numbers of changes and pet projects. The agenda ensures that adequate attention is given to prioritizing projects, aligning them to what is needed to implement business strategy, ensuring capacity and adequate resources to succeed, and minimizing the negative impacts on operations and the people who have to implement the changes while doing their "day jobs." Establishing an enterprise change agenda ensures that change does not get out of control in your organization and enables greater strategic oversight and accountability for priority changes. It also helps the leaders weave a cohesive story to communicate to stakeholders and the workforce about where all of the change activity is leading and what it needs to produce.

The agenda assists your organization and executives to ensure five critical success requirements:

1. **The change efforts happening are the right ones to fulfill your business strategy.**

    Identifying all efforts enables you to stand back and assess priorities against both your business strategy and your resources.

2. **The efforts are prioritized, organized, assigned, and paced in the optimal way.**

    Each change effort is a piece of your organization's overall change strategy. Looking objectively at the whole picture reveals whether the picture is realistic, complete, and possible within a given timeframe. It also allows you to see where there may be conflicts, overlaps, interdependencies, or opportunities for integration and coordination.

3. **The organization has the capacity to actually carry out—and succeed in— these changes.**

    Defining the entire change agenda is the only way to obtain realistic data on capacity, including workload, stamina, capability, and the best use of your in-house change resources.

4. **You are effectively managing your external consultants to help with the range of change efforts underway.**

    The agenda enables an enterprise look at the use of these resources, and supports leveraging them, coordinating them, and ensuring you have all of your needs covered to produce your outcomes in the most cost-effective and timely ways without duplication, loss of strategic oversight, or excessive expenditures.

5. **Your change efforts are aligned to support your desired culture.**

    Most if not all change initiatives on your agenda will have an impact on the organization's culture and be affected by leadership style and competency. Coordinated, overt attention to changing culture and realigning leadership style in *each* effort is essential to producing and sustaining overall culture change and collective tangible results from these critical efforts.

The organization's change agenda is built by identifying change initiatives currently underway or planned in four categories, from the most strategic to operational:

▶ Strategic importance to business success
▶ Enterprise-wide impact
▶ Functional or business-line specific
▶ Operational requirement

You identify the change efforts within each category, cluster them to assist with prioritization, review your available resources and contracted services, and ascertain if you have adequate capacity for the change efforts within each level.

The creation of the enterprise change agenda typically follows on the heels of the organization's strategic planning process and precedes your operations planning cycle. Because new change efforts may arise in any of the categories throughout the year, you must revisit the agenda periodically to ensure that it is still relevant and accurate. Having one executive oversee the agenda and coordinate its use and accuracy throughout the year is the best way to ensure it supports economies of scale and minimal negative impact on the organization. Organizations that have large autonomous business units have each business create and monitor its own change agenda, aligned with enterprise requirements. This makes reporting on each business unit's annual change priorities, progress, and resource usage very easy. These issues can and should be added to your scorecard.

The agenda is also the basis for leaders deciding how to allocate the organization's in-house change-related resources to the highest priority efforts. These resources and services might include project management, organization development, change management, LEAN management, training and development, quality improvement, and so on. They also include the change leaders and team members you take from operations. The use of resources and oversight of the enterprise change agenda can be handled by creating a strategic change office, described later in this chapter.

In most organizations, the decision to establish the discipline of an enterprise change agenda belongs to the senior executive team. Ideally, you would recognize its value before its absence overwhelms the organization. Consider the following Case-In-Point.

Exhibit 5.1 provides an assessment to identify the need you have for establishing an enterprise change agenda and the degree of benefit it will provide you. It asks you to identify the number of major initiatives you have going on, which indicates your basic need for this strategy. It then asks you to assess your organization against

---

CASE-IN-POINT

We worked with a federal government agency that was undergoing a major transformation. We began our work with an Executive Change Lab, a one-and-a-half day session where the senior leaders were briefed on the requirements of leading transformation and determined their risk of failure. One of the outcomes of the session was a mapping of their existing change efforts. Three things became clear as a result of this exercise. First, they had over 40 initiatives on their "priority" list, which had been honed down from 100. Secondly, many of these efforts were good ideas, but not driven by the immediate needs of the agency's transformation or its mandate. Thirdly, they had nowhere near the capacity to address these efforts successfully and maintain their operational standards.

The executives created an enterprise change agenda of seven top transformational priorities and focused their attention on the success of these. They were able to staff, train, and support these efforts to be successful. In the three years since this work, their change agenda has enabled them to review and adjust each year as new priorities have surfaced and change efforts were completed. Their success catalyzed them to initiate a formal process for adding to or reducing their enterprise agenda, resourcing the initiatives, and monitoring progress and ongoing capacity. This has had huge positive impact on their agency in terms of fulfilling their mandate of achieving citizen outcomes, employee engagement, and morale. More results have been produced with better efficiency and use of resources. They have also created a number of the change infrastructures we discuss in this chapter, all to their organization's change leadership benefit.

Exhibit 5.1. Enterprise Change Agenda Needs Assessment

WORKSHEET

How many major* change efforts are underway in your organization or planned to begin within six months? _____ *(*Major* refers to scope, complexity, impact, necessity, scale, and demand for significant resources and capacity.)

Consider the implications of having the number of major change efforts you have:

< 5: no need for an enterprise change agenda

5 to 10: slight need

11 to 15: moderate need

16 to 20: high need

Over 20: critical need

Rate the following statements using a scale of 1 -5, where 1 = Strongly Disagree and 5 = Strongly Agree.

_____ 1. We effectively use mechanisms to identify and track all of the significant change efforts in our organization.

_____ 2. We effectively use a process to ensure that we have the right change efforts to deliver our business strategy.

_____ 3. All changes currently underway are necessary to executing our business's strategic direction.

_____ 4. Our change initiatives are sponsored and resourced according to their priority.

_____ 5. We effectively use a mechanism to identify and assess our organization's capacity to succeed with all our changes while continuing to operate effectively.

_____ 6. We have the capacity to undertake—and succeed in—the key changes currently underway without major negative impacts on people and operations.

_____ 7. Our operational plans reflect the requirements and demands these changes have for the organization.

_____ 8. We have and effectively use a formal protocol for adding/dropping/ modifying/reprioritizing initiatives on our agenda as priorities shift.

_____ 9. We have an effective process to ensure that high priority changes get resourced ahead of low priority ones.

_____ 10. We are effective at managing resource expenditures to ensure best and highest use across the organization.

_____ 11. We are effective at managing our in-house change-support expertise and services to ensure best and highest use across the organization.

(continued)

Exhibit 5.1. **Enterprise Change Agenda Needs Assessment**

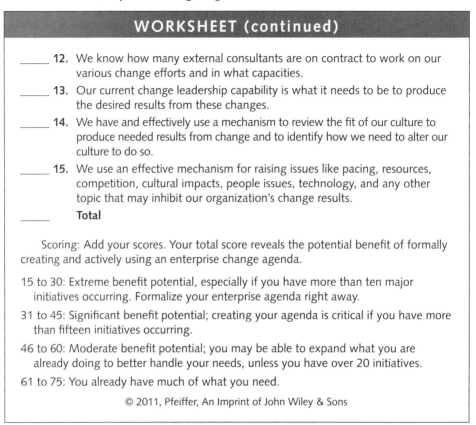

	WORKSHEET (continued)

_____ **12.** We know how many external consultants are on contract to work on our various change efforts and in what capacities.

_____ **13.** Our current change leadership capability is what it needs to be to produce the desired results from these changes.

_____ **14.** We have and effectively use a mechanism to review the fit of our culture to produce needed results from change and to identify how we need to alter our culture to do so.

_____ **15.** We use an effective mechanism for raising issues like pacing, resources, competition, cultural impacts, people issues, technology, and any other topic that may inhibit our organization's change results.

_____ **Total**

Scoring: Add your scores. Your total score reveals the potential benefit of formally creating and actively using an enterprise change agenda.

15 to 30: Extreme benefit potential, especially if you have more than ten major initiatives occurring. Formalize your enterprise agenda right away.

31 to 45: Significant benefit potential; creating your agenda is critical if you have more than fifteen initiatives occurring.

46 to 60: Moderate benefit potential; you may be able to expand what you are already doing to better handle your needs, unless you have over 20 initiatives.

61 to 75: You already have much of what you need.

© 2011, Pfeiffer, An Imprint of John Wiley & Sons

fifteen criteria that describe the benefits an enterprise agenda can produce. These criteria reflect the five success requirements of having an agenda described earlier. Your data—the amount of change you have occurring and the potential benefits you are currently realizing or not—will determine how important having an enterprise agenda would be to your organization right now.

Engage your executives in this exercise and discussion. First, have them complete it individually; then compile the numbers, average them, and review your results collectively to determine the value of establishing and working an enterprise change agenda.

2. Common Change Process Methodology

We are not surprised when we do change audits for clients and discover that they have multiple change methodologies being used across their organization. Often, when new leaders come into an organization, they bring their familiar approaches with them. Some models address start-up, some people issues, some just implementation, some engagement, and some communications. All are pieces of the overall picture that a change process methodology needs to provide. Intentional or not, these various change models, concepts, and terms end up competing and conflicting, confusing both employees and change leaders who work on multiple efforts, making it very difficult to coordinate across initiatives and measure progress in common terms.

We must also note the organizations that have no distinct approach to change at all. With each change effort, they reinvent their process, waste enormous effort, often create greater confusion, and lose all opportunity to learn from and expedite their changes. The absence of a shared process model is costly.

A common change process methodology overcomes these challenges and produces many positive outcomes that you cannot achieve with multiple approaches to change, such as the following:

- Increasing change capability, through a common language, skill set, process roadmap, and tool kit
- Sharing best practices across initiatives because of shared approaches
- Sharing work products across change teams to increase speed; for example, multiple initiatives borrowing from a standard template for writing their cases for change, designing their change solutions, or creating their implementation master plans
- Moving people to different change teams with rapid start-up and little disruption
- Collaborating effectively across functional areas on enterprise-wide initiatives
- Managing capacity
- Integrating initiatives to minimize overlaps and gaps and reducing impact on the organization
- Communicating effectively to stakeholders about all key change efforts
- Monitoring progress of different initiatives
- Using a phase gate approach to decision making and resourcing

Using a common change methodology across your organization is critical to building change capability. We will discuss change process methodologies more extensively in Chapter Eight. Our companion book, *The Change Leader's Roadmap*, describes Being First's change process methodology in great detail. You can also get more information at www.changeleadersroadmap.com.

3. Change Infrastructure

Change infrastructures are standard structures and practices for designing, implementing, and monitoring your organization's change efforts. They underlie the work, making it clear, consistent, and manageable. All strategic functions in your organization have such infrastructures. Think about your IT, finance, marketing, or HR functions. They all have standard practices, methods, templates, and ways of ensuring high-level performance and outcomes. Those methods and practices are structured, overt, accessible, understood, and used. Each of the professionals in those functions are trained and held accountable for applying those standard practices to their areas of responsibility. Over time, those "infrastructures" are refined and developed to produce best practices to ensure the highest results. This is all possible because the methods and practices are common to everyone engaged in that function.

The purpose of developing change infrastructures is identical to these other strategic disciplines: to support your organization to deliver results from change by establishing and using overt, commonly used structures and practices that optimize change execution, accelerate time-to-results, and build capacity. Once established, these infrastructures become the baseline for people to increase their change leadership effectiveness. They provide a foundation for building your organization's change capability.

Change infrastructures include standard roles, templates, and methods for governing your change initiatives, as well as common practices for setting up, orchestrating, and overseeing their effectiveness. When you establish a common change process methodology, it will become your most significant change infrastructure. For example, in our change methodology—The Change Leader's Roadmap—each task can become a change infrastructure because it provides guidance on best practices for executing that task. Our clients use these to standardize and optimize how their change leaders and consultants then apply them. Over time, these become best change practices for their entire organization. Standard change tasks are included in the following sample list of change infrastructures:

SAMPLE CHANGE INFRASTRUCTURE ELEMENTS

▶ Standard practices for creating your case for change

▶ Standard templates for building change strategy

- Standard change governance, including roles, team charters, and decision making

- Standard conditions for success and ways of measuring success

- Standards for change communication plans and stakeholder engagement strategies

- Expectations and methods for rapid course correction

- Expectations and requirements for multiple project integration ("air traffic control")

- Change leadership competencies: skills, knowledge, behaviors, and mindsets

- Roster of best practices and change tools for all key tasks in your common change process methodology

- Universal support mechanisms for communications, feedback, and information management, such as intranet sites, project software, and communication protocols

Make key change infrastructures known and available to anyone involved in leading change in your organization. However, beware of the fear of mandated standards. Leaders and change consultants can easily balk at the idea of standard approaches unless you demonstrate the wisdom in using them. Make the enterprise benefits overt, and engage users in helping develop and refine your infrastructures. Ultimately, your change leaders and consultants should "own" these infrastructures and be held accountable for making them "best-in-class."

4. Strategic Change Center of Excellence

Many organizations have internal change consultants. These professionals are found in different departments in different organizations, including organization development, organization effectiveness, change management, quality, process improvement, LEAN and Six Sigma, IT, HR, and project management. Each adds its own value in its own way, depending on the discipline.

The most common scenario we see in organizations is that leaders call on these services when they happen to see a need, often too late in the process to ensure clear foresight or prevent predictable people or process problems. Many leaders, operating on autopilot, simply do not see the need very often, and when they do, miss significant opportunities for how best to apply these talents. Most of the existing services offer a piece of what is needed, but challenges arise because no one is looking after all of what is needed. To make matters worse, these resources often compete among themselves to be engaged on major change efforts. The end result is that the organization does not get its full value from these resources.

Consider: Who has their eye on the organization's strategic change needs? Who keeps conscious, proactive attention to ensuring that the organization sets up its mission-critical change efforts for success from the very beginning? Who oversees that the level of change expertise needed is being developed and used in the best way? Who ensures that there is effective collaboration among these various change resources for the good of the change efforts and the entire enterprise? Someone must, or breakthrough results can never occur.

These issues and the complexity, cost, and potential benefit of enterprise transformation have generated a need for a *Strategic Change Center of Excellence*. This Center of Excellence is comprised of the organization's major change support resources, many of which were listed previously. Likely, your organization has all of this consulting expertise in place, at its headquarters and in its business lines. The Center is a way of organizing, networking, and training them for the best and highest use. It need not house all of these resources; rather, it supports them, accesses them, and develops them. The Center's charge is to create a "new breed" of change consultant, devoted to the overall success of the business, no matter what their expertise or where they live in the businesses.

The Center can play several value-added roles:

▶ Provide the central pool of the most highly skilled consulting resources for use on major change efforts.

▶ Determine complementarities and ensure consistency among all of the change resources and their approaches, thereby providing the best and most aligned guidance on change.

▶ Provide temporary or "loaned" resources where the organization most needs them.

▶ Be a vehicle for developing the highest level of change leadership and consulting that the organization needs to succeed.

▶ Identify, build, teach, and use the organization's change process methodology and change infrastructures on major change efforts.

- Identify, build, and distribute best change practices.
- Pilot new change practices before rollout.
- Provide "case management" learning clinics and showcases for others (consultants and leaders) during any phase of change.
- Help address cross-boundary/cross-business integration needs relevant to producing the highest results from change.
- Help match resources to demand and be a voice for change capacity reality checks.
- Surface critical risk factors, issues, and needs for course correction from all levels of the organization engaged in major changes.
- Advocate for realistic conditions for success on how changes are set up and led.
- Input to and look after changes in culture and leadership style affecting key change efforts' success, including coaching executives as they lead their change efforts.

The Center's consultants advise and support the executives in charge of the enterprise change agenda and can be a central resource within the strategic change office (SCO, described later), strategic planning, or HR. Their function is to provide the best resources and services on major change efforts—for start-up, change strategy development, planning, design, implementation, and consultation on the multiple project integration requirements among all priority initiatives. They ensure effective stakeholder engagement and change communications. They also input to and facilitate essential course corrections to the change agenda and its priorities, and work toward creating full organizational alignment in the design and execution of all change efforts in support of the business strategy.

These consultants also provide high-level change education and coaching for executives, change sponsors, and leaders. A critical role they can play is to help identify the organization's past practices and patterns that inhibit its ability to succeed in change. They can use change history audits to surface this data and then work with key executives to determine how to prevent these negative practices and embed better ways to oversee change.

The Center can be structured and run in a number of ways. It is a convener, organizer, developer, and orchestrator. It can host periodic face-to-face meetings and trainings, work virtually, provide Web-based education and support, and use an interactive intranet site for meeting, learning, project or issue tracking, logistics, and communications. When working on key change initiatives, Center consultants will partner with business line or headquarter change sponsors to provide the best change consulting from the very beginning of the effort, which is the heart of strategic change consulting.

The Center's role, in whole or in part, is a necessary investment in ensuring that your organization can actually achieve results and create the value it needs from its most important change efforts over the long term. Building strategic change consulting expertise within such a Strategic Change Center of Excellence is the next edge of organization development and change management. It expands the role and positioning of these services to focus on the organization's most important changes, using and teaching the strategic disciplines for change the organization chooses to create. The Center is one of the first steps that you should consider in creating change as a strategic discipline because it builds on your current expertise and successes in leading change and takes them to new levels—levels required for breakthrough results. Because the Center works as a network and does not require changes in organization structure, it might be the best place to begin. (See premium content: Upgrade Your Organization Development and Project Management Staff to Strategic Change Consultants; www.pfeiffer.com/go/anderson.)

5. The Strategic Change Office (SCO)

Approaching change as a strategic discipline to build superior change capability all comes together in establishing a strategic change office. This is a pioneering concept that we have yet to see in full application. A few of our clients are experimenting with aspects of this function. Others are becoming more and more interested in it and seeing its potential value. We believe establishing an SCO represents the current cutting edge of change disciplines—a wave of the future that will become more common over the next decade. We introduce it here because it is a key strategic discipline for ensuring results from change, managing your enterprise change agenda, building superior change capability, and sponsoring your Strategic Change Center of Excellence. As you read about this function, imagine having an SCO in your organization and its impact on change results, change leadership, and change capability.

The SCO is a senior executive function that oversees the success of change across the entire enterprise. It is led by the Chief Change Officer (CCO), who sits on the executive team. This enables the SCO to be positioned to ensure that major change initiatives are the right ones to drive the business strategy, advocating for what is needed to maximize results on these mission-critical initiatives, and ensuring strong change capability throughout the organization.

The SCO is the primary vehicle for making change a strategic discipline in your organization. It is responsible for building and monitoring your organization's enterprise change agenda, raising the priority level of the oversight and support of change from somewhere down in the organization—usually in a Program Management Office—up to the "C" Suite. It also promotes consistent and rightful use of your change process methodology and change infrastructures, housing your Strategic Change Center of Excellence, which enables it to access the best resources, services, and methods for every phase of change.

The SCO does not "own" all of the priority change initiatives; it creates the conditions for them to be optimally successful. The SCO leader and consultants partner with the executive sponsors of key initiatives to support those leaders to accurately scope and launch their change efforts successfully. The executives still own the decisions about what needs to change to implement their business priorities and the strategic decisions about how they are run. But instead of simply naming change projects and handing them off to their line organizations, the executives first engage with the SCO.

SCO consultants work closely with each executive sponsor to create a change strategy that clarifies change governance, potential integration with other initiatives, scope, pace, and a true picture of the resources and time required for the change effort to deliver on its promise. The SCO also helps assess the impact of the change on current operations and people, so other executives can know early on what impacts they will have to deal with and when. The SCO then secures professional change support from the Strategic Change Center of Excellence, the organization's content experts, and/or external resources to define and mobilize the effort according to its priority, desired outcomes, resourcing, and requirements.

The SCO enables change leaders and project team members to have far greater access to the executive suite when critical issues emerge. Being knowledgeable about all the large change efforts in the organization, the SCO can more easily get the right senior leaders to engage in key strategic change issues, such as the impacts of taking on any new change, how it will or will not tax capacity and resources, what priority and level of urgency it has, what organizational activities can be stopped or modified to address capacity constraints, issues with external consultants, and what will be required of the executives collectively to ensure results. The SCO has the authority to get the executives' attention when any changes—or the organization's capacity to deliver on them—are at risk. With this intelligence, the executives have far more capability to ensure the effective implementation of their own individual initiatives, enterprise-wide efforts, and, more importantly, the organization's collective business strategy.

Recall that successful change leadership requires competent attention to the three key areas of content, people, and process. Typically, executives focus on content and delegate the people and process issues to others. The SCO ensures that the change leadership teams of the major initiatives build change strategies that can deliver the best *content* solutions, and simultaneously engage *people* in the change process in such a way that they develop commitment, ownership, and skill in implementing the desired state effectively. The SCO is not in charge of any content decisions but influences the *change process* so it generates the best content solution and proactively handles the people and cultural dynamics to deliver on it. It contains the organization's highest change process expertise, including how to deal with all of the people requirements from the beginning of the effort. This is key to the SCO providing its strategic value as a standard-setter and an advisor to executive change sponsors. The SCO advocates for the importance of people and process, and places both on par with content, which is what makes establishing an SCO so critical to your organization's success with change.

The SCO is also in charge of ensuring that the organization has the change capability that it needs to succeed at long-term change. It partners with your training functions—in particular with your corporate university, executive, and management development groups—to ensure the right change training and development occurs at all levels of your organization, for all of the groups who have a role in making change successful.

FUNCTIONS AND BENEFITS OF THE SCO

1. **The SCO can increase speed and lower the cost of change.** Every executive wants change to happen faster, with less financial and human cost. Establishing the SCO supports those results. The SCO is tasked to ensure that each new change fits within your enterprise change agenda. It reduces duplication of effort; ensures that the outputs from one project flow seamlessly as timely inputs to others; ensures effective integration and pacing across projects; and stops competition and clashes among them. It increases people's understanding of the big picture of change and how all change efforts work collectively to implement the organization's business strategy, thus lowering resistance and

building commitment in stakeholders. This alignment speeds up change by removing so many classic barriers to implementation.

2. **Ensures major change efforts are directly linked to business strategy.** Ultimately, all major change is strategy execution; the primary reason you do change is to enable implementation of your organization's strategy and goals. With the SCO leader at the executive table co-creating the business strategy and overseeing your Enterprise Change Agenda, this link is ensured. Each of the other executives, including the other "chief officers," relies on the oversight of the SCO and the competency of the Strategic Change Center of Excellence to support them to successfully launch and implement their major changes. The SCO helps ensure the success of *their* changes to achieve the organization's collective business strategies and goals.

3. **Ensures the Enterprise Change Agenda is appropriate, realistic, and vital to identifying and driving the right strategic changes.** As described previously, the SCO plays the oversight role for ensuring that the organization has the right change efforts in place to be successful and has the capacity and resources to succeed in them.

4. **Ensures your organization has the capacity to succeed in its agenda's change efforts.** Far too often, the executive team initiates major change efforts without assessing whether the organization has the workload capacity to succeed at the changes without negatively impacting people or operations. This is especially true if you do not have an Enterprise Change Agenda. Always remember this: All internal resources for change are borrowed from operations, so there is always some level of impact on operations. How much impact can you tolerate? How much impact will your changes have? With the SCO, the "get real" conversations about capacity can happen among the executives before they initiate major changes, not later when those efforts are spiraling out of control, operational goals are not being met, or your best talent is burning out.

5. **Ensures executive accountability for proactively leading change efforts until full ROI is achieved.** A major source of failed change is change sponsors not seeing changes through. They delegate responsibility and go on to new things before the changes have been fully absorbed into operations and are delivering their full ROI. Sometimes leaders reduce resources too early; other times, they quit championing, monitoring, and holding people accountable for an effort's full success. The SCO, linked to the executive team, minimizes

these shortcomings. The SCO does not run the change efforts; it oversees their effectiveness and integration, ensuring their optimal results.

6. **Ensures that top change efforts get priority selection of staff and resources.** With executives fully informed about the purpose and role of all major change efforts in executing strategy and achieving key goals, the resource allocation conversation becomes much more pragmatic and hard-hitting. With the SCO facilitating, they can talk through the trade-offs around staffing and resourcing to ensure each effort gets its proper due. They can take a stand against "pet projects" that bleed off resources and capacity needed for higher priorities.

   Often, executives commit to a significant enterprise transformation, as in cultural transformation or ERP implementations, but months later when they must provide necessary resources from their organizations to the change, they balk. They say, "I never agreed to that" or "I didn't know you would want *those* people." The SCO can ensure from the beginning that all executives understand the downstream resource implications on their operations of any enterprise change and then hold them accountable at those later dates to earlier commitments made to support the change. This causes the executives to listen more completely when enterprise efforts are being discussed and produces deeper commitments that will sustain when challenges arise.

7. **Ensures effective course corrections.** With the SCO at the executive table holding a place on the executive agenda, course corrections are more easily made. The required executive discussions regarding the trade-offs, costs, and benefits of different scenarios in response to emerging dynamics can occur more thoroughly and in a timely manner to generate alignment and a sustainable course of action.

8. **The SCO owns your change process methodology, change infrastructures, and best change practices, and ensures effective dissemination of these throughout your organization.** With focused commitment to a common methodology and change leadership standards, executives and line change leaders can more readily build superior change capability.

9. **The SCO houses your Strategic Change Center of Excellence, and ensures efficient access and best use of your organization's change expertise and resources.** The SCO does not necessarily house all of the resources that may be required for a change to succeed; it may simply know where they are and how to access them as needed. It has a dotted-line relationship to the myriad types of expertise and resources in the organization, and it has the authority to mobilize the right resources and skills for any given change that it supports.

The consultants who live inside the SCO include master-level change consultants. They should be trained as highly skilled consultants to your line executives, being the super users of your common change process methodology and champions of your best change practices and infrastructures.

Consequently, the SCO must be staffed by people who understand how to scope and prepare for all types of change and how to bring the right people together so change is set up for success from the beginning. The SCO can request to hire more of these resources to ensure adequate capacity and capability. People and process resources are usually tougher to secure and are far less developed in most organizations than their content counterparts. The following list shows people and process expertise that may be needed for any type and size of change.

People and Process Expertise

▶ Build the case for change.

▶ Establish shared vision.

▶ Scope change accurately.

▶ Develop change strategy.

▶ Design change governance.

▶ Address leadership mindset and style requirements; develop and lead leadership breakthrough processes.

▶ Develop stakeholder engagement and change communication strategies.

▶ Create change initiative integration strategies.

▶ Coordinate the logistics of projects.

▶ Conduct organizational assessments for content designs, readiness, and capacity to change.

▶ Conduct impact analysis.

▶ Create culture change strategies.

▶ Provide organization development; team building; new team start-up.

▶ Deliver change leadership development and executive coaching.

▶ Audit and measure individual change efforts.

▶ Develop rapid course correction systems.

▶ Deliver HR support services.

▶ Provide plans for and/or facilitate key meetings.

10. **The SCO oversees the best use of external consultants.** Managing change-related vendors is a very high-leveraged use of the SCO. The SCO can create preferred vendor relationships with the various types of external experts your organization needs. It can be particularly helpful in selecting contractors for the full range of services that support your change agenda. It can align the external consultants with your internal resources, coordinate efforts across multiple consulting firms, and renegotiate agreements and deliverables to better serve your needs as they change over time. This oversight can greatly reduce fees, confusion, and redundancies, as well as ensure that external firms deliver their services in ways that align with your organization's cultural requirements, common change process methodology, and change infrastructures.

11. **The SCO can oversee enterprise culture change and leadership style strategies.** Given that so many strategic initiatives require the organization's culture and leadership style to change, enterprise oversight of this complex and sensitive imperative can be effectively provided by the SCO. Cultural transformation requires a multi-pronged approach, touching most areas of the organization. Success requires master-level skill and attention. For all the reasons stated, the SCO can be the best facilitator of cultural transformation. Not the owner, but the facilitator! The executive team must own culture change, just like they own content decisions. The human resources department has a huge role, but in many organizations, they are not positioned to own culture change either. An SCO/HR partnership is critical to support executive-owned culture change. The areas of responsibilities between them must be diligently negotiated. With both the EVP of HR and the SCO leader at the executive table, they can have the appropriate influence on the executives to be models of the new cultural mindsets, behaviors, and norms.

12. **The SCO ensures that your organization takes an integral view and promotes a conscious approach to (change) leadership.** These five strategies for creating change as a strategic discipline will bring benefit to your organization. But real breakthrough happens when they are founded on the wisdom of operating consciously and approaching organizational performance and change from an integral perspective. We know of no better initial starting point to champion this approach enterprise-wide than through a formal SCO structure. The positioning of the SCO, and in particular the Chief

Change Officer, can influence leadership throughout the organization to wake up, operate more consciously, and unleash human potential throughout the organization.

Leading the SCO: The Role of the Chief Change Officer

The head of the SCO is the Chief Change Officer (CCO), who is a member of the executive team and ultimately in charge of creating change as a strategic discipline for the organization. This puts the SCO in its proper place in your organization, on par with your chief strategy, chief financial, chief information, and chief technology offices. Placing change leadership in the executive suite—where it belongs—secures all of the benefits provided earlier in the "Functions and Benefits of the SCO" list.

To get the full benefits of conscious change leadership described in this book, your CCO will need to embrace, model, and effectively promote a conscious, integral approach to transformation. He or she will need to be—by their own will and choice— a conscious change leader themselves. They will need a level of personal development that enables them to champion these ideas successfully with their executive peers and throughout the organization. They will need to model a conscious approach.

Creating a CCO role will require an adjustment in your organization's executive ranks. Because this role does not typically have line authority, the person in it must have strong influence skills and full legitimacy. The role, and the SCO, must be seen as advocates for corporate success, not as the "change police." Our first CCO met with confusion about his role because his peers only understood line authority, not this type of "people, process, and standards" authority. They had not made the mindset shift necessary for this to work. The senior team must have the foundational understanding of the value of the SCO, and of conscious change leadership, for this approach to take hold. This understanding can be aided by generating accurate data about the real risk factors the organization has in leading—or failing to lead—its strategic changes. Performing a change audit can generate this data. The best scenario is that you can proceed in this direction before your organization faces a major crisis in change and that this can be done in a conscious, proactive way, not as a reaction to failure.

Creating a SCO is a bold move. Some of our clients have established their enterprise change agenda and then ensured that change project leaders have access to the executives when issues of pacing and capacity surface. Others have established a change oversight function or Center of Excellence that supports strategic initiatives in their use of The Change Leader's Roadmap methodology. Others have established key change infrastructures and published best change practices.

An example of a less formal approach to the SCO function is occurring with one of our hospital system clients. They have established a person (not a senior executive, but one level down) who oversees many of the functions of the SCO without naming them. She just does the work. Over the course of three years, she has demonstrated to the executives the strategic advantage of being smarter about how they define and lead their key changes. She does not have much staff but does have influence over the use of the organization's change-related resources and their use of The Change Leader's Roadmap methodology. She guides the change initiative leads and the senior Change Leadership Team's work, and surfaces key issues of pacing, change strategy, capacity, and timing. So without a title or a department, she accomplishes many of the important functions of the SCO. Her level of influence with the senior team is unique and grows with every critical course correction she names and oversees. Over the next decade, we expect that a major aspect of our consulting will be helping visionary companies develop an SCO and a Strategic Change Center of Excellence, and that the CCO role will become more common.

If you establish an SCO or CCO, please let us know about your experience and outcomes. We would appreciate adding your insights to our research.

SUMMARY

Developing change capability requires a significant investment in training and developing people, but it also requires building the organizational infrastructures, systems, and processes that support change execution. This means treating change as a strategic discipline within your organization and giving it the same type of study, standards, and application you give to other strategic functions such as finance and HR. In this chapter, we addressed five key strategies for establishing change as a strategic discipline to build your organization's change capability.

We introduced the enterprise change agenda as a vehicle for executives to create a strategic—and realistic—view of the change priorities they require for business success. We discussed the benefits of using a common change methodology across your organization. We described the various elements of a change infrastructure that can drive best practices and consistency in the leadership of all of your change efforts. We discussed the value of a strategic change center of excellence, the services it would provide, and why it is the next evolution for how OD, OE, and change management consultants can contribute to their organizations. Lastly, we introduced the SCO and the role of the CCO as a senior-level function chartered to ensure that the organization has the capability, conditions, and vehicles to succeed in its mission-critical change efforts. All of these strategies push the envelope of change leadership, and all of them drive toward greater leadership attention to consciously succeed at change.

Conscious change leaders embrace building change capability as an outcome of their work. They integrate the activities required into the normal course of leading their change efforts, consciously using their change projects as laboratories of development for all involved. They build and use their organization's strategic change infrastructures and systems to continually expand their organization's ability to change successfully, always seeking to improve the way their organizations improve. And most of this moves conscious change leaders far beyond the realms of change management.

SECTION ONE SUMMARY

We are at the close of Section One: A Call to Conscious Change Leadership. Throughout this section, we have been building an understanding of what conscious change leadership entails beyond traditional change management. Fundamentally, conscious change leadership is about how to achieve breakthrough business and cultural results, while *simultaneously* building superior change capability in our organizations (Success Levels Three, Four, and Five).

So far in our discussion, we can conclude that concious change leaders:

▶ Are accountable for both business and cultural outcomes, and pursue breakthrough results in each.

▶ Know the type of their change effort and build a change strategy suited for that type.

▶ Integrate attention to content and people into one unified change process.

▶ Address all seven drivers of change to pursue the full scope of change required.

▶ Take an integral view, attending to all quadrants and levels. In their change processes, they attend to individual mindset and behavior as well as collective (organizational, team, and relational) culture and systems.

▶ Integrate ways to build change capability into their change initiatives and their organizations.

- Approach change as a strategic discipline, building where possible organizational infrastructures, functions, and systems to support that end.

- Choose to operate consciously, intentionally turning inward to become increasingly self-aware of their own mindset and autopilot functioning in how they lead their change efforts.

- Choose to grow personally to become better models of the changes they are asking of their organizations.

Fundamentally, conscious change leaders need a thorough understanding of both how human beings function and the change process so they can unleash the human potential in their organizations as they go through change. We now turn to Section Two: People Dynamics, where we will explore Chapter Six, Human Dynamics: From Resistance to Commitment; Chapter 7, The Role and Impact of Mindset; and Chapter Seven, The Role and Impact of Culture. We will then take this comprehensive understanding of people into Section Three: Process Dynamics, and apply it to designing change processes that deliver extraordinary outcomes.

People Dynamics

Human Dynamics: From Resistance to Commitment

Understanding human needs is half the job of meeting them.

—Adlai Stevenson

In Section One, we presented the possibility and hope of achieving breakthrough results from change. In this section, we go deeper into the key lever for delivering those results: people. Our intent is to help you avoid the common mistakes regarding people that we outlined in Chapter One, as well as help you capitalize on more of the change capability you currently have in your organization. Our discussion will look at how people function from the perspective of individual mindset and behavior, as well as collective culture. We will look "under the hood" to discover what makes us behave and act as we do. For conscious change leaders, this is vital information. We like to think of this as practical psychology. "Practical" because understanding it leads to greater outcomes from change. And you won't need a degree in psychology to apply these insights. We draw on Being First's *Leading the Human Dynamics of Change* and *Self Mastery* training programs for this information.

There are four very compelling reasons to become competent in leading the human dynamics of change:

1. **Better change results:** From the most practical results-oriented perspective, conscious change leaders attend to human dynamics because they need people to be fully committed and contributing to the positive outcome of their

change efforts. Rule #1 as it relates to human dynamics in change is *the greater the commitment is in your people, the greater the results will be from your change efforts.* Breakthrough results only become possible when you unleash the human potential in your organization in extraordinary ways.

2. **A more committed and aligned workforce/healthier workplace:** Happy and committed people are more productive; they learn and adapt faster than resistant, defensive, and angry people.

3. **More sustainable operational performance:** Change efforts supported by committed people have less negative impact on operational excellence and cause less wear and tear on the organization.

4. **Greater change capability:** Your organization will become more change ready and capable, more able to quickly adapt and respond to emerging dynamics in your market, and more able to capture market opportunities others miss.

Our investigation of human dynamics is all in the context of how we can minimize resistance and maximize commitment in each change initiative we lead. To this end, we will explore the following in this chapter: (1) the complex and multi-dimensional nature of human beings and how it requires our attention to go beyond mere intellectual approaches; (2) that we each have both an ego and a higher self, and that both must be addressed to effectively engage stakeholders; (3) the core needs that influence levels of resistance and commitment in stakeholders; (4) the emotional transitions stakeholders go through during change; and (5) the moment for each of us when resistance shifts toward commitment, the dynamics of this transformational shift, and how to support it in ourselves and others. All of this will take us beyond change management into the deeper reaches of human excellence that conscious change leadership catalyzes.

PEOPLE ARE MULTI-DIMENSIONAL

We are all comprised of a body, emotions, mind, and soul. Our bodies are all similar but uniquely different. We all have bones, muscles, skin, internal organs, and vascular, neurological, and endocrine systems. All of our lungs breathe air, and all of our hearts pump blood. In the end, our bodies turn into the same dust.

We all have a similar palette of emotions—fears, doubts, grief, anxieties, as well as happiness, joy, and love—yet we express these emotions in unique ways.

We all have minds that have an ego, conscious and unconscious functions, beliefs and worldviews, ideas, and opinions. And we all have a soul, a spiritual element that connects us to something greater than ourselves. Based on differences in cultural and religious beliefs (mind), we may use different words to describe our soul and our God, but universally, across humankind, the majority of people acknowledge that Spirit exists, and is a part of who we are.

All four dimensions are interconnected, interdependent, and form one integrated system. The state of each dimension mirrors the others, so when there is a change in one dimension, the others also change. For example:

▶ When we perceive (mind) something as a threat, and our emotional and physical states change: We become afraid and our hypothalamus initiates a sequence of nerve cell firings and chemical releases of adrenaline, noradrenalin, and cortisol; our heart rate goes up, blood is shunted away from our digestive tract and directed into our muscles and limbs.

▶ When we feel inspired (soul), and our emotion turns toward joy, our thoughts become positive, and our body secretes "happy" hormones.

▶ When we eat too much sugar, and our mind gets unclear; our body energy first goes up, then down.

We can shift our whole system in a positive direction with a positive intervention in one area. If we change our perception and see the threat as neutral, our physical and emotional state will change. When we smile instead of frown, our emotional state is uplifted in a matter of seconds. If we stop slouching and stand more upright and robustly, we immediately feel more capable.

These four dimensions—body, emotions, mind, and soul—form the basis of who each person is. When we were born, we were not given a manual for how this incredible miracle called the human being works, but it does. Regardless of what continent we were born on, what religious beliefs our parents had, or what color our skin is, for each of us, these four dimensions have similar laws, principles, and "mechanisms" that govern their functioning. How much do we each understand these human dynamics? Who taught us and helped us develop this understanding? Is it complete and accurate? What more can we learn, and how would we apply that new wisdom to make the transformational change efforts we lead more successful? From our perspective, the more we understand human dynamics, the more we can unleash our potential and support others to do the same.

Each of us has an ego (mind) and a being, or higher self (soul). Understanding these two core functions is vital to developing insight about human dynamics and behavior. Let's explore each in turn.

Ego

A fundamental function of our mind is the ego. If you do an online search, you will find many definitions of the ego. Here is a simple, direct, and practical way of thinking about the ego.

The ego is our sense of individual self, distinct from everything else; it is our personal self, our sense of "I" that generates in us a perspective that we are "in here" and everything else is "out there." It conjures our personal identity—unique, different, and separate from the rest of reality and everyone else.

The ego has gotten a bad rap in many circles. Some people treat it as something to overcome or get rid of, but we need a strong and healthy sense of self to lead a productive life. It is not that the ego is bad, but simply that it must be managed and developed like all other aspects of ourselves if we want to excel.

The purpose of the ego is to establish our unique identity and sense of self by creating boundaries between us and everything else. The primary boundary the ego creates is "this is me" and "that is not me." Here I am. There you are. This primary boundary of self/not self establishes the inner perspective of separation between us and everything else. This sense of separation is fundamental to how the ego experiences life. When the ego says, "I," it refers to *my* thought, *my* idea, *my* need, *my* desire, *my* want. This is my position; that one is not. I am a Democrat, not a Republican. I am a meat eater, not a vegetarian. I am a blue collar worker, not a white collar professional. But are all of these personal identities and labels really me? Are they *who* I am, really? Are they the essential me?

A core function of the ego is to protect us, to keep our unique self physically alive and psychologically feeling good about ourselves. The ego generally hates failure because failure makes us look bad. To the ego, failure is psychological death, so it attempts to avoid it at all costs.

The core tool of the ego in avoiding failure is fear, otherwise known as the fear of failure. The ego uses fear to protect us from failure in three primary ways. First, it can drive us toward success by generating in us extreme dedication, focused concentration, disciplined practice, and one-pointed perseverance to achieve goals. Fear-based dedication can deliver great success but often at a price, such as work and family life imbalances, stress-related diseases, myopic self-interest, and loneliness. Over time, the ego creates a sense of identity and mindset around this success-oriented way of being, such as the following:

▶ "I am a hard worker."
▶ "I never give up."
▶ "Success is more important than relationships."
▶ "I am always the one carrying the load."

This identity then becomes a major piece of who we are.

The ego's second way of using fear of failure to protect us causes us to avoid situations where failure is a possibility. The problem with this strategy is that great opportunity usually exists in these situations. We have to take the risk to get the gain, but with this orientation, our ego keeps us out of the game to protect us from the potential failure that exists there. With this way of being, the ego creates a self-identity and mindset that sounds like the following:

▶ "I am not a risk-taker."
▶ "I don't like new situations."
▶ "I don't go first; I let others lead."
▶ "I avoid being put on the spot."

Our behavior then revolves around this identity.

The ego's third way of using fear is to cause us to hold back our effort (performance) so if we do fail, it has an excuse. It can tell itself, "I would have succeeded if I had really tried." The fear, doubt, or anxiety it produces in a challenging or difficult situation are its excuses for not achieving. The personal identities in this orientation become something like the following:

▶ "I try hard but it never works out."
▶ "Oh well, at least I am a person who gives it a shot."
▶ "I could have done better."

Another notorious strategy the ego uses to protect us from feeling like a failure is blame. It blames both people and external circumstances, stating things like the following:

- "We would have met the goal if Bill and his team had done their jobs."
- "If it weren't for our competitor's new product, we would have hit our sales numbers."

With this ego orientation, it then relies on finding external reasons why things are not going as well as hoped.

The identity the ego creates for who we are becomes the central organizer of everything in our lives. Each of us has a blueprint in our unconscious minds for who the ego says we are, and most of our decisions and actions stem from this picture. As conscious change leaders who introspect, we can begin to spot our ego's identity by paying attention to the stories it tells. Listen to your internal voice when things do not go right. You will find a consistent story that you are telling yourself, a consistent way your ego makes sense of its "reality" and how you fit in it. This story is your ego's identity, but is it really you?

Our egos create problems for us through the various dysfunctional ways it plays out our identities and seeks to protect us from failure. For example, Dean once worked with a professional tennis player who was trying to break through to a significantly higher level world ranking. Her ego kept "stopping her" in key matches. She would get ahead and then lose in the last set. By turning inward and listening to the previously unconscious stories in her mind, she realized that she was holding back because she did not want the other person to lose. Her ego's conditioning had it wired that it was a bigger failure for her to make someone else look bad than it was for her to look bad. Her ego identity was, "I am a person who does not cause discomfort for others." That is a noble trait in certain situations, but not on the tennis court—if your intent is to win. After she reprogrammed this conditioned ego response (only as it applied to tennis, of course), she started winning more matches, and her world ranking went up. Our ego creates all kinds of unique defenses to live out its identity and keep us feeling good about ourselves. What are yours?

Our ego functions as our inner judge and generates our conditioned ways of responding to reality, based on what it believes is right or wrong, good or bad. The playing field of the ego is the mental, emotional, and physical planes, where duality rules; for example, this feeling is good to have, that one is not; this idea is right, that one is wrong; this circumstance is good, that one is bad. And as we know from our earlier discussion, after the ego judges a situation or phenomenon, our minds, bodies, and emotions all respond accordingly. Ultimately, where the ego places the boundary of what is good and should be included, and what is bad and should be excluded, generates our thoughts, feelings, and behaviors in any situation. If it judges a circumstance as bad, then our thoughts, feelings, and actions all reflect that position.

The ego "fights or flights" whatever it perceives as bad in order to keep things good for us. If someone challenges your idea in a meeting, you may find yourself lashing out at that person in defense or withdrawing in a sulk and participating less. Your identity as a "competent leader" has been attacked, and your ego is responding accordingly.

These fear-based, fight or flight ego reactions occur on autopilot. They happen automatically and unconsciously. For example, if failure occurs in your functional area of responsibility, you may automatically and unconsciously jump in and start telling staff what to do to fix it. As an isolated event, this may not present a problem, but if you are in a cultural transformation trying to build more empowerment in your organization, your behavior and modeling may set your team's progress back. Our ego needs to be monitored constantly for whether its automatic and unconscious conditioned responses fit the situation and promote the positive outcomes we seek. The more we understand our ego, the more easily our conscious awareness can spot these reactions before they derail us.

The ego is often called the "false self" because it generates an illusory sense of identity based on its desires and fears. It feels good when its desires are being met, which keeps its identity intact, and badly when they are not. The reference to "false self" suggests that we have another more authentic self that exists beyond the realm of desire, evaluations, and judgments. Is there more to us than our ego's desires and labels—something deeper that is more essential? The fact that we can observe and be consciously aware of our ego's wants, desires, and positions about things reveals that something other than those wants, desires, and positions exists within us. What is it that is beyond your ego? Are you aware of it?

Being

Being is the unbounded, unconditional Self of pure awareness within us. It is our internal witness, the observer that can watch our ego or mind in action. Being is our authentic self, the Self beyond our ego's desires, wants, and attachments. It is our connection to that which is greater than our personal or ego identity. It is the link between our separate self and Spirit. Being is another name for our soul.

Where the ego operates in the gross, conditional world of body, mind, and emotions, our being is of the subtle, spiritual dimension. It is the unconditional awareness within us that is present to all things. As such, being does not judge. It holds no right or wrong. It simply observes and witnesses, accepting without commentary whatever condition reality is manifesting. Where our ego generates thinking and judgment about reality, being is pure awareness of reality.

Regardless of circumstances or our ego's judgment and story about them, being is steadfast. Anytime we become consciously aware, there being is, ever present. It does not fluctuate, think good or bad thoughts, or have good or bad feelings. It simply is; always available and always accessible.

Being is the source of breakthrough and the foundation of personal excellence. It transcends the ego's bounded and constrained perspectives and opens new doors of possibility. It is our deep sense of centeredness that enables us to move outside our ego's comfort zone. It is the calm within us that we sometimes find, and always rely on when we do, in the middle of stress or breakdown. Being is the source of our intuition and the quiet voice or hunch inside that leads us to a solution we could not previously see. It is the source of the courage we have felt to persevere through extremely difficult times. Being is the flow of awareness we experience when performing effortlessly and things get extraordinarily clear. It is the source of the tender, heartfelt moments we experience when observing a baby sleep, or listening to the birds sing in a quiet reflective moment, or talking late in the night with a friend in need. Being is where we are operating from when we realize our full potential in anything.

Ego ignores being because it cannot comprehend it and because being threatens ego's existence. As you develop your inner witness through observation and engaging conscious awareness, being reveals what your ego's attachments and conditioned ways of perceiving are—not *truths* as ego would have you believe, but *perspectives* that may or may not be accurate or useful in any given situation.

Being "holds the space" for everything else, regardless of what it is and whether our ego judges it as positive or negative. It does not react but rather accepts whatever shows up, bringing a neutrality and centeredness that enables us to better discern the right response in any challenge. Lacking emotional reactiveness, our being enables clear conscious awareness of what is and identification of what actions are called for to deliver desired outcomes.

Leaders operating on autopilot are controlled by their egos and are relatively out of touch with their beings. Their responses to situations are governed by their ego's identities and conditioning, by what makes them feel okay, and by what preserves their sense of (false) self. Their ego's conditioning creates the story of what they believe and perceive. Their ego's "positions" are their only positions. The voice in their head is their only voice. Their ego's wants, desires, and judgments are relatively fixed the way they are—immovable and making change difficult.

Conscious change leaders are more in touch with their beings and authentic selves. They access their being through their enhanced conscious awareness. This engages more of their potential, and makes them more flexible and able to operate outside of their conditioned styles. It empowers them with more choices. In transformation, where the change process is nonlinear and answers are emergent, operating from our being is far more trustworthy than only having access to our ego.

Transcending ego limitations to operate more often from our being is key to our success as a change leader. This level of personal development makes conscious change leaders better leaders of people. Let's look at how this relates to helping us manage core needs—in ourselves and others—so we minimize resistance and maximize commitment in our change efforts.

CORE HUMAN NEEDS

We each possess six primary core needs (see Exhibit 6.1), all of which can be triggered by events in transformational change. We each have all six needs to some degree, but one or two are always dominant and drive the majority of our behavior. You could say that these one or two are where we live internally most often. They represent our "hot buttons," our most sensitive issues as human beings. When our core needs are threatened, we react to protect ourselves. When we are emotionally hurt or upset—or resistant—it is usually because one or more of these core needs have been triggered by events around us.

DEFINITIONS OF CORE NEEDS

▶ **Security**: Needing to feel secure and physically and emotionally safe, cared about.

  ○ "I need to know things will be okay. I need to feel physically and emotionally safe, without threat."

Exhibit 6.1. Core Human Needs

- Security
- Inclusion and Connection
- Power
- Order and Control
- Competence
- Justice and Fairness

- **Inclusion and Connection**: Needing to be invited to join the group, be part of what is happening and in relationship with others.
  - "Will I be on the team that is doing this work or overlooked as a result of this change? Will I keep my relationships intact? Will I be selected?"
- **Power**: Needing to have direct influence over the outcome and process of the change; needing things to go as I want; needing to maintain power or influence as a result of the change.
  - "Will I lose power through this change, or will I gain it? Will I be able to influence things to go the way I want?"
- **Order and Control**: Needing to know what is going on at all times and have things be predictable, structured, and planned; needing logic and order in the change, with minimal surprises.
  - "I need a clear plan so we know what is happening and can minimize disruptions and chaos."
- **Competence**: Needing to feel capable, effective, skilled, and right.
  - "Will I be able to perform and succeed in the new organization and be seen as competent and 'in the know'? Will I get adequate training before I am held accountable to produce?"
- **Justice and Fairness**: Needing things to be fair and equitable.
  - "Will the decisions of this change and their implications for me be just and equitable? Will politics or nepotism rule over fairness and equality?"

These six core needs (First Tier) are ego needs, the ego's way of feeling okay, and that all is good. In transformation, when our ego perceives that these core needs will be met, then it judges the change as good. When our ego perceives they are at risk, then we believe that we have a problem.

HOW WE DISCOVERED CORE NEEDS

We came to identify these six core human needs after a number of years doing extensive work with our clients on their core beliefs as they went through various forms of our *Self Mastery, Leading the Human Dynamics of Change*, and *Executive Team Development* and *Coaching* programs. The same core issues kept surfacing for people across race, level in the organization, and personality type. After a number of years, we saw that people's core needs fell within these six categories.

Then we discovered the work of Clare Graves and his "Level of Existence Theory," and the work of Don Beck and Christopher Cowen, two of Graves' dedicated students who evolved Graves' work into their Spiral Dynamics model.[1] These researchers found that people across cultures operate from different value systems or worldviews, which they call *memes* (rhymes with themes). They differentiate eight worldviews, six in what they call First Tier, and two in Second Tier. The six in First Tier corresponded significantly with the six core needs that our findings produced. Our research base was approximately 2,000 people; theirs was 50,000 worldwide. We were convinced we had a glimmer into a fundamental fact of human existence and that as pragmatists, we could apply this key understanding: *These six core needs are operative in people going through change and need to be attended to in order for change efforts to succeed*.

While these needs are universal among people, how they manifest and the degree to which they are present and felt can be culturally and socially biased. We acknowledge that we are discussing core needs here from our own Western mindset and culture. If you are of a different nationality, please adapt these ideas to fit your culture's norms and understandings. But also know that these core needs have been researched and found to be present across cultures. It is how they are expressed that is culturally influenced.

Change, especially transformational change, because of its chaotic, nonlinear, and "march into the unknown" nature, frequently triggers these core issues in people. When unresolved, they manifest as resistance. You may hear people disagreeing with the direction of the change, see them not contributing to it, or see them intentionally trying to sabotage it. Sometimes, they just disagree with the direction or content of the change. But usually, under their resistant behavior is an unresolved or threatened core need, a fear that the change will lead to bad results such as (1) not being safe; (2) not being included or connected; (3) losing power; (4) being out of control; (5) being seen as incompetent; or (6) not being treated fairly.

These ego reactions are almost always unconscious. Sure, people feel and express them, but the source of their uneasiness is almost always unconscious. They are not aware that their ego is fearful that one of their core needs will not get met. Operating on autopilot, they simply resist and think that the "bad, misdirected" change is their valid reason for reacting negatively and not committing. They blame the external situation for their internal resistance, not realizing that it is self-generated by their ego's core needs. This unconscious ego reaction usually keeps them from accurately perceiving the positive aspects of the change effort.

People operating consciously, with a fair amount of self-awareness, will realize that their resistance is self-generated as a consequence of one of their ego's core needs being triggered. Because they are better able to connect with the neutrality and centeredness of their own being, they will be able to sort out for themselves if they are resisting something "out there" (content) that is valid to resist, or whether they are simply afraid "in here" that something their ego does not want might happen.

Core needs can generate positive and negative responses—commitment and resistance—depending on a stakeholder's perspective, conditioning, and what is happening to the stakeholder in the change. As a change leader who is aware of these human dynamics, you can help "manage" people's resistance by attending proactively to their core needs. For instance, if people with a high ego need for power are taken out of the decision-making loop or not given any choice about their future, they will predictably react negatively. But if you ask for their input to decisions, they will feel they have more power over their fate and be more positive about the change. Similarly, if you put people with a high ego need to be seen as competent into unfamiliar, visible roles that they are not yet prepared for, they will be very concerned about failing and looking bad publicly—and will resist. However, if you let them know well in advance that they will receive significant training and coaching and the time to learn their new responsibilities before being held accountable for high performance, they will feel far more positive about the change.

Remember this: If people fear (even unconsciously) that their core needs will not get met, you will see resistance. If they believe that their core needs will get met, you will see greater commitment. Change leaders operating on autopilot trigger resistance in stakeholders by inadvertently designing change processes that trigger that resistance. Conscious change leaders, with their deeper understanding of people, intentionally design change processes that build commitment by overtly planning actions that enable stakeholders to see that their needs will get met. The results between the two are night and day. So, rather than have your own ego react negatively to stakeholder resistance, engage your being and accept their natural reaction. And then put in place change strategies that minimize and neutralize their resistance and turn it toward commitment.

Exhibit 6.2 outlines typical examples of change leadership behavior that triggers stakeholders' core needs and the resistance that goes with them. Review them as examples of what to avoid.

When you are creating your change strategy and plan, think about the core needs your key stakeholder groups have, particularly the targets of your change. While the mix of every individual's core needs may be different, you will notice themes or generalizations of the needs within any given stakeholder group. For

---

Exhibit 6.2.   How You Might Inadvertently Trigger Core Needs

SECURITY

▸ A large percentage of employees have received termination "pink slips," and you have not told those remaining anything about their futures.

▸ You communicate that if people do not get on board with this change quickly, they will be let go.

▸ You announce a downsizing without any other information.

INCLUSION AND CONNECTION

▸ You do not ask for people's input on matters that are important to them, especially if you have had an ongoing work relationship with them.

▸ You move people to new work teams where they know only a few people.

(continued)

- You create an exclusive group of people to help shape the change and exclude many others for no apparent reason.
- You avoid responding to people who make requests of you.

POWER

- You announce position changes without warning.
- You change your normal decision-making process without notice for key decisions affecting the outcome of your change effort.
- You reorganize, shifting people's relative power in the organization, and provide no clarity about the influence authority of people's new roles.

ORDER AND CONTROL

- You engage people but provide no direction for their work.
- You provide no change roadmap or process plan to stakeholders impacted by the change.
- You do not make the impacts of the content changes overt, and people are left to worry about how they might be negatively affected.

COMPETENCE

- You impose a change that requires new skills or knowledge and do not provide adequate training or learning time before people are held accountable to perform in the new system.
- You place key leaders in very visible new roles requiring their immediate action with no room for error or course correction.
- You lay the expectation for accomplishing this change in a very short time period on top of people's already excessive workloads.

FAIRNESS AND JUSTICE

- Without explanation, you overlook people with seniority or expertise when staffing new, higher positions.
- You decide to split up long-standing work teams with no logical rationale, with some of the people being seen as winners and others as losers in the change.
- You do not make the criteria used for staffing decisions overt.

example, your finance group will likely have far bigger control needs than your sales group, whose issues may be primarily about competence. Your HR department may likely have greater fairness issues than your risk management team, who may be predominantly concerned with order and control. Health care clinicians will be very concerned about competence. With clearer understanding of your stakeholder groups, you can then design your engagement strategy and communication plan to help resolve predictable issues. You will notice far greater commitment to the content of your change effort and far less resistance when you take these predictable human dynamics into account.

The content of your change can influence what core needs get triggered in people. For example, during an acquisition, employees of the acquired company will more than likely have *security* needs (Will they dismantle our division?), *inclusion and connection* needs (Will I have a job after they weed out duplicate roles?), *power* needs (Will we have any authority?), and *fairness* needs (Will nepotism determine job selection?). Big software implementations that force work flow and job redesign often trigger power, control, and competence issues in people. Predictably, they feel victimized by not having much say, if any, over how their work will be done, and whether they can be successful using the new systems, processes, or technology.

Your organization's overall culture has dominant core needs. High-tech companies often are driven by competency; banking institutions by power and control; NGOs by inclusion, fairness, and justice; and government agencies by power and control.

What are the core needs of your culture? Be aware of them because you will want to address them in your change strategy. If your organization revolves around competency, for example, then announce training and development plans early in your process reengineering effort, or you will face resistance you could otherwise have mitigated early. If you work in a bank, lay out a clear and structured change process plan, or all the people with high control needs will be up in arms about your change effort, even if they agree with the content. In health care, communicate overtly to clinicians how you will "stress test" your medical records hardware and software under load so they do not become resistant because of a valid fear that patients may be harmed or that they will not have accurate information from which to make sound decisions.

Culture is a powerful force and will always resist a transformation that triggers its core needs and ways of operating. This creates challenges for leading transformation, which by its very nature confronts the existing culture. No matter what your type of change, always design your change strategy to work with the culture you have, even as you plan to change it. We will discuss culture change in Chapter Eight.

Exhibit 6.3.   Assessing Your Change Strategy and Plan

Instructions: For each core need, assess how your existing change strategy and plan will likely trigger resistance, and then determine how you can alter your strategy and plan to minimize resistance and maximize commitment by resolving that core need issue.

Core Needs	How our existing change strategy and plan likely threatens core needs and triggers resistance:	What we need to add, remove, or modify in our change strategy and plan to minimize resistance and maximize commitment:
Security		
Inclusion and Connection		
Power		
Control		
Competence		
Justice and Fairness		

HIGHER CORE NEEDS

You are likely familiar with Abraham Maslow's work[2] on human needs, which most of us learned in high school. Maslow was a true pioneer, and interest in his work is coming back once again. Maslow identified five core needs: (1) physiological needs of hunger and thirst, (2) safety needs of security and protection, (3) social needs of belonging and love, (4) esteem needs of recognition and status, and (5) self-actualization needs. Maslow suggests, then, that the ego has needs for security, belonging and love (our inclusion and connection need), recognition (our competence need), and status (our power need). We add the distinctions of control and justice, as does Spiral Dynamics. These distinctions give us greater effectiveness in creating change strategies that minimize resistance and maximize commitment to change.

Maslow also identifies self-actualization as a core need, calling it a "desire for self-fulfillment" that surfaces when our more basic needs are satisfied. Other psychologists see this not as a desire but as an "intrinsic motive," a "compulsory urge to grow," or an "evolutionary drive." However you view it, it is extremely important for us as change leaders to understand that *we are all hard-wired to want to actualize more of our potential.* This yearning comes from our being. It dominates our focus when our six ego needs are fulfilled, and expresses in a constant desire to learn and do better. This inner calling of our being has been the catalyst of human development for thousands of years, pulling us forward into more of our potential. The drive to self-actualize is a core part of our human nature.

Bev Kaye and Sharon Jordan-Evans, in their research of 17,000 people for their great book on retaining top talent, *Love 'Em or Lose 'Em*,[3] support this in their findings. Table 6.1 highlights the top ten reasons they found people stay in their jobs, with the top two clearly being self-actualization needs. In the table, we correlate their findings to our list of core human needs.

Conscious change leaders help others self-actualize by engaging them in their organization's change efforts. They promote people to grow through change and provide opportunities to explore, experiment, make decisions, test, and refine. They provide challenges and give stakeholders the time, information, and resources to solve them. By providing opportunities to stretch, grow, and learn, they consciously engage people's beings because they know that is a prime way to catalyze commitment.

Conscious change leaders do not overly control or mandate change processes because that predictably triggers ego resistance and stifles stakeholders' higher need to grow. Autopilot leaders, especially those with high power and control needs,

Table 6.1. Employee Retention Research

Why Most Employees Say They Stay	Human Need
1. Exciting work and challenge	Self-actualization
2. Career growth, learning, and development	Self-actualization
3. Working with great people	Inclusion and connection
4. Fair pay	Justice and fairness
5. Supportive management/good boss	Inclusion and connection
6. Being recognized, valued, and respected	Competence; inclusion and connection
7. Benefits	Justice and fairness
8. Meaningful work and making a difference	Self-actualization
9. Pride in the organization, its mission, and its products	Inclusion and connection
10. Great work environment and culture	Self-actualization; Inclusion and connection

CASE-IN-POINT

To pick up where we left off in two previous Case Studies, after we conducted the *Leading Breakthrough Results: Walking the Talk of Change* program for the Detroit Edison executive team, they decided to provide that same personal and interpersonal development opportunity to the top 300 leaders in the company. Those sessions culminated in the Visioning Retreat described in Chapter Three, where the company re-created its purpose, mission, vision, and goals. Because of the impact of these programs, the executives then decided to provide that same four-day development opportunity to their top 1,500 leaders, and then a one-day version to their 8,000 employees.

It took three years to complete these sessions. All were overtly tied to the transformation the organization was undergoing, in particular, to overtly exploring the mindset, behavior, and culture required to achieve the vision and goals they agreed were paramount. This was clearly a monumental undertaking, but as Tony Earley, current CEO of DTE Energy (Detroit Edison's parent company) said years later, "Not a week or month goes by without me hearing someone reference what they learned in the *Walking the Talk of Change* program, and how it informs our current culture and successes." Conscious change leaders make these investments because they know the impact of inner human development on people's commitment and performance.

make this mistake frequently. Give up some control, and make available numerous opportunities for people to get involved. Yes, they will make mistakes in these new opportunities, but these will be small compared to the extraordinary results they will produce. Use your change efforts to support people to actualize more of their potential.

As part of your transformational change strategy, consider providing personal growth and development training to both leaders and staff. This is a major way in which conscious change leadership provides far deeper attention to human dynamics than change management. Change management specialists would typically use tools and techniques to overcome resistance by sharing more information and getting people more involved in implementation. They attempt to shift stakeholder behavior from the *outside*. Conscious change leadership, of course, does all of this as well, but also provides guidance, training, and coaching—a practical "owner's manual" for how people function internally—so they can become more aware of their own ego's functioning and recognize the core needs that are limiting their contribution and commitment to the change effort. The context of this personal development is maximizing results from the change effort and transforming mindset, behavior, and culture as the Drivers of Change model demonstrated was necessary. Conscious change leaders support this growth from the *inside*, knowing that it will naturally shift stakeholder behavior toward commitment and sustain it over time.

EMOTIONAL TRANSITIONS

People have emotional reactions to change. With our understanding of ego, being, and core needs, we see that reactions of fear, doubt, anger, sadness, or confusion are the basis of resistance. If stakeholders are to get through these emotions and "overcome" their resistance, they will move through a process of acknowledging and releasing these feelings.

Numerous emotional or psychological "transition models" exist that attempt to describe this process. The most widely known is the William Bridges model.[4] Most, if not all, of these models owe much to Elizabeth Kübler-Ross'[5] early research on grief, formalized in her Five Stages of Loss. Another very useful model is John Adams and Sabina Spencer's[6] Seven Stages of Transition.

If you research these and other models, you will notice significant similarity. We are not here to promote one or the other; they are all valuable in their own ways.

Figure 6.1. Resistance to Commitment

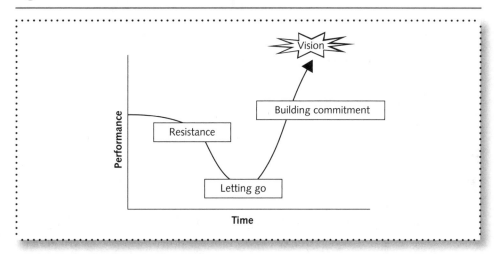

Instead, we want to share conclusions about emotional transitions and how you can use your awareness of them to best lead your change efforts.

When change is introduced, many people will go through a natural emotional response. In the simplest of terms, it starts with initial resistance, then moves through a letting go phase and ends in commitment (Figure 6.1). Notice how there is a drop in performance shown in the figure. This is natural. You should expect this and not be concerned by it, unless it goes on for a long period of time.

Getting to commitment, of course, assumes people get through their resistance. They may get emotionally stuck there and not move forward. Your job as a conscious change leader is to support their emotional transition so their natural resistance can turn into commitment. The more you understand core needs, ego, and being, and the process of going through emotional transitions, the better you will be at this.

Our exploration of emotional transitions and supporting people to move through their resistance to full commitment assumes that the content of the change effort is right for the organization. It will generate positive outcomes that the organization needs and that are aligned to the organization's strategy. If that is not true, then stakeholders should resist it, and the only way to get them to full commitment is to alter your content. This is one reason to always ask people about the nature of their resistance. They may have invaluable insight about how the direction of change needs to be course corrected.

Figure 6.2. Comparing Transition Models

Kübler-Ross
Denial → Anger → Bargaining → Depression → Acceptance

Bridges
Letting Go → Neutral Zone → New Beginning

Adams-Spencer
Losing Focus → Minimizing the Impact → The Pit → Letting Go of the Past → Testing the Limits → Searching for Meaning → Integrating

Review the models in Figure 6.2 to discover their similarities. Notice that each model reveals that there is a point when the tables turn, where a shift happens, where resistance turns toward commitment. In the Kübler-Ross model, it is in *acceptance*. In the Bridges model, it is the *neutral zone*. In the Adams-Spencer model, it is in *letting go of the past*. No matter what model you use, this is the moment of truth you should most concern yourself with. With this shift, commitment and transformation are possible. Without it, people stay stuck in resistance. So how do you promote this transformational shift?

THE TRANSFORMATIONAL SHIFT: FROM RESISTANCE TO COMMITMENT

Acceptance is the essence of the transformational shift. Kübler-Ross made this fact well known through her work with the grief associated with death and dying. People have to get to a place of acceptance if they are going to move beyond their resistance and emotional upset.

To accept, we first have to be aware of the emotion that underlies our resistance. We have to recognize and acknowledge it. Denying the emotion, or pretending that it is not there, keeps us stuck in it.

After we are aware of the emotion, we have to *feel* the emotion. Every psychologist will tell you that a person cannot fully let go of a "negative" emotion until they allow themselves to feel it. Understanding people as multi-dimensional beings, you can see the wisdom in this. We cannot just think our way to acceptance. An emotional reaction remains stuck in our bodies until it is fully felt. Once felt, it *naturally* releases, like the steam that comes out of a kettle when you take the top off. Being mentally aware of the emotion, and then feeling it in our body, transforms the emotion. Remember, body, mind, and emotion all work together as an integrated system.

Most of us have been taught by social norms that anger, fear, doubt, sadness, anxiety, and other "contracted" emotions are bad, whereas confidence, excitement, and joy are good. In other words, we unconsciously judge the emotions that underlie resistance as bad. Most of us, especially men, are also taught not to feel those emotions. Common dictums from parents are, "Don't cry," "Don't be sad," and "Don't be angry." These early admonitions created a very strong denial mechanism in most of us. When we are angry, sad, fearful, or doubtful (resistant), we do not let ourselves fully feel those emotions because our ego judges them as bad and judges us as bad if we have them. Automatically and unconsciously, we set about complaining about the situation that triggered them. We go into our heads, give over to our egos, and generate self-talk about "how bad it is" (out there), rather than drop our awareness into our bodies and feel the feelings (in here). Our ego, with its conditioning that these feelings are bad, keeps us from feeling them. We "push them away" by turning our attention to the external world and how to get it to stop "making us upset." This blocks the emotions from releasing. This is how people stay stuck in resistance and exacerbate it over time: They do not allow themselves to feel the emotions of the resistance because they orient to complaining about the content that triggered them, which is the ego's way of justifying the resistance.

Change managers, or change leaders operating on autopilot, exacerbate stakeholder resistance with well-intentioned attempts to "overcome" it, which triggers the ego to dig in its heels even more. Techniques to "overcome resistance" are usually applied from the "outside" by the change manager and often, at best, quell it without resolving it. Change managers, of course, do not intend the resistance to get stuck, but that is what often happens. The manager's ego judges the stakeholder resistance as bad, so their autopilot response is to attempt to put a boundary around it to "contain" it. This is 180 degrees from what works.

Methods such as listening sessions work because with leaders, by "holding the space" for employees to air their upset, allows them to feel their feelings. This is key: *When people can express their feelings and have them be fully heard without judgment, rebuttal, or defensiveness, they feel "gotten" and can let their feelings go.* By being seen and accepted, received as a whole human being, their ego has nothing to fight against, no battle to wage to claim its identity. Holding the space for someone

A client of ours had a very public ethical crisis, sparked by actions of its CEO. Stakeholders, including employees, were up in arms, writing negative comments on the Web, in the newspapers, and in the business press. The executives thought that a strategy of containment and distance was the best option. They hoped that "time would heal" and that they could just let the episode blow over. When they realized that the anger and resistance were not going away, they responded by sending out an email assuring people that "this is not a problem, and we are on track to have a great business year." In essence, they were saying, "Just get over it and move on." Nothing could have been further from what was needed.

Luckily, we were able to influence the leadership team to introduce an alternative strategy of engagement and active listening—opening up rather than shutting down communications. We designed a series of small, cascaded "listening sessions" conducted face-to-face, during which each and every employee had the opportunity to speak directly to their executive. Prior to executing the listening sessions, we coached executives in how to listen unconditionally to what employees had to say, inviting all responses in confidence and without recrimination. The executive team then compiled all of the sessions' comments and personally visited each site to convene large groups of employees for a dialogue on what they had heard and what actions they were committed to taking in response.

The results were phenomenal. Over three months, trust was regained in the company because the leaders showed up as authentic—really hearing and responding to people's pain, anger, and loss of faith. Employees, in turn, took it upon themselves to restore the faith and confidence of their customers and communities in the organization. The entire crisis became a major catalyst for a companywide values clarification and alignment process that engaged all employees.

to express their emotional upset enables the upset to dissipate. This is 180 degrees opposite from what our ego wants to do. It wants to suppress, contain, or overcome the upset. By strengthening your conscious awareness and ability to connect to your own center and being in the midst of crisis, you can remain centered and model a more effective behavior of unconditional listening.

Think of this dynamic another way. Remember that the ego judges, creating mental boundaries of right and wrong: "these thoughts, feeling, or actions are good"; "those thoughts, feelings, and actions are bad." Where the ego sets these boundaries establishes the point of conflict and what needs to be fought or fled from. At first, the executives in the Case-In-Point above drew a line and labeled our proposed listening sessions as bad because their egos feared getting out of control, being incompetent, and being powerless in the face of employee animosity (their core needs were triggered). After educating the leaders about human dynamics, they realized they needed to expand their thinking, remove their judgment, and engage in the listening sessions. This internal shift in their perception allowed them to do what they at first perceived as negative. In similar fashion, employees at first judged the executives as untrustworthy, creating their own boundary for conflict. When they experienced the executives as real people who listened unconditionally without defensiveness or rebuttal, their judgment lifted, and trust was rebuilt.

Transformation always comes from expanding the ego's boundary further out and perceiving as positive what you initially were holding as negative. And this includes how you treat "negative" emotions. Rather than hold them out, let them in. Perceive them as neutral, not negative. Allow them to exist. Feel them and support others to do the same so the emotions can be released. Holding the space for others so they can be heard and felt in the middle of their emotional upset is transformative. And it is one of your primary responsibilities as a conscious change leader.

Acceptance is a moment of neutrality where ego stops fighting, our awareness opens, being emerges, and commitment can begin to grow. By holding the space for contracted emotions to exist, you enable commitment to be born.

Another very key point to keep in mind: *Your job is not to get the resisters to commit.* That will happen on its own accord as resistance diminishes, if the content of your change is viable. Your job is simply to help employees get to neutral, to a moment of acceptance where their mind, body, and emotions can relax and open. Then their being can show up, and commitment will grow naturally. Once that begins, put them to work. Engage them in the challenges of the change effort. Give them opportunities to learn, grow, and develop; allow opportunities to self-actualize. You will be pleased with the outcome.

Be very aware here. Your ego—in the face of their initial resistance—will likely subtly try to manipulate stakeholders from their position of resistance to commitment. But your manipulation, no matter how disguised and covert, will be felt by them. It will cause them to further resist. Resistance is a contracted force and when you push on it, no matter how minor, it contracts further. To be effective, you have to keep yourself connected to your own being, not your ego, operating from center rather than your own emotional reaction. Do not manipulate; simply accept them as they are, and they will change of their own accord.

Next is an overview of how to support the transformational shift in others. As you read it, remember that remaining centered in your being is more important than any of these steps.

Guidelines for Supporting the Transformational Shift

Many approaches and tools can support people to make the emotional shift out of resistance. Two-way, face-to-face conversation is vital, either with an individual if the issue only pertains to them, or in a team or larger group setting if the upset is pervasive. Structured and cascaded team meetings can work. No matter what methods and tools you use, here are guidelines that will help you succeed.

1. How you contextualize the conversation, invite people into it, and set up the process is critical!

    ○ Make sure participants know that this is not a "usual" business meeting of a one-way tell, a sell, or a contrived question-and-answer session.

    ○ Make overt the expectation that you want to hear the full scope of what they think and feel.

    ○ Make it clear that no matter what is said, there will be no recrimination or retribution.

    ○ Tell them that you will repeat back to them what is said to ensure you understand correctly.

    ○ Let them know when you will get back to them and how, and that you will be making commitments for action based on what you hear.

2. Hold the space for their resistance and call it forth by making space in yourself.

    ○ Remain conscious of what occurs in your own mind, body, and emotions.

    ○ Remain as centered, consciously aware, and operating from your highest self as you can; be observant of your own ego reacting negatively to their resistance. If you react and get upset, you will only make matters worse. There is no place for defensiveness or aggressiveness in this process.

○ Accept them, and do not make them wrong for their thoughts and feelings. Their reactions are valid and real for them. Do not judge them.

○ Do not try to convince, manipulate, or subtly coerce them into perceiving things differently. Just let them be where they are.

○ Listen, listen, listen. Hold the space for them to vent into, without defensiveness or attack on your part. Simply receive what they say and do.

3. Open a two-way dialogue. Begin by stating your observations that you see that people are concerned and that you want to hear their concerns first hand. Then ask them about their general concerns about the change, using questions such as the following:

○ How are you doing?

○ How is this change impacting you and others? What concerns, issues, or questions do you have?

○ How do you think this change will benefit or cause problems for our organization? (Let them challenge the content.)

4. Ask them questions that might surface their deeper concerns. Do not label these as "core needs" or anything else. Simply inquire from the perspective of trying to understand them. If you are convening a very large group, you might want to first ask these "deeper" questions in smaller groups so participants feel more emotionally safe. Plus, more people will get to speak. This will help more people to have the courage to bring their concerns to a larger group dialogue.

○ What concerns do you have that things won't work out in the end, or that your personal job security is threatened?

○ What concerns do you have about being included or having a part to play on the team as a result of this change? About potentially losing the relationships you have valued in your work?

○ What concerns do you have about losing power and influence over the work we do as a result of the change?

○ What concerns do you have that our plan going forward is not clear, structured, or organized enough?

○ What concerns do you have about your ability to perform and succeed in the new state?

○ What concerns do you have that you or others may be hurt by the change or that decisions will not be fair?

○ Which of these concerns are the most important to you during this change?

Be sure to reflect back to them what you hear them say in their answers. Use active listening to ensure they are heard and that you interpret what they say accurately.

5. Provide information about the change, but do not attempt in any way to convince them that your perspective is right and theirs is wrong. Stay in neutral, and simply discuss the following:

   ○ Review and discuss the case for change, the desired outcomes, and the current timeframe for the change.

   ○ Talk about what is not changing to provide reassurance that not everything is falling into "chaos."

   ○ Emphasize the strengths they bring that will help them succeed.

   ○ Discuss scenarios and possibilities you see for the future.

   ○ Ask them to identify any potential benefits they see for themselves coming out of the change. Share the benefits you anticipate for yourself and the team's work from the change.

   ○ Let them know where there are opportunities to become involved and participate.

   ○ Acknowledge what you don't know and when those things are likely to be worked out and clarified.

   ○ Explain how you will inform them on updates and new developments; schedule specific times for this.

6. Ask them what they *can* support about the change right now, and what they need to become fully engaged and committed. Do not promise anything, except what you know you can deliver. Make a request for a time-bound grace period, where they consider the possibility for the change, its overall value for the organization, and how they might support it.

   ○ Request that they do not promote resistance in others during this time, and that they simply think about the change with fresh eyes.

7. Ask them how you can support them and what further information they might need. Make commitments to each other for a follow-up discussion.

The emotional shift from resistance to neutral is the birthplace of commitment. It is truly an inner dynamic. You cannot force it from the outside. But you can support it, first by being in real, authentic relationship with the person or people who are resisting. Secondly, by bringing to the interaction your highest self that does not judge or make others wrong. In essence, your being holds the space for their ego's resistance and by doing so, exerts a transformational influence. When a person complains, disagrees, or vents into such an unconditional, accepting space, there are no boundaries there for their resistance to hit and trigger more conflict, attack, or manipulation. There is no fight to be had, so their resistance, once heard and acknowledged, dissipates naturally. This provides an inner release to the charge their ego was carrying, enabling their awareness to clear. A level of openness emerges, and the inquiry into the value of the transformation takes on a very different tone. If the direction and content of the transformation have merit, they will now perceive it, and their commitment will grow all by itself—not because of what you did, but because of the "presence" you brought to them. When you put your being first, breakthrough can happen.

SUMMARY

In this chapter, we uncovered critical human dynamics that need to be fully understood to design and lead change efforts that generate stakeholder commitment and breakthrough results. Key points include the following:

1. Resistance is caused when a person's core needs are triggered, and their ego perceives that their needs will not be met.
2. Resistance is unconsciously generated by the ego; resistance is seldom an intentional ploy by stakeholders to sabotage your change effort.
3. Stakeholder resistance is not to be feared but expected.
4. Emotional transitions are natural, predictable, and manageable, and drops in performance are normal during these transitions.
5. You have key responsibilities as a conscious change leader to design change strategies that minimize the threat to stakeholders' core needs and to support people through their emotional transitions when they are triggered.
6. There is a tipping point, a moment when people make an internal "shift" out of resistance and into a neutral state of acceptance. Making this shift is a requirement of their developing commitment. Supporting the shift is a primary responsibility of all conscious change leaders.
7. Conscious change leaders are not responsible for "overcoming" resistance. Rather, their job is to hold an accepting space for others to express their resistance into so it can be fully felt and resolved by them.

8. Commitment is developed as a natural outcome when people come to accurately see the value of a change effort and are engaged in solving its challenges to ensure success.

You can see that conscious change leadership approaches resistance from a deeper, more fundamental perspective than change management. Conscious change leaders see stakeholders as co-creators of the change and accept them onto the "change team" in whatever state they are initially in, no matter how resistant. The intent of conscious change leaders is always to assist stakeholders to grow and develop as people, to transcend their ego limitations to engage their higher self, and to further self-actualize as part of the organization's transformation. Simply quelling resistance is not an objective they hold. Rather than try to avoid resistance or push through it when it occurs, conscious change leaders greet and engage it. They invite it out because they have the skills to hold the space for it so it can release. What emerges in its place is deeper trust, connection, and commitment from all involved, and, therefore, more potential to succeed. Increased self-actualization emerges out of the place where resistance once resided.

In the next chapter, we turn our attention to the role and impact of mindset, continuing our inquiry into critical human dynamics in change.

ENDNOTES

1. Beck, D., and Cohen, C. *Spiral Dynamics: Mastering Values, Leadership and Change.* Cambridge, MA: Blackwell, 1996.
2. Maslow, A. *Motivation and Personality* (2nd Edition). New York: Harper and Row, 1970.
3. Kaye, B., and Jordan-Evans, S. *Love 'Em or Lose 'Em.* San Francisco: Berrett Koehler Publishers, 2005.
4. Bridges, W. *Managing Transitions: Making the Most of Change* (2nd Edition). Cambridge, MA: Da Capo Press, 2003.
5. Kübler-Ross, E., and Kessler, D. *On Grief and Grieving.* Scribner, 1997.
6. Adams, J., and Spencer, S. *Life Changes: A Guide to the Seven Stages of Personal Growth.* Paraview Press, 2002.

The Role and Impact of Mindset

The universe is transformation; our life is what our thoughts make it.

—Marcus Aurelius

A number of years ago, a university professor conducted an experiment in his Introduction to Psychology class. The class was held in a large auditorium with more than 300 students present. As the professor was standing at his lectern on the stage, a large man ran aggressively toward him. The man was tall and burly and was dressed in black leather pants and a pair of black motorcycle boots. His dark hair was long and greasy, and he sported a black stocking cap pulled low over his brow. He wore large chains that dangled from both his belt loops and his boots.

As the man reached the professor, he withdrew something from underneath his jacket. The crowd gasped as the man pointed the object at the professor's chest. Simultaneously, a teaching assistant, who was hidden behind the stage curtain, fired a 22-caliber pistol loaded with blank cartridges. The students screamed and ran as the professor fell to the stage floor, and the man escaped offstage.

From behind the stage, the teaching assistant spoke over the loudspeaker to bring calm to the class, "The professor is all right. This is a simulation. Please calm down and return to your seats."

The professor stood, and asked the class, "What did you just see occur?" The majority of the class reported that they saw a hoodlum shoot the professor with a large caliber pistol. Why do you think they saw a pistol, when in fact, the man was wielding a large yellow banana?

The majority of students saw a false reality because of their mindset and the erroneous assumption it formulated from the data they had. Their mindsets constructed the sights and sounds to mean "hoodlum" and "murder." They reacted to dynamics that weren't actually there. They reacted with fear and attempted to run for the exits, neither of which was factually called for. This happens all too often in transformation and is a major cause of failure.

In this chapter, we investigate the human dynamic at play in this example: mindset. We further define mindset and specifically highlight how it determines the following:

- Our perceptions of reality
- Our internal experience
- Our level of achievement
- Our personal responsibility and empowerment
- How well we walk our talk
- How well we design our change processes

WHAT IS MINDSET?

Mindset is represented in the upper left quadrant of our Four Quadrants of Conscious Change Leader Accountability Model (refer to Figure I.2 in the Introduction), representing the inner dimension of individuals.

Mindset is our worldview, the place or orientation from which we experience our reality and form our perceptions of it. The cornerstones of our mindset are our core beliefs and values we hold about ourselves, others, and life in general, that is, our fundamental assumptions about reality. Many of these (mostly unconscious) beliefs pertain to our core human needs. Our ego creates its identity around these beliefs, which are a part of our mindset and influence how we see the world. Our mindsets contain the core constructs of our ego's mental conditioning that organize incoming sensory data to create *meaning* out of the sights, sounds, smells, tastes, and sensations that we experience through our interface with reality.

Many leaders were first introduced to the notion of mindset and how it impacts leadership performance through Joel Barker's video series on "paradigm shifts," which was based on Thomas Kuhn's ideas (1962).[1] Then Peter Senge (1990)[2] popularized the concepts of personal mastery and mental models in his bestseller, *The Fifth Discipline*. "Mental models" are similar to our definition of fundamental assumptions and core beliefs. Senge's work helped legitimize this concept for leaders and consultants and furthered the understanding of mindset in organizations. The discussion of mindset—given its impact on results—now needs to move onto center stage in leading and consulting to transformation. The current failure rate of change demands it.

Mindset is different from awareness.[3] Metaphorically, awareness is the blank canvas upon which our perception draws our reality. Mindset is the filter through which we perceive, determining what gets drawn and how it is interpreted.

Mindset is different from knowledge. Whereas knowledge can be seen as the *content* of our mind, mindset is the mental framework that constructs a particular meaning from that content.

Mindset is also different from thinking, which can be seen as the overt *process* of our mind. There are different types of thinking, such as rational thinking, strategic thinking, intuitive thinking, visual thinking, or linear thinking. No matter what type of thinking we are engaged in, mindset is the context within which all of our thinking occurs.

We also differentiate mindset from emotions and behavior. Webster defines emotions as "the affective aspect of consciousness; feeling; the state of feeling; a psychic and physical reaction subjectively experienced as strong feeling and physiologically involving changes that prepare the body for immediate vigorous action." From our perspective, emotions are the qualitative descriptors you place on the sensations caused in your body by your mindset. When your mindset perceives an event as "threatening," you experience certain associated emotions—fear, stress, anxiety, sadness, doubt, frustration, nervousness, and so forth. Some people label these emotions as negative, but we see them simply as "contracted," causing certain responses within your body to prepare you for handling a threat: muscles tighten, breath shortens, heart rate and blood pressure increase, specific hormones flood your body, and your nervous system becomes more excited. These emotions are simply your mindset's way of sounding the battle cry.

When your mindset deems an external event to be valuable or supportive, you experience "expanded" emotions—confidence, excitement, happiness, pleasure— and your body responds accordingly. Your breath gets longer and deeper, your muscles relax, and different sets of hormones are triggered. The point is that emotions are neither good nor bad; they are simply the bodily sensations that correlate to and are produced by certain mindsets. "E-motions" are simply the energy in motion in your body based on how you are interpreting reality at the time.

Webster defines behavior as "the manner of conducting oneself; the way in which something behaves." Behavior is both the action we do and the tone or quality we place into that action. Behavior is the bridge between the inner world of our thoughts and emotions and the outer world of our actions and results.

Formally addressing the topic of mindset supports change leaders to ask critical questions of themselves, such as the following:

▶ How does my mindset influence my decisions, actions, and results?

▶ What aspects of my mindset contribute to my ability to lead transformation, and what aspects of my mindset limit my success?

▶ What role does my mindset play in who I am as a change leader today and in becoming the change leader I want to be?

▶ What beliefs and assumptions exist in my mindset that I am not even aware of, yet limit the quality of my performance and life?

Mindset Is Causative

A fundamental premise of conscious change leadership is that *mindset is causative*; it directly influences and impacts our internal experience and our external behaviors, quality of performance, and results. The Self Mastery Model (Figure 7.1) graphically displays this fact. Let's go through the model step by step.

There is a two-way relationship between the external environment and leaders' mindsets, or fundamental beliefs and assumptions about reality—events happen in the external environment (a: facts), and they influence and affect leaders' mindsets; leaders' mindsets about reality determine (b: interpretation) what they perceive (c) in reality. The interface between what happens in reality and leaders' interpretation of it "causes" their internal state—their thoughts, decisions, sensations, emotions, and energy (d). Leaders' internal states then determine their behavior and the manner in which they conduct themselves (e). Their behavior in turn shapes their actions and quality of performance (f), which impact their results (g). Leaders' results then become a part of their external environment (h), and the process continues as they perceive their new reality.

Figure 7.1. The Self Mastery Model

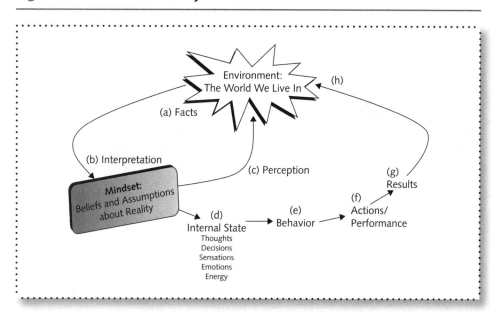

The Self Mastery Model shows that the results we create in the world are rooted in our mindset and way of being. Everything—our attitude, feelings, behavior, actions, and results—stems from our mindset. This does not mean, as some theorists might suggest, that altering your mindset automatically produces a concomitant shift in results. You still have to deal with the forces of the external world and the need to *do* something to impact them. Believing you can fly does not mean that you can fly. However, transforming your mindset does increase the probability of success because an optimal state of mind enables you to manifest more of your ability as you engage in the actions required to produce your desired outcome.

The Impact of Mindset on Perception

Many of us confuse the events that happen around us with our mental constructs of those events. The two are so intricately woven that we often do not realize the impact our mindsets have on determining our perceptions of reality. Because reality and perception are so seamlessly intertwined, we don't see that they are in fact two distinct phenomena. We commonly make the mistake of assuming that our perception of reality is objective, when it seldom is.

Figure 7.2. The Seamless Connection Between Mindset and Reality

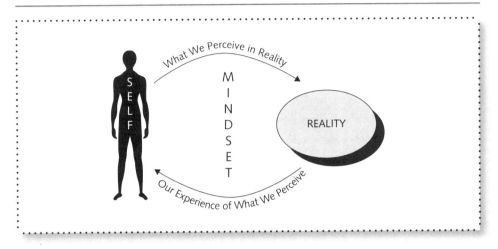

Figure 7.2 demonstrates this dynamic. What we perceive in reality is influenced by our mindset, just as our mindset determines our experience of what we perceive. Again, notice the two-way relationship; mindset influences what we perceive "out there" and what we experience "in here." Therefore, mindset impacts both our external reality and our internal reality. This will become clearer as we proceed.

Our mental constructions of reality often cause us to see a world that doesn't really exist. Mindset is extremely powerful; it can construct whatever "objective" reality we want to believe. People once thought that the world was flat. This belief did not make the world flat. It did not change the empirical evidence. It simply determined the meaning that was made of the empirical evidence of seeing a ship go off the edge of the horizon. And with that meaning made, sailors acted as if the world was flat and mostly sailed close to shore.

Because of this seamless connection between reality and mindset, it is very difficult to know what is reality and what is interpretation or a mental construct of reality. Is the world flat, or do you just see it as flat? Are your employees resistant, or do you just see them that way?

Here are some amusing, very public misinterpretations leaders have made in the past. Think about the major impact these errors in judgment had, and you can easily see just how important a role mindset plays in leading transformation successfully.

This 'telephone' has too many shortcomings to be seriously considered as a means of communication. The device is inherently of no value to us.

—Western Union internal memo, 1876

The wireless music box has no imaginable commercial value. Who would pay for a message sent to nobody in particular?

—David Sarnoff's associates in response to his urgings for investments in the radio in the 1920s

We don't like their sound, and guitar music is on the way out.

—Decca Recording Company, rejecting the Beatles, 1962

There is no reason anyone would want a computer in their home.

—Ken Olson, president, chairman, and founder of Digital Equipment Corporation, 1977

Drill for oil? You mean drill into the ground to try and find oil? You're crazy.

—Drillers whom Edwin L. Drake tried to enlist to his project to drill for oil in 1859

The observer (me in here) and the observed (it and them out there) are deeply interconnected. Change leaders who operate on autopilot consistently slip into the delusion that reality and their interpretation of it are one and the same. Because they do not see and understand the difference between "out there" and "in here," between external reality and internal meaning making, they cannot strategically address how mindset influences perception, either their own or anyone else's. Consequently, mindset—the most powerful of change levers in all human systems, from individuals to societies—goes unattended. As we stated earlier, confusing reality and our interpretation of reality is one of the most debilitating errors we can make as change leaders, and when we operate on autopilot, we do it consistently, often causing us to perceive our change efforts' content, process, and people issues inaccurately.

Conscious change leaders, because they explore their own internal dynamics, are aware of the influence of their mindset on their perception and consider it in every critical decision or action they take. Because they realize that mindset influences their own and others' perceptions, conscious change leaders ensure that they and others explore their mindsets as a central strategy of their organization's transformation process. They seek out and name the mental models that influence their assessment of data, their change process design decisions, and their implementation plans. Executives have been doing this since the 1970s as part of strategic planning when they define the assumptions they hold about their marketplace. In conscious change leadership, we take it further.

The Impact of Mindset on State of Being

The reticular activating system (RAS), which lies at the base of the brain stem, is among the most primitive parts of the brain, sometimes referred to as the "reptilian brain." The RAS is the gateway for incoming sensory information, sending it to either the conscious mind or the subconscious mind (see Figure 7.3).

The RAS sends both valuable and threatening information to the *conscious* mind; we then become aware of it and can respond appropriately. The RAS sends information that is neither valuable nor threatening to the *subconscious* mind. Because this information is insignificant, the RAS does not bother us with it. Because we are not made aware of this information, we do not know it is being inputted into our brains. It simply is recorded as an unconscious memory.[4]

Figure 7.3. Reticular Activating System

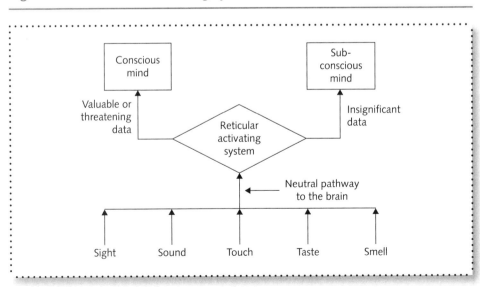

What tells the RAS how to process the information we receive? What determines whether the incoming data is perceived as valuable, threatening, or inconsequential? Our neocortex does—the programming and conditioning of our mindset (ego)!

For example, events happen: The stock market goes up; your customer service rating goes down; your biggest client orders $10M worth of product; your idea is rejected in the staff meeting; your child's soccer team wins the tournament; your mortgage check bounces. Some events you label as "good," and you react favorably to them. Other events you label as "bad," and you react negatively to those. Your reaction is determined by your mindset: how you perceive and judge what you experience. It is not determined by the event itself, which we demonstrated in the psychology professor's experiment at the opening of this chapter.

Most of us believe that events in reality have inherent value. In other words, some things are positive while others are negative. However, most of reality is comprised of "neutral" events, which are not good or bad in themselves. They just are. We register these neutral events through our senses of sight, sound, taste, smell, and touch.[5] Our mindset then adds meaning to these events, evaluating them as valuable, threatening, or insignificant. The "valuable" data triggers an "expanded" state of being; the "threatening" data triggers a "contracted" internal state; and the "insignificant" data produces no reaction at all. Specific information, valued or feared by our mindset, then becomes the trigger of an expanded or contracted emotional and behavioral response within us. Our state of being, moment by moment, is thus determined by our mindset. The *source of our reactions, whether positive or negative, is the meaning made by our mindset.*

Way of Being

Mindset, emotions, and behavior are intricately linked and interact with one another as an interconnected system we refer to as one's *way of being*. For example, if leaders possess a mindset that "change should be fast and painless," when complex, long-term change is actually required, they may feel impatient and frustrated at the slow pace. Behaviorally, they may become controlling, domineering, and autocratic. Their mindset, emotion, and behavior are triggered as one unified shift reflected in their way of being.

Way of being is a powerful concept. It can be used to describe how leaders are "being" and expressing themselves at any point in time or how they are relating to others in various circumstances and situations. While mindset causes emotions and behavior, the combination is the source of leaders' way of being.

Over time, all leaders acquire a habitual change leadership style. This style is their way of being applied in their role as a change leader. Their change leadership style is an outgrowth of their mindset and emotional and behavioral patterns. At times, however, a leader's way of being can change in different roles or under different circumstances, but generally, it is relatively consistent and reflects the deeper dimensions of their ego's conditioning.

People make reference to others' ways of being frequently. An example that illustrates this pertains to Sue, the senior vice president of manufacturing in one of our client organizations. When John, one of her direct reports, returned from a meeting with Sue, his team immediately asked, "How did Sue respond to our issue?" John replied, "She was responsive and concerned about fixing the problem." John's answer revealed Sue's "content" position about the problem, while simultaneously alluding to Sue's way of being.

In our change leadership coaching practice, we often ask change leaders to make clear distinctions between their ways of being and what they do—their actions. Usually, leaders focus primarily on what they do and pay little attention to how they are coming across to others; they focus only on the external world at the expense of their internal world. This creates numerous problems. For example, when leaders take action, they assume they will have a certain impact or produce a specific outcome. However, taking action with different ways of being can create very different results. In the preceding example, if Sue had been defensive and hostile, even though she may have ultimately agreed to resolve the team's problem, her confrontational way of being would have had a much different impact on the team than if she had been positive and genuinely concerned. Way of being is a powerful force in human interaction, often far more impactful than the content. In the guidelines for supporting others to make a transformational shift outlined in the previous chapter, way of being is the key factor in "holding the space" for others to release their resistance and build commitment. What you say often matters less than how you say it and where you come from in yourself. When you are caring, compassionate, and present, almost any content you deliver will "land" better with the recipient.

The Impact of Mindset on Performance

Mindset not only influences our perception and internal experience but also our external performance and results. A very simple equation called the Fundamental Law of Individual Success (Anderson, 1986) clearly demonstrates the impact of mindset on performance. This law is stated as:

$$\text{Ability Level} \times \text{Mental State} = \text{Performance}$$

Our ability level establishes our *potential* for success. It is a product of our experience, training, and genetics. Ability increases or decreases based on your practice routine, but at any *point in time*, we have a distinct ability level in any task we undertake.

Ability does not guarantee success. Ask any athlete. Sometimes the most skilled athlete loses, or the less skilled wins. Herein lies the impact of mindset on performance. Mindset, which directly influences the inner state we are in when we are performing (or at any other time, for that matter), determines how much of our potential we actualize.

As Table 7.1 illustrates, if we are 100 percent focused, then we perform at 100 percent of our ability level. We reach our potential because we are fully present and engaged. This is the internal "flow state" or "being in the zone," as many high performers describe it,[6] where we are operating from our being and not blocked by our ego's fears. People often call this an "altered state" because it is nonordinary. But it is always available if we know how to quiet our ego to access it. This is the competitive edge that most elite performers possess.

If we are distracted or preoccupied, then our performance suffers because we are performing at less than 100 percent focus. If 20 percent of our mindset is occupied elsewhere, then only 80 percent of our ability can manifest. We underperform by the 20 percent that is engaged elsewhere. This phenomenon is true whether we are leading transformation, playing golf, or nurturing our children.

Table 7.1. Fundamental Law of Individual Success

	Ability Level		Mental State	Performance
Person A	Trial 1	10	100% Focus	10
	Trial 2	10	80% Focus	8
	Trial 3	10	60% Focus	6
Person B	Trial 1	8	60% Focus	4.8
	Trial 2	8	80% Focus	6.4
	Trial 3	8	100% Focus	8

In the early stages of Dean's career, he founded and ran the Optimal Performance Institute in Oakland, California, where he trained elite performers how to manage their internal states of being to perform optimally. Dean learned these methods early; he was a world-class swimmer in his youth, being the first ten-year-old boy to break one minute for the hundred-yard freestyle and the first twelve-year-old to break two minutes in the two hundred. He went on to become an All American swimmer and water polo player at Stanford University, where he began formulating his Optimizing System for managing inner states for high performance.

Dean witnessed numerous success stories at the Optimal Performance Institute. The CFO of a Fortune 500 company won his country club's golf tournament after years of barely making the top 10. Three young figure skaters who never contended for gold at the U.S. Nationals went on to get first, second, and fourth places three months after learning his system. And Kristi Yamaguchi and Debbie Thomas, both students of his when very young, went on to win gold medals in figure skating at two different Olympics. Did these athletes succeed because they managed their internal states better? We will never know for sure. They clearly all had superior talent. This was the early 1980s, when mental training for athletes was only seriously pursued in eastern bloc countries such as Russia. Dean had been using these techniques since the age of 10. When he was in Moscow competing in the World Student Games at the age of 20, he had some very informative conversations with Russian trainers who were using advanced "accelerated mental training" techniques, which he later successfully adopted at the Optimal Performance Institute. Now, mental training is common with athletes, but the same techniques are equally powerful in business. They are just not used very often.

In 1990, an IBM subsidiary hired the Optimal Performance Institute to train its 300 top salespeople. Dean instructed them to bring a client problem they could not solve into the one-day session. After learning and just beginning to practice these techniques, 83% of the participants said they had discovered the solution to their problem during the session. These same high-performance techniques for athletes can provide solutions for conscious change leaders to the complexities of leading transformation.

We tend to perform best when we are confident, calm, and centered because that "expanded" state of being makes it easier to focus 100 percent on the task. When we are in a "contracted" state—experiencing fear, doubt, or anxiety—we tend to lose focus because we are mentally and emotionally preoccupied with our internal upset. Our egos are engaged rather than our beings operating in pure awareness of what is happening around and within us. However, the best performers in any discipline, from sports to acting to leading transformation, are those people who have developed the ability to manage their internal state and can maintain 100 percent focus on the task, regardless of their emotions. For these "masterful" people, contracted emotions don't distract them. When their ego is triggered and they feel fear, but they are able to remain consciously aware, operating from their being with one-pointed concentration, and they can take the energy of the fear and apply it to their performance.

In Table 7.1, notice how Person A's performance suffers as he loses mental focus over the three trials. See how Person B's performance improves as she increases her focus over the three trials. Notice also that a lesser-skilled person can actually perform better than a person of greater skill—if the lesser-skilled person is in a more "centered" and "focused" state of mind. With all of the distractions and dynamics of leading transformation, this is an essential skill to master as a conscious change leader.

SELF-MASTERY

Self-mastery is the process of turning inward and engaging your conscious awareness to discover the patterns in your mindset, emotions, and behaviors; transforming those patterns that are limiting, and engaging ones that model your chosen ways of being and deliver your desired results. Self-mastery is personal development in all four dimensions of ourselves: physically, emotionally, mentally, and spiritually. The pursuit of self-mastery lessens the control your ego has and places it with your authentic self—your being.

Conscious change leaders pursue self-mastery in two ways: self-management and personal transformation. Self-management is the ability to manage your internal state of being in *real time* so you can be more focused and centered as you perform. Self-management skill is learning to manage your ego's fears to maintain 100 percent concentration. Personal transformation is the process of overcoming historical or conditioned fears, doubts, and self-limiting ways of being that keep you from being fully focused in present time or cause undesirable behaviors. Personal transformation is a longer process that takes place *over time*.

Notice the relationship between self-management and personal transformation. Self-management is what change leaders do "online" to adjust their internal state during real-time activities to maximize their performance. Personal transformation is what change leaders do "off-line" over time to manifest more of their potential. It is how they overcome habitual ego reactions so they won't need to *manage* them in real time. Both of these skills begin with conscious awareness and a strong ability to witness what is going on inside of you. Both enable conscious change leaders to operate from their beings more and their egos less. Doing so dramatically raises their effectiveness.

The key to self-mastery, as with any skill set, is *practice*. It is relatively easy for us to break a behavioral habit in an isolated situation but far more difficult for

SELF-MASTERY TECHNIQUES

There are many self-mastery processes, tools, and techniques that you can use to improve both your self-management and personal transformation skills:

- Breathing techniques (See premium content: How Developing Breath Control Can Make You a Better Leader; www.pfeiffer.com/go/anderson.)
- Body awareness and relaxation techniques
- Mental rehearsal tools, including visualization and affirmations
- Emotional release techniques
- Focusing techniques
- Behavior pattern reprogramming
- Personal visioning and purpose identification
- Energy management
- Diet and exercise
- Values clarification
- Core belief identification
- Behavioral style assessments

Our role in this intervention was to help the executive team transform the plant from "worst-in-class" to "best-in-class." Early in the change effort, Henry, the team leader, committed himself to taking a conscious approach and pursing his own self-mastery with our assistance. Henry was the new facility manager, a young upstart recently out of business school who thought he knew all the latest management approaches to improving work processes. Joe was the production superintendent of the facility, a hard-nosed, long-term employee with twenty years of service who was the technical expert in running the manufacturing facility's machinery. Both Henry and Joe were loyal employees who wanted to contribute the most they could to the organization.

Joe, who represented the "old guard," resisted Henry's new ideas and refused to implement them fully. Henry felt threatened by Joe's resistance, for he realized that the entire facility was swayed by Joe's opinions. For three months, Henry and Joe went at it toe-to-toe, with no resolution in sight. As a result of their constant bickering, the plant's executive team was in disarray, divided along party lines between the "newcomers" and the "old guard." The plant's performance continued to deteriorate, primarily as a result of the leaders being unable to agree to a change strategy.

Henry, in exasperation, requested some coaching from us. We taught him a number of self-mastery tools, which he began to practice and apply effectively. As a result, he began to explore his fundamental assumptions and core beliefs about the situation. With some assistance, Henry began to realize that he was assuming that Joe was a threat, perceiving Joe as inherently obstinate, and battling with Joe from the belief that if he, Henry, didn't "win," he would lose face and credibility with the other managers. Looking deeper within himself, Henry saw that his hostility toward Joe was driven by his own desire and need to be seen as competent, which he saw as his path to being included and liked by the other leaders. Henry realized that this competency issue came from his own deep-seated doubt in himself and his desire to make a real contribution. When he wasn't sure that he was capable, Henry usually felt that others saw him as incapable, and that frightened him because he had such a high need to be included and liked.

(continued)

Henry's new awareness of his previously unconscious mindset enabled him to begin a personal transformation process. He began to acknowledge his own competence separate from what others thought of him and began to view Joe as an ally who held the shared vision of making the facility as successful as possible. This shift of mindset, along with breathing and centering techniques, enabled Henry to behave and act differently toward Joe in real time. Rather than tell Joe how his old ways were wrong, Henry began to listen to Joe more, to entertain Joe's views rather than pontificate his own. Over the course of a few weeks, Henry's change in behavior and performance began to alter his results with Joe. Joe began to tone down his own hostility toward Henry; Joe had less reason to fight because Henry was no longer his adversary. Soon Joe began to listen more himself and was surprised by the good ideas he heard coming from Henry. As Joe warmed to Henry's innovations, he tried a few of them, and their successes helped Joe build further trust in Henry.

Over time, Henry and Joe's bond strengthened as the performance of the facility improved. The rest of the management staff began to temper their own hostilities as they saw their leaders cooperate more. Soon they had a collaborative solution for transforming the facility. In the end, Henry and Joe formed a tight partnership based on mutual respect and open acknowledgement that each brought different and equally essential pieces of the facility's overall formula for success. The team excelled, and the plant emerged twelve months later to become "best-in-class."

us to sustain the new behavior over time. The processes, tools, and techniques in the sidebar are only effective if you use them regularly. In our change leadership development work, we consistently see that those change leaders who establish and maintain a daily practice of self-mastery become the most masterful. No ifs, ands, or buts: practice makes perfect.

Committing to a daily practice of self-mastery is a natural by-product of choosing to live and lead transformation consciously. It begins with your choice to turn inward—to reflect about who you are, how you are in the world, and what impact you aspire to have on those around you. In choosing a conscious approach to change leadership, you will naturally begin to self-manage in real time and personally transform over time. And like wine, as you age you will just keep getting better.

The Case in Point demonstrates the importance of self-mastery in action and its ability to help change leaders recognize and change their mindsets and behavior through both self-management and personal transformation processes and tools. The case illustrates the basic behavioral tenet of self-mastery:

Fix yourself first, and then others, and the environment.

By "fix," we do not mean that you are broken. Remember, we all have conditioned egos that cause undesirable ways of being in us and lesser results than we want. By "fix," we simply mean attend to and manage your own self and mindset first. Engage your conscious awareness and return to a clear and centered internal state so you are better able to deal with the external situation and people. Put your "being first."

In Henry's case, he was able to create a powerful partnership with Joe because he saw how his own mindset was creating the hostile relationship with Joe. He owned that he was responsible for contributing to their conflict. Yes, bull-headed Joe also contributed, but Henry realized that he could not change Joe. He could only change himself. Consequently, he "awoke" to his previously unconscious mindset and antagonistic way of behaving toward Joe and altered himself accordingly. When he shifted his mindset about Joe, his feelings, behavior, and actions began to change. Because he was relating to Joe in a different way, it set up a different dynamic between them. Over time, these new conditions between Henry and Joe enabled Joe and the rest of the management staff to alter their own mindsets and behavior. Henry modeled the fundamental way of being of a conscious change leader: He turned inward and "fixed" himself first. Recall the guidelines for supporting the transformational shift: When we operate from our own being and hold the space for others to be how they are, it sets up the conditions for them to begin to shift out of their own ego reactions.

Our abilities as change leaders expand the moment we realize that the leverage point for transforming external events (our organizations) is transforming our own internal mindset about those events. When we take responsibility for the self-generated constructs of our own limiting mindsets and transform them, we acquire the potential to relate to the external situation in ways that enable the situation to change. It is difficult for us to see a solution to a change-related problem without first altering our mindset. Albert Einstein said it best in his now-famous quote: "The problems that exist in the world today cannot be solved by the level of thinking that created them." To solve or change anything of significance, we must first transform our mindsets to operate from a higher level of being and thinking. Pursuing self-mastery unleashes this capability.

From our perspective and the empirical evidence we have from thirty years of delivering to our clients the Being First Approach, self-mastery training should be a core component of all organizational transformations. It is the foundation of unleashing the human potential in an organization and the primary generator of breakthrough results.

PERSONAL EMPOWERMENT AND RESPONSIBILITY

For many of us, the fact that we create our own experience of reality based on how we see the world is difficult to accept, for it means that we are responsible for our own reactions, behaviors, and results. It is much easier for us to assume that we are not responsible, that we are somehow victims of the external forces around us. The belief pattern of this victim mentality goes something like this: "Events happen and they affect me; I cannot control how I feel or react. Since the events 'caused' me to feel and behave the way I do, I am not responsible." This "victim" mindset results when we do not understand the influence of mindset on our perception of reality.

When we are operating on autopilot, this victim mentality is the norm for most of us. It is the identity the ego crafts to keep us feeling okay about ourselves in the face of an undesirable situation. Recall that the ego thinks it is bad to experience contracted emotions, so when they are triggered, it simply takes the position of labeling the circumstance as the cause of them, absolving itself of any responsibility.

This victim orientation is the biggest drain on the human potential in organizations. It is the exact opposite of personal empowerment and responsibility, which are cornerstones of highly functional people. *Personal responsibility*, ultimately, is acknowledging that we are the source of all of our internal reactions and the behaviors, style, and outcomes they produce. It is the natural orientation we take when we fully understand and embrace the fundamental fact that "mindset is causative." *Personal empowerment* is the outcome of taking personal responsibility. It is accessing the source of our personal power—our *being*—through consciously observing our ego's limiting reactions and transcending them. *Personal empowerment* is the ability to step outside of our ego's comfort zone to make positive things happen and deliver results.

Conscious change leaders seek to operate with personal responsibility and empowerment, but they also consciously set up the conditions to support stakeholders in their change efforts to do the same. As we learned in the previous chapter, they interface with people who are in resistance in ways that assist those people to take personal responsibility by expressing their resistance, which of course starts to resolve the resistance. They also provide training and development where feasible to teach stakeholders the human dynamics we are discussing in this section. After this level of understanding is present in an organization, ego-activated issues get resolved quickly because people spend their time solving them rather than blaming, defending, or attacking each other. They become better performers and contributors, and better able to produce real results. Daily issues in transformational change efforts such as process breakdowns, role and decision making confusion, power and control issues, communication problems, interpersonal conflicts, and performance issues no longer cause major roadblocks.

Initially in their relationship, Henry and Joe each held onto a victim mentality, blaming one another for their conflict. They were each giving up their personal power to change and create the results they wanted. They focused more on complaining about each other than the source of the problem they could actually influence and fix—themselves. It only takes one side to generate a shift in an interpersonal dynamic. In this case, Henry "woke up" first.

Co-Creative Way of Being

As we pursue self-mastery and transform our ego conditioning to transcend (fulfill) our core needs, we express more of our beings. This generates new, more "evolved" ways of being in us. We *fight or flight* less and support and include more. Our hearts open because they contain less pain about our core needs not being met. We think more about others and what is best for the organization as a whole because we have less need to focus on our ego's self-interests. We become more compassionate, supportive, and cooperative. We become open to feedback, learning, and course correction. We become more flexible. We look for and accept others' input to our ideas. We engage in two-way communication, with as much or more attention on listening than speaking. We lessen our need to dominate and replace it with a sincere desire to collaborate.

The really great thing is that all this comes naturally. It takes attention to transform our egos, but what emerges out of that transformation takes no major effort because it is a natural outgrowth of our self-mastery. When we quiet the voices of our egos, our automatic and unconscious way of being becomes more "co-creative" (Exhibit 7.1).

Exhibit 7.1. Co-Creative Ways of Being

- Attend to the needs of others and the organization as a whole
- Personally empowered and responsible
- Collaborative and supportive
- Caring and considerate of others' needs
- Authentic; operating with high integrity and transparency
- Flexible
- Learning and development-oriented; passionate about improving

These attributes are "co-creative" in nature because they establish in us a greater ability to work in collaboration with others in pursuit of what is best for the larger organization. With a co-creative mindset and behavior pattern, we become capable of extraordinary results. When large numbers of people in an organization develop this way of being, breakthrough becomes far more probable.

Leaders and trainers take note: A very important point to understand here is that training and development in these types of *behaviors* can be very useful. However, behavior training will never be the source of people operating co-creatively. The source is their own inner awareness—their being—that emerges naturally when they personally transform the limitations within their egos. This makes personal transformation training, especially when coupled with behavior training, a very powerful intervention; and made even more powerful when overtly linked to transformation of your organizational systems and culture. Again, an integrated—and integral—approach to change in all quadrants and all levels produces maximum results.

Awareness: The Foundation of Self-Mastery

Exhibit 7.2 offers a simple but very effective way to help you identify your habitual reactions and patterns. Make copies of it, or create a spreadsheet like it, and use it for a week as a daily log to record your experience. Fill it in as soon as possible after leaving situations in which you were very "centered" and effective, or in which you reacted negatively in ways you would like to change. Describe what occurred in the situation that "triggered" your positive or negative reactions. Be specific, especially about your physical sensations, emotions, and internal

Exhibit 7.2. Assessing Your Ways of Being

WORKSHEET						

SELF-LIMITING

External Situation	Emotional Reaction	Physical Sensations	Mindset and Self-Talk	Behaviors	Actions	Results

OPTIMAL

External Situation	Emotional Reaction	Physical Sensations	Mindset and Self-Talk	Behaviors	Actions	Results

© 2011, Pfeiffer, An Imprint of John Wiley & Sons

"self-talk." In just a couple days, you will begin to see patterns across the columns. You will notice that similar situations trigger similar mental, emotional and physical states; behaviors; actions; and results. As you become familiar with both your self-limiting and optimal internal states, you will recognize them more quickly so you can either course-correct or reinforce them. Over time, your physical sensations and thoughts will become wake-up calls that activate your inner witness for real-time self-management and off-line personal transformation work.

WALKING THE TALK OF CHANGE

A critical change leadership behavior is for leaders to walk the talk of their change effort, to model the transformation they are after in the organization. The "talk" denotes their vision of desired behaviors, and the "walk" denotes their the behaviors and actions they actually model. Leaders who do not align their walk and talk, and consistently say one thing and do another, establish a predictable path to failure. This breeds distrust and dissention, increases employee resistance, and damages all hopes of building employee commitment for the transformation.

Walking the talk of change essentially means leading from the way of being that is aligned to, promotes, and demonstrates your desired culture. This aligns your individual behavior and mindset to the desired culture and models it into existence. Of course, you will need to align systems, structure, processes, and technology as well, but we will come to that in the next chapter. All things being equal, change leaders operating consciously have greater ability to walk their talk of change than those operating on autopilot because of their increased awareness and sustained focus and commitment to their own self-mastery process.

Walking the talk does not mean that you need to be perfect all the time. Mistakes are expected and quite acceptable as long as you do three things— (1) acknowledge your incongruent behavior to yourself and those it impacts; (2) make overt amends for it as appropriate; and (3) become more consistent in your talk and walk over time.

You may initially resist the idea of overtly acknowledging negative behaviors, especially to subordinates, but you will be amazed at how powerful this simple act is in building trust and establishing a cultural norm of personal responsibility throughout your organization. We are all human, and we all make mistakes. The mistake is seldom the real issue. Covering it up or not acknowledging it creates the problem because it establishes by default a cultural norm of inauthenticity. Inauthentic behavior stifles openness, truth telling, and learning. By being vulnerable and taking responsibility when you do not model your desired culture, you will promote others to do the same. This "bad" modeling can be equally, if not more important than the times when you do model desired behaviors. Your humbleness about your own imperfections and your openness to reveal and acknowledge them to others encourages them to do the same. It establishes cultural norms of self-reflection, learning, and course correcting (self-mastery!). With these norms in place, your culture will unleash more of its human potential, making breakthrough results a greater possibility. It all starts with you modeling what it means to operate consciously, making inner dynamics and self-development an overt and legitimate aspect of your organization's culture.

SUMMARY

In this chapter, we have demonstrated that mindset is causative. The mindsets we hold as change leaders influence (1) what we see in our transformations; (2) our internal experiences; (3) our decisions; (4) our impact on others; and (5) our performance and results. We showed that the significant impact of mindset calls for the ongoing pursuit of self-mastery; that learning, self-management, and personal transformation are critical aspects of successful organization transformation. We also suggested that we as conscious change leaders, have a critical role in modeling desired ways of being in our organizations and to bring those to life as desired cultural norms.

In the next chapter, we will explore culture: its critical role and impact on change leadership success, and how positive cultures unleash greater human potential and results.

ENDNOTES

1. Kuhn, T. *The Structure of Scientific Revolutions* (1st Edition). Chicago, IL: The University of Chicago Press, 1962.
2. Senge, P. *The Fifth Discipline: The Art and Practice of Learning Organization*. New York: Doubleday, 1990.
3. There are other, more subtle processes of your mind whose descriptions go beyond the scope of this book. See Ken Wilber's books for superb discussions of these more subtle dynamics of human awareness and consciousness.
4. Penfield, W. *Mystery of the Mind: A Critical Study of Consciousness*. Princeton, NJ: Princeton University Press, 1975.
5. In this explanation, we are using a mechanical description of brain functioning to simplify our point. Please note, however, that current brain/mind research reveals a much more complex and holistic functioning of the brain (see Grof, 1993; Pribram, 1971).
   Grof, S. *The Holotropic Mind: The Three Levels of Human Consciousness and How They Shape Our Lives*. New York: Harper Collins, 1993.
   Pribram, K. *Languages of the Brain: Experimental Paradoxes and Principles in Neuropsychology*. New York: Brandon House, 1971.
6. Csikszentmihalyi, M. *Flow: The Psychology of Optimal Performance*. New York: Harper & Row, 1990.

CHAPTER

8

The Role and Impact
of Culture

The only thing of real importance that leaders do is to create and manage culture. If you do not manage culture, it manages you, and you may not even be aware of the extent to which this is happening.

—Edgar Schein

We started this section by addressing the human dynamics of commitment and resistance. In the previous chapter, we explored the role and impact of mindset and saw how it is key to optimizing human performance and establishing a person's readiness to change. In this chapter, we explore culture—an often elusive component of transformation—from the perspective of how it can unleash (or stifle) human potential and performance. We address different types of cultures and explore the fundamentals of transforming culture.

WHAT IS CULTURE?

Culture is to an organization as mindset is to an individual. Culture is the way of being of the organization—its character or personality. Within culture lie the company's core values, its norms and operating principles, and its myths and stories. It determines what types of individual behaviors are acceptable or not, and shapes the behaviors and style exhibited by the organization in the marketplace. Culture infuses "*how* work gets done around here" and how the organization behaves in relation to its customers. Culture is the interior dimension of the collective.

Culture has impacts on an organization qualitatively similar to those that mindset does on an individual. Culture impacts the organization's "perception" of its reality, how it pursues opportunities, responds to competition, or deals with product recalls and downturns in the market. Culture impacts the state of being of its employees (morale) and sets the tone for people's emotional experience at work. Culture impacts the organization's performance and results and determines how much of the human and organizational potential actually gets released into the marketplace. Culture establishes the norms regarding personal responsibility and empowerment, and it impacts the organization's orientation to learning (organizational mastery). Culture determines the level to which the organization "walks the talk" of its espoused values. It is a pervasive force—a key factor in leading successful transformation.

Culture is initially formed as the organization takes on the mindset, behavior, and style of its founders. It is embedded over time into the very fabric of the organization through its formal and informal policies and procedures, methods, practices, and ways of operating. The leaders, consciously and overtly or not, ensure that their own worldviews, beliefs, values, and work ethic are infused into how the organization operates. Think about Hewlett and Packard in their company, Steve Jobs at Apple, Larry Page and Sergey Brin at Google, and Bill Gates and Paul Allen at Microsoft. Each of these leaders put their own cultural mark on their organization while it was in its early, formative stages. There is nothing wrong with this; it is just what happens when people organize and work together over a period of time. Culture forms whether we want it to or not. The only variable is what it forms into, which we will address later in this chapter.

Indicators of Culture

Not too long ago, Dean was riding an elevator with a client named Jim, who was the CIO of a large multi-national company headquartered in Chicago. They were riding the elevator down from the twenty-fifth floor executive suite to the lobby of the headquarters building at the end of a long work day. Dean noticed that everyone in the elevator was carrying a briefcase. When they arrived, the lobby was bustling with activity as people were leaving their offices for the day.

It then struck Dean that nearly everyone in the lobby was also carrying a brief-case. Surprised, Dean pointed this out to Jim, asking, "Does everyone bring work home at night?"

"Oh, no, few people work after hours," Jim replied. "You have been work-ing with our CEO long enough to know that he is a workaholic. He is here early and stays late. People carry their briefcases home to demonstrate their work ethic, but few actually do any work. It is just part of our culture to look extremely dedicated."

Culture is hard to see, hear, or touch. In itself, it is not tangible. It is very difficult to see the "mindset of the organization," unless we look at how the orga-nization behaves and how it operates. We find culture by peering into the other three quadrants, as it is always reflected there to a significant degree. We see culture in people's *behavior*, as in carrying a briefcase home after work, how decisions get made, or how information is shared. We see culture in an organiza-tion's *systems*, structures, policies, technology, hiring practices, reward mecha-nisms, and business processes because they are all established as a reflection of the culture. And we see culture in the *mindsets* displayed by the majority of the organization's employees, manifested in the patterns of their attitudes, comments, emotional reactions, and decisions. Remember: All four quadrants reflect each other.

We are strong proponents of assessing your culture at the beginning of a trans-formational change effort so you have objective data about it and its impact on organizational performance and employee behavior. But even if you do not for-mally assess your culture, you can quite effectively get a sense of it by observing what we call "indicators of culture" (see Exhibit 8.1).

Seasoned change leaders and consultants can very quickly and accurately assess the basic culture of any organization by gathering information about a handful of these key indicators. For example, assume an organization has numerous levels of hierarchy with strictly enforced privilege policies, like who parks his or her car where or who gets what size office. Also assume that in this organization, information is protected and closely held as a sign of power, and that when information is shared, it flows generally from top to bottom in the form of announcements about corporate policy decisions. Assume also that the highest ranking person in a meeting makes all of the decisions, that mistakes are punished heavily, and that no formal structure or process for learning or feedback exists.

Exhibit 8.1. Typical Indicators of Culture

- Leadership style
- Communication patterns; tone of typical conversations
- Decision-making styles
- Use of information
- Use of electronic communication as a vehicle for information sharing, decision making, and relationship building
- Level classifications and privileges
- Monitoring systems
- Performance standards and expectations
- Consequences of failure and orientation to learning
- Space/layout
- Norms and behavior
- Stories, myths, traditions, and rituals
- Heroes and heroines
- Symbols (brand, logo, motto, language, relics)

These indicators of culture are its overt expressions. They reflect culture in the other three quadrants of mindset, behavior, and systems. They make culture visible. Indicators of culture are like signposts, the tell-tales that collectively reveal the personality or character of an organization.

Given these indicators, what is the culture of this organization? You can safely bet that this is a "power and control" culture in which rank delivers significant privilege and authority, leaders solicit little employee input and make all key decisions, employees are disempowered and reactive, and people "cover their butts" rather than take risks. You might expect the organization to be highly unionized, with poor customer service ratings, and a traumatic track record of change. Certainly you would have to dig a bit deeper to check out these assumptions, but these few key indicators would give you a fairly accurate first assessment of the culture and its underlying design principles.

Exhibit 8.2 lists the typical indicators of culture. Use it to make an informal assessment of your current culture, and compare that against the culture you believe is needed to succeed in your market. Recall your drivers of change and reflect on what ideal culture your market is "suggesting" you need to excel. Is a culture change required in your organization?

Exhibit 8.2. Indicators of Culture

	WORKSHEET	
Indicator	Common Examples in Your Organization	What This Infers About Your Culture
Leadership style		
Decision-making styles		
Distribution of influence		
Degree of autonomy		
Level of employee involvement		
Frequency, tone, style, and direction of communication		
Use, flow, and availability of information		
Level classifications and privileges		
Job design		
Use of rewards and punishments		
Monitoring systems		
Performance standards and expectations		
Goal clarity		
Consequences of failure and orientation to learning		
Space, layout of offices		
Norms and behaviors		
Stories, myths, traditions, and rituals		
Heroes and heroines		
Symbols (brand, logo, motto, language, relics)		

THE IMPACTS OF CULTURE ON PERFORMANCE

In developmental and transitional change efforts, leaders can under-attend to culture and still achieve their desired business results. But in transformation, we have already established that culture change is critical. Before you decide to ignore culture in nontransformational change efforts, keep in mind that culture is a primary force that either limits the performance of your people—and, there-fore, the results in the organization—or unleashes their full potential. You cannot achieve truly breakthrough results without creating a culture that promotes human excellence in both individuals and the collective. The fact that culture change is such a hot topic these days is testimony to the impact of culture on organizational performance. We all intuitively and experientially know that culture impacts how people behave and perform, and the organization's results.

The Fundamental Law of Organizational Success (Table 8.1) establishes this premise at a theoretical level. It provides insights about the impact of culture on organizational performance similar to those the Fundamental Law of Individual Success (Chapter Seven) revealed about the impact of mindset on individual per-formance. In Table 8.1, notice that we replaced the "mindset" column from the earlier table with "culture," and we replaced the "ability level" column with "core competencies." Our core competencies label refers to the organization's total capa-bility for results—its full potential—as determined by its products and services, their quality and fit with customer's needs, its marketing and customer awareness and evaluation of its brand, as well as how it is designed organizationally (its struc-ture, business processes, technology, systems, skills, etc.). The rating simply shows that Company A has more "competency" than Company B.

Table 8.1. **Fundamental Law of Organizational Success**

Company	Core Competencies	×	Culture	=	Performance
Company A	10		100% Constructive		10
Company A	10		80% Constructive		8
Company A	10		60% Constructive		6
Company B	8		60% Constructive		4.8
Company B	8		80% Constructive		6.4
Company B	8		100% Constructive		8

Assume two companies have similar core competencies, missions, strategies, systems, staffs, and skills. One has a culture that is co-creative: vibrant, empowered, collaborative, supportive, results and learning oriented, information sharing, and passionate about serving customers. The other company's culture is staid and static, based on entitlement, risk aversion, information hoarding, and an attitude of "we know what is best for the customer." Whose stock are you going to buy? Clearly, the organization whose culture unleashes its people's potential will win in the market every time, as long as it possesses and applies capability near commensurate with its competitors.

Culture is a determining factor in every organization's success. In Table 8.1, notice how both companies achieve more of their potential the more co-creative their culture becomes. Notice also how Company A, which has more competency, could actually be beaten in the marketplace by its competitor with less competency (potential) if its competitor had a more co-creative culture.

Some cultures release more of an organization's human potential than others. They enable and catalyze greater results. Let's investigate what these cultures look like.

Types of Cultures

Culture is like an unconscious design requirement. Everything tangible in the organization is inadvertently built off its template. If the culture is high performing in its nature, then most likely so will the organization's systems (content) and its people (mindset, behavior, and performance) be. But which types of cultures are high performing, and which types are not?

Before we share our experience and present some research, let's start with your own experience of teams (a collective that has a culture, just at a smaller scale than an organization). Think of the highest performing team you have ever been a part of. It may have been a team related to work, sports, your church group, a service organization, or any other group that had a common purpose. You may have been on this team recently or years ago. What were this high-performing team's attributes? What made it so special? How did it behave and operate that set it apart and led to its superior results? What was its character and way of being?

We have asked many teams this question over the years, and the answers are always very similar (Exhibit 8.3). In this exercise with teams, we also ask, "What attributes that you commonly experience in low-performing teams were absent from the highest performing team?" This question also generates consistent answers.[1]

Exhibit 8.3. Commonly Stated Cultural Attributes of High-Performing and Low-Performing Teams

HIGH-PERFORMING TEAM CULTURES

▸ Aligned intent and purpose; common *known* goal
▸ Unconditional trust, mutual support, and collaboration
▸ Friendly give-and-take among members; a sense of equality; "we are all in this together"
▸ Extraordinary commitment and passion to deliver results
▸ Personal initiative and responsibility; can-do attitude
▸ Open flow of information
▸ Fun
▸ Clear roles and decision making
▸ High personal integrity of members
▸ Learning-oriented; forgiveness of mistakes; dedication to improvement

LOW-PERFORMING TEAM CULTURES

▸ Confusion about goals and roles
▸ More attention on personal power and status than performance
▸ Opposition and conflict among members
▸ Compete with each other rather than cooperate
▸ Disempowerment: wait for others to act rather than take initiative
▸ Blame and finger-pointing
▸ Low flow of information
▸ Not much listening; lots of telling
▸ Defend positions and mistakes rather than be learning-oriented

The majority of us seem to have a common perspective and experience—regardless of our role or status in the organization—about what type of team culture unleashes the greatest human potential and what types stifle human performance.

In Exhibit 8.3, notice the strong correlation between our collective experience of high-performing cultures and the description at the end of the previous chapter of the co-creative way of being. High-performing team cultures get generated when members are operating "co-creatively" from their beings rather than through the fight or flight behaviors of their egos. Team members are not clamoring to look good, gain power, or stay in control. They are not worried about who is included or not, or who is in charge and making decisions. Their egos are strong (they each know who they are) and healthy (not lost in fear of their needs not getting met). Consequently, the group dynamic (culture) takes on a unique tone. Each team member displays strong individualism (presence) while simultaneously looking out for each other and the team's achievement. Each brings their full capabilities to the endeavor without diminishing anyone else. Each individual's way of being brings out the best in their teammates. There is much connection, collaboration, alignment, and support. Collectively, they unleash the cumulative potential of the whole team. What could be better? This raises the question: What types of organizational cultures deliver the greatest results? The most obvious answer is to say that positive organizational cultures will look a lot like positive team cultures and the mindsets of effective individuals. They will be "co-creative."

There is great research on this topic performed by Human Synergistics, a leading leadership and culture assessment firm operating for more than forty years. The firm's findings parallel our own. They identify three different types of cultures they call (1) constructive; (2) passive/defensive; and (3) aggressive/defensive (see Table 8.2, Three Types of Organizational Cultures).[2]

The Human Synergistics' "constructive" culture is similar in nature to what we call a co-creative culture. Notice how their four norms of a constructive culture—achievement, self-actualizing, humanistic-encouraging, and affiliative—and the corresponding sample of behaviors reflect our previous discussions of being and higher core needs. In constructive cultures, people orient to excelling and being their best, achieving, growing and developing, being open and caring, participating with each other, learning, and sharing their inner, personal selves. This produces a high level of trust, alignment, and collective support of common goals, and enables people to co-create together.

Passive/defensive and aggressive/defensive cultures reflect states in which people's lower core needs are not satisfied, and their egos dominate in unhealthy ways. Passive/defensive cultures take on the *flight* reaction of the ego, and aggressive/defensive cultures embody the *fight* dynamic. "Power over and control of" become central themes in these cultures, as do emotional insecurities, needs for inclusion and approval, fear of failure, and needing to be right, which are all ego dynamics. People tend to operate as victims, disempowered and blaming others for problems rather than jumping in and solving them. Learning is limited as people cover up mistakes rather than proactively and communally solve them. Dominance and control dictate much of the relationship across boundaries of hierarchy and function, and collaboration and support are minimal. In these cultures, people

Table 8.2. Three Types of Organizational Cultures

Types of Culture	Norms	Behaviors
Constructive	Achievement	Pursue excellence; be enthusiastic; establish clear plans of action
		Value members who set and accomplish own goals
		Challenge yourself, but be realistic
	Self-Actualizing	Value creativity, quality over quantity
		Balance task with personal development
		Learning oriented; be unique and independent thinker
	Humanistic-Encouraging	Person centered; participation
		Supportive; help others grow
		Open to influence; be constructive
	Affiliative	Positive interpersonal relationships; share feelings, thoughts
		Friendly and open
		Support others' satisfaction
Passive/Defensive	Approval	Conflict avoidance; get agreement; be liked by others
		Superficial "pleasant" interpersonal relations
		Go along with; seek approval
	Conventional	Conservative and traditional
		Bureaucratically governed and controlled
		Conform and follow the rules; make a good impression
	Dependent	Hierarchically controlled; lack of empowerment of others
		Do only what you are told; do what is expected
		Clear decisions with superiors; please those in authority positions
	Avoidance	Punish mistakes; fail to reward success
		Shift responsibilities to others; avoid being blamed for mistakes
		Risk avoidance; wait for others to act first
Aggressive/Defensive	Oppositional	Confrontational; oppose ideas; point out flaws
		Negative rather than positive reinforcement
		Gain status by being critical of others; be hard to impress

(*continued*)

Table 8.2. Three Types of Organizational Cultures (continued)

Types of Culture	Norms	Behaviors
	Power	Nonparticipative; control subordinates; demand loyalty and followership
		Authority by position; be responsive to demands of superiors
		Take charge; build power base
	Competitive	Winning is valued; members rewarded for out-performing peers
		Win-lose; work against, not with peers to be noticed
		Show strength; never appear to lose
	Perfectionist	Persistence and hard work valued; work long hours to meet narrowly defined objectives
		Avoid mistakes; keep on top of everything
		Detail oriented; miss nothing

tend to operate on the surface, both by being superficial with each other and by not addressing deeper mindset and cultural "causes" of problems and challenges. Digging deep is generally not an option because ultimately that unveils how one thinks and feels. These are externally oriented cultures, and as we have repeatedly demonstrated, they insufficiently attend to the inner domains of how people think and feel. Consequently, ego dynamics rule because leaders do not "look inside" to understand and transcend them.

Constructive, co-creative cultures operate from higher internal states of being, whether in an individual, team, or organization, and this leads to higher performance and better outcomes. We all know this intuitively, but a study by Cooke, and others[3] of more than 60,000 respondents to Human Synergistics' Organizational Culture Inventory (OCI) corroborates our collective professional experience. This study assessed five individual and five organizational outcomes of culture that can drive the performance and long-term effectiveness of an organization. Regarding individual outcomes, their study demonstrated that "constructive cultural norms are positively and significantly associated with members' reports regarding role clarity, quality of communications, 'fit' and job satisfaction, and negatively related to members' reports of behavioral conformity." Regarding organizational outcomes, they found that "constructive norms are positively associated with quality of products and services, commitment to customer service, adaptability, and the quality of the workplace, and negatively associated to employee turnover intentions."

Another qualitative research study[4] of Australian and New Zealand companies found that transformations from defensive cultures to constructive cultures produced numerous positive business outcomes, including (1) increased profit, (2) increased employee engagement, (3) greater customer satisfaction, (4) business growth, (5) reduced operating costs, (6) increased staff retention, (7) increased market share, and (8) increased service quality. This should be no surprise to any of us who have lived inside different organizational cultures over our careers.

So, we know that culture matters, but if the culture is not what it needs to be, how do you change it? How do you transform culture from defensive norms of behavior dominated by ego conditioning to constructive norms where people individually and collectively excel and work together to co-create breakthrough results?

TRANSFORMING CULTURE

How to transform culture is one of the cutting-edge challenges in most organizations today. We have been studying and developing methods for successfully meeting this challenge for nearly thirty years, since about the time the organization transformation movement began in the early 1980s. We are proud to say that much of what we felt in our guts back then about what was needed to transform culture was accurate. We are also embarrassed to confess just how naïve we originally were about what it really takes to implement those methods. Now, thirty years later, we are both wiser by the trials of experience and clearer about how organizations can transform their cultures to unleash unheralded levels of performance in their people.

Given the intended scope of this book, we are not going to explore in depth specific culture change strategies but will instead highlight some of the key principles and approaches that we believe are fundamental to your success. We will also introduce you to Being First's approach to transforming culture. Let's start with highlighting the six conditions that must be in place for your culture change to succeed.

CULTURE CHANGE CONDITIONS FOR SUCCESS

1. **Culture change must be relevant to the business.** It should be an answer to the organizational changes that your marketplace is signaling that you need to make to be successful (remember the drivers of change). The case for culture change must articulate that a change is required to deliver greater customer

and marketplace outcomes. Culture change is not just a good idea; it's a business necessity. This point must be made clear throughout the organization. It should be made relevant to all levels of your business—enterprise, business lines, teams, relationships, and individuals—as well as all functional and geographic areas.

2. **Culture change must be explicit and legitimate.** Leaders should make the business case overt. Culture change should be governed and led as a legitimate change initiative, included in the enterprise's strategic change agenda, and sustained until your desired culture is fully embedded and alive in your organization. It should receive adequate leadership attention, with resources, time, and capacity allocated to the work required. When leaders treat culture change as vital, surfacing what is out of alignment with the desired culture becomes expected and encouraged rather than minimized or admonished.

3. **Culture change must include personal change.** Both leaders and employees should have opportunities to identify the behaviors that will both support and hinder the desired culture. Conversations, training, and other opportunities to support personal change should be provided so both leaders and employees can consciously engage in the personal changes required. We have described providing widespread personal transformation and leadership breakthrough training to shift mindset as a recommended and proven vehicle for accomplishing this.

4. **Culture change must have a champion and be modeled by leadership.** A prominent executive, often the CEO, should sponsor the culture initiative to make it clear to everyone that it is a critical change initiative. New culture messages and behaviors should be embedded in all communications, HR systems, and employee interaction processes. All change initiatives should be consciously designed and run in ways that model the new culture, as distinct from the old. Leaders should be involved in teaching and modeling new cultural norms and practices. Performance management systems should support effective leadership modeling.

5. **Culture change must engage a critical mass of your employees.** You cannot change culture by executive order. Culture change must be nurtured, developed, and brought forward through the interactions of people, both within levels and across levels. It is catalyzed through conversation, discussion, and the give-and-take of ideas. It is nonlinear and moves forward in spurts, with some areas of the organization changing their way of being, working, and

relating faster than others. This path of organization-wide culture change can only be sustained by engaging the entire organization in *consciously* addressing "who we collectively are and why."

6. **All aspects of the organization must be realigned to the desired culture.** Organizational structures, systems, processes, and technology should be evaluated for which support and reflect the desired culture, and which do not, and then appropriate change efforts put in place to realign those that do not. HR systems and policies, including hiring practices, succession planning, compensation, and performance management should be realigned to support the new culture. Leader and employee mindset and behaviors must also align with the new culture, especially how people relate and operate across boundaries of hierarchy and function.

Culture Change and the Conscious Change Leader Accountability Model

What does the Conscious Change Leader Accountability Model (refer to Figure I.1 in the Introduction) tell us about transforming an organization's culture?

Organizational culture change requires a process to attend to all quadrants within all levels, from individuals to the marketplace.

In other words, culture change is not just change in some cultural norm. It requires a transformation of the entire integrated system of quadrants and levels. It touches individual mindset and behavior; relationship and team norms and work procedures; the organization's systems, structure, business processes, and technology; and how the organization interfaces with its marketplace. In cultural transformation, we must realign all these dimensions to the new organizing principle that the culture seeks to embrace. All must be included as part of a successful culture change process.

This is no small undertaking. The good news is that a "tipping point" exists, and that when "adequate" change is underway in "enough" of these quadrants and levels, the gravitational force to remain the same will be outmatched, and the whole enterprise will tip toward the new direction being established. Getting to critical mass is essential. A key is to address where your leverage points are and ensure adequate attention to them so you can efficiently and effectively apply your limited resources to get the overall transformation you seek. Change in certain quadrants and levels in your organization will generate greater influence on the overall transformation than others. Identifying those leverage points early is an important aspect of building an effective culture change strategy. One way to do this is to do an initial impact analysis of the overall direction of the transformation. Keep in mind that leverage points for culture change are different in every organization, which is why there is no cookbook or formula.

Here is the critical understanding: All quadrants and all levels must be consciously addressed in one way or another no matter what initially catalyzes your

CASE-IN-POINT: HOSPITAL SYSTEM

In one hospital system client, the transformation was focused on increasing patient outcomes and lowering costs by becoming a more integrated system. This was initially conceived of as a restructuring effort, but after assisting executives to address the impacts of such a change, major discoveries surfaced, including the most profound—that this fundamentally required a cultural transformation. Certainly, the new direction required shifting many external systems: altering case delivery procedures, roles, and responsibilities to become more evidence-based and multidisciplinary team oriented; aligning numerous financial systems across regions; and implementing technology and infrastructure to build common, systemwide support operations. None of this could happen without addressing the culture: The competitive, uncooperative relationship between regions had to transform to collaboration to build the needed cross-boundary teams for many core functions; between the system office and regions trust was required to successfully shift the resource allocation and decision-making models throughout the company; and the norm of each doctor doing procedures his or her own ways rather than based on evidence-based best practices had to change. This transformation obviously required a very significant mindset shift in doctors and nurses who were used to using their own care delivery protocols, which were now going to be determined by cross-regional best practice teams. The executives also realized they would need to heal old, historic, emotional wounds in their largest medical group. After a full day of assessing the impacts of the transformation, the executives realized that changes in all four quadrants at all five levels were required. Their effort would never have had a chance of success unless they included all these areas in the design of their change process. By the way, this became a three-year effort, not the six-month effort originally conceived.

CASE-IN-POINT: ELECTRIC UTILITY

We were called into an electric utility because a structural reorganization in the service department was having numerous problems (systems). When we inquired, we discovered that this reorganization was part of a larger culture change effort occurring across the organization to become more customer focused and service oriented. At the time we entered the client system, this connection had not yet been overtly made to the people in the service center. Consequently, the culture change work being done at the enterprise level had little current impact, bearing, or integration on the work being done in the service center. That was soon to change.

The service department had previously been organized by function, so when a customer called with a repair request, the order would pass across five different desks before being executed, causing unacceptable delays, great expense, and tremendous customer dissatisfaction. The service department had been structured this way for thirty years and reflected the old command-and-control, silo-oriented culture. Over these years, tremendous competition, frustration, and blame had mounted across functions.

The reorganization had created service teams, with members from each function now working together serving a specific customer area. We did an assessment and quickly discovered that the post-implementation work of developing these new teams to be able to work effectively together was completely neglected. We created a team development process that healed old personal wounds (mindset/behavior at relationship level), clarified new roles and responsibilities (team systems), built team decision processes (team systems/behaviors), and made the journey to a collaborative culture overt and achievable (team norms). We integrated this work with the collaborative culture work being done by human resources at the organizational level and created an integrated design team from across functions to redesign enterprise processes and systems. By addressing all quadrants and all levels, our client was able to see where change was most needed and could prioritize it to reach the tipping point of transformation. The original reorganization effort quickly went from looking like a complete failure to one of great success.

need to transform. Whether your starting point is content or culture, you must look up, down, inside, and across to see how the "whole, integral system" needs to transform together. What you leave out will be your path to failure; what you include will be your foundation for possible breakthrough.

Note the similarities and differences in the Hospital System and Electric Utility Cases-In-Point about the initial catalysts for transformation and how the quadrants and levels were consciously attended to in different ways.

BEING FIRST'S APPROACH TO TRANSFORMING CULTURE

Attending to all quadrants and all levels, more or less together, seems impossible if you view this requirement through a mindset of separate parts; for example, addressing content in isolation or trying to manage human resistance to the change separate from the design and implementation of content. We need to somehow integrate all the work required, in all the levels and quadrants, into a unified change process. And we need to somehow know if our efforts are delivering the results we want.

We solve the major challenges of transforming culture using a seven-phase approach (Exhibit 8.4).

1. Secure Executive Commitment and Alignment

This initial step is of paramount importance. Executives must understand why they are seeking to transform culture, the results and level of success they are after, what it will take to be successful, what it requires of them, and approximately what resources and timeframe it will take to sustain it through to success. They should

---

Exhibit 8.4. Being First's Approach to Transforming Culture

1. Secure executive commitment and alignment
2. Assess current situation and culture
3. Determine desired culture
4. Identify leverage points for culture change
5. Apply The Change Leader's Roadmap to build change strategy and process plan
6. Implement culture change strategy and process
7. Model, reward, and reinforce desired culture

---

understand that a successful culture change strategy will require work in many quadrants and levels, that they must behaviorally model the change they are asking of the organization, and that they are ultimately accountable for the transformation's success. This is not something that can be delegated. They must champion it and sustain its energy and direction over time.

2. Assess Current Situation and Culture

A culture assessment is critical so the executives and entire organization can objectively perceive who they collective are. In essence, a culture assessment enables the organization (the totality of its members) to self-reflect and know itself as a whole. As in any transformation, "self" awareness is the starting point.

A cultural assessment is different from an employee satisfaction, morale, or engagement survey. These all measure outputs of culture. They are the results of culture. A true culture assessment actually describes the norms and behaviors that predominantly exist as patterns within the culture. The Human Synergistics' Organizational Culture Inventory is a great example of an effective culture assessment.

This assessment provides baseline data that enables you to monitor progress over time. It also enables more truthful conversations and evidence-based decisions about the culture, both at the executive table and throughout the organization and its change process. We *always* hear executives describe their cultures as different (and more constructive) than the indicators we observe. Formally assessing the culture provides a needed dose of reality to build an effective culture change strategy.

3. Determine Desired Culture

This step makes overt the desired cultural norms and behaviors the organization will be developing. In many companies, the executives ask their HR departments to determine these. In others, the executives do that work. In a few, a high-engagement process is developed to get input from throughout the organization. Our experience makes it very clear that the more people you involve in articulating the desired culture, and the more you tie this outcome to the market's drivers and the evidence of high-performing cultures, the more successful you will be.

An ideal way to determine your desired cultural norms and behaviors is to use the same assessment, or at least its framework, that you used to assess your current culture. This provides you with a clear articulation of what culture you collectively seek to co-create, contrasted against what you currently have. You can then re-assess your culture to monitor progress as you execute your culture change strategy.

4. Identify Leverage Points for Culture Change

With a clear understanding of your current culture and articulation of your desired culture, you can step back and identify what quadrants and levels are your leverage points for change. What specifically needs to shift throughout all these dimensions that will bring the desired culture to life?

Your desired outcomes will provide the context for this determination. Keep in mind that culture change is Level Four Success, and it includes Level Three Success (business outcomes). This means in any culture transformation, you should also be seeking specific business outcomes as well. These "ground" the culture change effort and make it relevant to the business, not just the people. These business outcomes provide motivation and the ability to measure real business impact.

Some of your leverage points will be at the organizational systems level. You may need to restructure areas of the business and reengineer core processes, including HR practices of how you hire, train, promote, and reward people. Other leverage points will exist within key operational teams, including how they collaborate with other teams, make decisions, and share information. Other leverage points will be within individuals, including how they think and perceive their roles, accountabilities, and desired behaviors.

Mapping your leverage points provides your initial "best guess" at how to exert the greatest amount of positive change in your organization. This clarity informs your change strategy.

5. Apply The Change Leader's Roadmap to Build Your Change Strategy and Process Plan

Now that you know your leverage points, you must take this "conceptual map" and make it real. You must build a change strategy and change process plan that will organize the work required in each of the quadrants and levels to impact these critical areas.

Here is where The Change Leader's Roadmap (CLR) is a godsend. It provides the strategic guidance for thinking through and deciding your overall change strategy, including what change initiatives you will need to best organize the work required, how to govern them, integrate them, resource them, sequence them, and engage stakeholders in them. With a clear change strategy in place, the CLR then provides the change tools your change project teams will need to execute all the key tasks in their individual change initiatives in an integrated way that builds momentum, accelerates outcomes, and minimizes costs due to inefficiencies or work redundancies. Our companion volume, *The Change Leader's Roadmap*, identifies where in the CLR specific guidance for changing culture is embedded. Chapter Fourteen of that book offers a specific map of the model calling out the tasks and work that you will likely need to address to create your culture change plan.

A key aspect of building your change strategy is taking your map of leverage points and perceiving them against the realities of your organization's actual readiness and capacity for change, and adjusting it accordingly. You will want to base your change strategy and process plan on accurate information about your stakeholders' emotional readiness (internal) and the available workload and resources (external) that they can expend without negatively impacting operational performance. Using the CLR enables you to create an initial change strategy and plan that is streamlined to consume as few resources as needed to succeed in your culture change. Then you can use the CLR to monitor implementation and easily add additional change tasks if needed.

6. Implement Culture Change Strategy and Process

You will need to continually monitor your change process plan's implementation and make adjustments as necessary. Culture change is never linear or certain; your initial plan will simply be your initial best guess at what is required. New information, dynamics within other change efforts affecting culture, and other challenges will undoubtedly surface in many quadrants and levels and require you to adjust as needed. You will find that using the guidance system of the CLR will enable you to spot required adjustments early and help you determine your best responses. If resistance or roadblocks occur, the CLR will help you quickly discover why.

7. Model, Reward, and Reinforce Desired Culture

Throughout implementation, you will want to overtly look for ways to best model, reward, and reinforce the desired culture as it manifests. The most critical is for upper-level leaders to conscientiously model the new ways of behaving, relating, and thinking. Some of the other ways will be formal, as in new reward systems, celebrations, and awards, and overtly announcing achievements and successes due to the new culture. Others will be informal, as in managers modeling or complimenting staff on their new behaviors. The point of this step is to make it everyone's job—at all levels—to overtly look for, point out, celebrate, and make conscious the new culture as it reveals itself in new mindsets, behaviors, and systems.

Pursuing Level Five Success: Change Capability

When conscious change leaders pursue Level Five Success, they build into their change strategy and process plans specific tasks to develop greater awareness, knowledge, and skill about leading change. One topic of great importance to achieving breakthrough results is helping leaders and the workforce understand the integral nature of the organization (all quadrants, all levels). Developing this understanding becomes a part of their culture change implementation. Strategies can include training and development, coaching and consulting support, as well as involvement in designing and executing specific change activities in an integral way.

Make conscious the focus on all quadrants and all levels. Make overt how your change strategy and process plan attends to both internal and external dynamics at all levels of the system. Keep this fact conscious and reinforce it throughout your change process. Engage people in the deeper conversations about human dynamics, including mindset and culture. Those involved will naturally begin to expand their awareness and understanding and be able to draw on that in the future as they lead other efforts. They will begin to see internal dynamics more clearly, including their own. They will develop a better understanding of stakeholder resistance and know how to support its transformation into full-blown commitment.

Engage people in broader conversations about how dynamics across levels impact each other. This will help them see the interdependencies across quadrants and levels and how to positively influence each as needed.

Making these dynamics conscious will establish a different topic and quality of conversation in your organization. It will begin to "wake up" your organization and the people in it to a broader and deeper level of awareness and understanding. It will generate greater conscious awareness and self-reflection in your stakeholders. And this, as we know, will establish a foundation for greater change capability and breakthrough results going forward.

SUMMARY

In this chapter, we defined culture, saw its relationship to mindset, and high-lighted its impact on organizational performance. We described the types of cultures that unleash human potential and those that stifle it, and discovered the similarities in attributes between constructive, co-creative cultures and high-performing teams and individuals. We saw how transforming culture requires us to attend to "all quadrants and all levels." We outlined six conditions for successful culture change and introduced Being First's Approach to Transforming Culture.

This concludes our exploration of people dynamics and sets up the discussion in the next section about process dynamics. In the next chapter, we will investigate the multi-dimensional nature of process and introduce the skill set of "conscious process thinking." In Chapter Ten, we will discuss change process models and how they guide successful transformation.

ENDNOTES

1. One deviation to these answers is that people sometimes say they have experienced that high command-and-control, authoritative cultures deliver superior team performance. In the vast majority of these cases, it was in teams that had short-term, very goal-oriented life cycles. The 1980 U.S. Men's Olympic gold-medal hockey team was a great example of this. Coach Herb Brooks was a master of motivation, using very strict discipline. If you listen to interviews of his players, however, they agree that his overt purpose was not to command-and-control them as much as it was to bring them together quickly and bond against him and his strenuous and disciplined workouts. He had *their* interests in mind, not *his* need for control or power. And it worked. His band of college upstarts "miraculously" upset the Russian team who had played together for eighteen years, were by far the Olympic favorite, and notably the best hockey team in the world at the time.

2. Cooke, R. A., and Lafferty, J. C. Copyright © 1973–2010 by Human Synergistics International. All Rights Reserved.

3. Balthazard, P. A., Cooke, R. S., and Potter, R. E. "Dysfunctional Culture, Dysfunctional Organiza-tion: Capturing the Behavioral Norms that Form Organizational Culture and Drive Performance." *Journal of Managerial Psychology*, 2006, Vol. 21 No. 8, 709–732.

4. Jones, Q., et al. *In Great Company, Unlocking the Secrets of Cultural Transformation*. Human Synergistics, 2006.

Process Dynamics

CHAPTER

9

Conscious Process Thinking

Indeed, to some extent it has always been necessary and proper for man, in his thinking, to divide things up. If we tried to deal with the whole of reality at once, we would be swamped. However, when this mode of thought is applied more broadly to man's notion of himself and the whole world in which he lives (i.e., in his world-view), then man ceases to regard the resultant divisions as merely useful or convenient and begins to see and experience himself and this world as actually constituted of separately existing fragments. What is needed is a relativistic theory, to give up altogether the notion that the world is constituted of basic objects or building blocks. Rather, one has to view the world in terms of universal flux of events and processes.

—David Bohm

The term "process" has many meanings in organizations. We have deliberated about using the term because it means different things to different people. However, we keep returning to the word because it most precisely describes what we mean when we refer to *conscious process thinking*, the subject of this chapter.

The purpose of this chapter is to describe the evolution taking place in our collective understanding of process, how the next breakthrough in our development is "conscious process thinking," and why it is necessary to lead transformation successfully. This inquiry will build on everything we have discussed so far.

We begin by differentiating our use of the term "process" from other uses. Then, we introduce "conscious process thinking" and contrast it with the more common "project thinking." We will describe its similarities to and differences from "systems thinking," and we will also discuss the tools that each of these thinking orientations use as they pertain to change leadership.

These discussions will set the stage for the next chapter, where we discuss change process models in general and introduce the specific change process model that we have built and refined over the past three decades, the nine-phase Change Leader's Roadmap.

DIFFERENTIATING AMONG USES OF THE WORD "PROCESS"

The term "process" has many different uses and meanings in the fields of leadership, management theory, and organization development. Reengineering, quality improvement, and team development all have different uses of the term. We need to differentiate these various meanings to ensure that we convey our specific meaning clearly.

Following is our view of the *other* uses. Notice that we have organized them in two categories: business processes and human processes. Human processes pertain to a person's mental processing and/or relational interactions. Business processes relate to actions taken by people to produce something. We encourage you to note your particular meaning(s) and uses of the word "process" from those listed next.

Business Processes

▶ **Business Processes:** Refers to what needs to occur to produce a specific organizational result. These include a hierachy of *levels* of process—core processes, their subprocesses, and more detailed procedures. Core processes often refer to "macro" processes that are "end-to-end" or cross functional, even reaching out of the organization to vendors, business partners, and customers. Subprocesses address the next level of detail and are functional elements of core processes. Procedures describe in operational detail how work should get done within a subprocess. Examples of business processes include product development, resource supply chain, customer service, and resource allocation.

▶ **Process Improvement:** The quality movement's practice of defining the action steps required to achieve an end and then refining those steps to achieve the outcome more effectively and efficiently. This work is applied to business processes to improve them.

▶ **Group Process:** The team-building related description of how groups of people operate together, relate to one another, and interact (e.g., the group's "way of being and operating").

▶ **Process Consultation and Observation:** The organization development practice of "objectively" observing what goes on when groups of people work together, then devising positive ways to influence their interactions, effectiveness, and relationships.

▶ **Process Facilitation:** The OD term for leading a predesigned experience or meeting agenda with the intent of achieving a desired outcome; observing and guiding the dynamics that occur during the rollout of the plan, and course correcting to enable the outcome to emerge; leading without controlling.

▶ **Processing Information:** The thinking and discussing a person or group does to understand, reflect on, make meaning of, or learn about something that has happened or that is needed from them. The information being processed may be about internal or external realities. Examples include debriefing an event, an interaction, or one's emotions.

▶ **Personal Process:** What an individual goes through as he or she grows emotionally or spiritually, becomes more aware, and learns from life's experiences; self-reflection; consciously learning from and course correcting one's life experiences, mindset, and behavior; self-mastery.

Clearly, the term "process" takes on many meanings in organizations. That in itself is a demonstration of the process nature of organizations. You may currently define or use the word "process" in one or more of the ways just listed. That is fine; all are useful distinctions and have beneficial applications.

We will now present a more global definition or treatment of process, and then apply it to a way of thinking and perceiving especially relevant to conscious change leadership.

OUR DEFINITION AND VIEW OF PROCESS

Webster offers two relevant definitions of process: (1) "progress, advance; something going on; proceeding"; and (2) "a natural phenomenon marked by gradual changes that lead toward a particular result; a series of actions or operations conducing to an end." The first definition is purely action oriented, while in the second, action leads to a result.

Webster's results-oriented definition is like our definition of process, which is: The natural or intentional unfolding of continuous events toward a desired outcome. The outcome, hypothetically, can either be one you desire or do not desire. We choose to orient our thinking about process as action *toward* a desired outcome. As Arthur Young (1976) would say, "process has purpose." It has a direction. It moves toward something. As conscious change leaders, we intend it to move toward what we want.

When most of us think of process, we think of a particular type of process, as in a business process or a particular work process. For change leaders, the most important type of process is the change process. That is the change leader's primary concern. But also important is the fundamental process nature of organizations and life. The more insight we have about the basics of process dynamics, the more effective we can be in all types of process applications.

Our mindset and perspective about process in general will determine what we perceive and see in our organization's or project's change process. It will determine our orientation to it, the tasks we design into it, and how we course-correct it when needed. It will influence whether we see key leverage points, and how to intervene with minimal disruption to get maximum results. The more conscious we are, the more we see process from a multi-dimensional, "integrated system" perspective. This is both a broader and deeper worldview than the common mindset leaders bring to managing a discrete business process, and is our next topic to explore.

We will begin this conversation rather esoterically as we seek an essential understanding of process, then we will turn our discussion toward action. Remember our orientation: We are after breakthrough results in our change efforts, and we are willing to go to the cutting edge of understanding to acquire greater insight. And then, with our feet firmly planted on the ground, we apply our new ideas in pragmatic ways to deliver greater outcomes.

THE MULTI-DIMENSIONAL NATURE OF PROCESS

Process is the essence of life because change is the essence of life. People have recognized this for thousands of years, as illustrated by these well-known statements:

All is flux; nothing stays still.

—Heraclitus

The only constant is change.

—Isaac Asimov

Change is the law of life.

—John Fitzgerald Kennedy

Life is a process. We are a process. The universe is a process.

—Anne Wilson Schaef

Life (process) continually unfolds, never stopping, leading from here to there and beyond, generating and constantly delivering circumstances, events, and results along the way. As results of process are achieved, process continually moves on toward the next result, then the next, and the next. This is the ongoing nature of process and is the essence of everything in life, including organizational transformation. So even if something looks static, it is not. At some level, it is process in motion.

Our twenty-first century science confirms this fact: All matter is energy, and energy is in constant motion.

When we discuss process with most people, they think of observable action, things they can see in external reality. But process is continually unfolding in all four quadrants of the Conscious Change Leader Accountability Model, including internal reality at all levels. Process is occurring within the *organization* itself, within the *teams and work groups* that exist in the organization, within the multitude of *relationships and interactions* that occur between people and within teams, within *individuals*, as well as within the organization's *environment or marketplace*. In all of these levels of the organization's reality, process is occurring within the internal dimensions of mindset and culture as well as the external dimensions of behavior and systems. All of life (including organizational change) is a multidimensional process in perpetual motion, an endless weave of processes intermingling with other processes across quadrants and levels, "the continuous dance of energy" (Capra, 1983, p. 91). As change leaders, we want to know how to most effectively influence this dance.

Key in this regard is realizing that all external results are temporary and unstable. All outcomes, structures, events, and tangible forms are simply snapshots of a continually evolving process. Their appearance of being fixed and permanent is an illusion, a perceptual "freeze frame" of external events in a moment in time. Take your organization's structure, for example. Today, it may seem fixed and firmly established. Yet last year it was likely different, and next year it will likely change again. If you widen your timeframe, the underlying evolving nature of your organization's structure becomes apparent. Over time, it continually changes between centralization and decentralization, local and global focus, business lines and functional services, standardization and autonomy, all the while evolving (one hopes) to a higher-order ability to serve the needs of your changing marketplace and customers. Even "fixed" structures are in dynamic flux.

There is usually a significant time delay between one "physical" change in an organization's structure and the next. Sometimes years can pass. This makes it appear that changes in an organization's structure occur in surges or jumps, rather than as a continual process. It looks this way if we attend only to the physical domain of systems at the organizational level. When we look more deeply, we can see that the change in an organization's structure is actually continuous and moving through other quadrants and levels.

For example, the marketplace is continually providing information that causes people within the organization to question the efficacy of the current structure. This promotes dialogue among teams of people—sometimes heated and sometimes harmonious. New ideas are generated by individuals. Studies are done. Conclusions are made. Debates continue. Some executives resist; others seek a structural change. All along the way, many people are involved personally, through dialogue with others (interpersonally) and in teams. They think, feel, debate, and argue, until finally, a decision is made to change the organization's structure by the person or people in power. At this point, new structural designs are created, debated, and further refined until finally one is chosen and implemented. Once implemented, we witness the new structure in place.

When did the process of changing the organization's structure actually begin? Was it when the person in power announced that a structure change was going to happen, or was the structure change going on long before via the many conversations and debates that were building momentum toward a formal change effort? And once the new structure was implemented, did the restructuring process really end? Or is there still conversation among employees in the hallways or among the executives at the board table about further refining the structure, or planning a possible future change to it given new directions in the business plan?

The process of change in the organization's structure is continually unfolding in various dimensions of reality, across levels and quadrants. This multi-dimensional process builds momentum, until finally, on the physical level, the change of structure manifests in a spurt. It looks like it happens isolated in some timeframe, but it is really an ongoing "process of continuous activity." Remember, all quadrants and all levels are interdependent, and process is continually evolving through them as an integrated journey forward to the next result.

Given this discussion, we need to further expand our definition of process as: the natural or intentional unfolding of continuous events, *within all dimensions of reality*, toward a desired outcome.

Taking a "process orientation," as we define process, means that conscious change leaders address the process dynamics of each of the quadrants at all levels relevant to their transformation, both the overtly seen external dimensions as well as the more subtle human dynamics. It also means perceiving the unfolding of process continually "across time," not just in a snapshot of time.

Why is this orientation so important? Seeing organizations and reality this way provides essential insight for change leaders into how and when to intervene in the change process to produce optimal results. When change leaders are conscious of the multi-dimensional aspects of process, they are able to "see" the interdependent process dynamics at play—how the occurrences in one dimension impact the other dimensions. This enables them to intervene where appropriate to influence the process in the direction of their desired outcomes. They can spot the leverage points.

Leaders operating on autopilot, viewing organizational behavior through their "traditional" lens, do not see the multi-dimensional process nature of transformation that we are describing. They perceive reality and organizations through their ego, which orients to separating wholes into their component parts. To this end, the ego generates boundaries, many of them artificially fabricated. This has autopilot leaders not see the continuous nature of process, flowing through all quadrants and levels, across time, as one dynamic stream. Instead, it has them fixated on static events and structures, and with their attention on the gross rather than more subtle levels of process, they must exert far more force to disrupt the current state and cause change. This limited perception of the reality of process (change) is at the heart of all transformational failures. It generates piecemeal, externally oriented approaches that consistently struggle.

Conscious change leaders can intervene in far more subtle and effective ways because their enhanced level of discernment gives them greater sensitivity for timing. Using our previous example, they know which conversations to influence about the organization's structure to move early dialogues forward. They can see when to influence someone's thinking with pertinent data, knowing that over time, that person's mindset will generate a positive conclusion that leads to action and then

In one manufacturing organization, the CEO was struggling with how to get the union to commit to the organization's transformation and become full players in it. The union's attitude was, "Our people will simply go get jobs in another company. You may go belly up, but our skills are in high demand throughout this industry." To further exacerbate the problem, a few years previously, the CEO and the union president had a very volatile and openly heated conflict. They had never laid the strike days to rest, and each carried personal grudges against the other.

But the company needed a partnership with the union to sustain its level of success. And the union, despite the union president's attitude, needed the company as well. Most of its members were long-term company employees and had little other work experience.

We suggested to the CEO that the company take a multi-dimensional process approach to the situation, and that rather than simply try to "contain" the problem, they use it as an opportunity to create a true breakthrough in union relations and collective outcomes. We had conducted a *Leading Breakthrough Results: Walking the Talk of Change* executive program with the leadership team, so they were beginning to see their transformation as multi-dimensional. This enabled us to help them see what was required for this breakthrough with the union. As you read the following list of the strategies they employed, notice how processes at various levels of organization and within different quadrants were employed:

- Breakthrough *mindset and behavior* training was provided for the executive team and for the union leaders, introducing both sides to how their assumptions about each other influenced what they saw about the other and cleared up significant emotional baggage.
- The executive team and union leaders were taught dialogue and interpersonal communication skills, using their live issues as the topics of conversational practice (*relational: behavioral*).

(continued)

▶ The union leaders were invited to the company's visioning conference and had an equal opportunity to influence the content and the emotional wording of the company's purpose, vision, goals, and system changes (*organizational; culture; systems*).

▶ A mid-manager who had a longstanding positive relationship with the union president became chair of a union-management partnership team, chartered to make changes in how the two entities worked together from both a cultural and operational perspective (*individual; relational; organizational; cultural; systems*).

▶ Coaching support was offered to the union leaders and the executives about their mindsets, emotions, and behavior to help them understand the impact of their styles on the union-management partnership (*individual; mindset; behavior*).

▶ The union's contract negotiations were begun a year in advance to ensure adequate bridge-building and to avoid a last-minute war (*organizational; culture; systems*).

▶ Union representatives partnered with company supervisors to conduct benchmark studies of best-in-class companies regarding union-management partnerships, giving both a shared purpose (*individual; relational; organizational; culture*).

▶ Plant managers invited their plant stewards to join the plant's change leadership team and influence the future of the plant (*organizational; culture; systems*).

After eighteen months of building momentum in many different dimensions, adequate momentum was created, and the desired changes in how the partnership operated were achieved. The next union contract was easily negotiated, employee grievances dramatically dropped to record lows, and union stewards and company supervisors developed effective working relationships throughout the company. However, at almost any time during that year and a half, there "seemed" to be minimal tangible progress in the union-management relationship, even though the internal dimensions of individuals and personal relations were being improved. Then, as if all at once, critical mass was reached, and the transformation occurred. Both the union and management were "suddenly" operating differently.

Taking a multi-dimensional process view, the conscious change leaders involved were able to turn their small wins and progress in the various dimensions (many of them internal) into a very significant and measurable outward achievement. They openly acknowledged that had they taken a more traditional (autopilot) view, the "lack of overt progress" would have caused them to "pull the plug" on every one of their individual, discrete attempts to influence the union-management relationship. They would have simply terminated the intervention. But seeing multi-dimensional process in action, continuous over time, gave them the wisdom and fortitude to continue until their desired result was achieved. They felt confident that it would ultimately occur because they could "see" the progress being made within the internal, relational dimensions that other autopilot leaders would have missed.

results. They do not just have to work at the gross levels where disruptions are more significant and resource consumption is greater. They see the possibilities of change earlier and are able to pull levers that autopilot leaders simply miss. They operate with greater finesse and produce far more significant results with less effort—all because they can see process at its most fundamental levels.

With this awareness, conscious change leaders discern how best to design, implement, and course-correct transformational change processes. Even though there are many different subprocesses to attend to, they know that all dimensions of organizational reality collectively comprise one overarching transformational process they must perceive and lead.

AN EVOLVING ORIENTATION TO PROCESS

Perceiving this multi-dimensional nature of the change process denotes an evolution in change leaders' perspectives. This evolution, again and as always, is toward greater span and depth, seeing across both space and time more conclusively, and seeing internal human dynamics at more fundamental levels.

This evolution is from linear thinking, to seeing interdependencies, to understanding process dynamics over time, to perceiving the role and impact of human consciousness; and it is well underway in business and industry and building steam. Critical mass has not yet happened, but it will. The current evolution of change leadership skill is about seeing the multi-dimensional aspects of process, broadening orientation to time, and consciously attending to mindset and culture as causative factors in behavior and results. We are, through this book, attempting to nudge this evolution along.

Let's look at this growth in perspective by addressing three thinking orientations that have evolved along this path: (1) project thinking; (2) systems thinking; and (3) conscious process thinking. All have their proper place and application, and all deliver value when their application fits what is needed.

Project Thinking

Project thinking is the mode of leadership thinking about how to execute projects that has dominated organizations over the past hundred years. Project thinking refers to the traditional linear, step-by-step, event-by-event thinking that leaders use to effectively design and manage developmental or transitional change projects. However, when used in transformational changes, it is often an autopilot reaction and inadequate to the requirements of the process.

Project thinking makes its greatest contribution to enhancing operational excellence. Project thinking has structured and organized the activities that have led to many of the significant increases in the production and productivity of the past century. As we describe project thinking as it pertains to leading change, you will notice the familiar attributes of how operational projects typically get implemented in organizations.

Project thinking is linear and sequential. One step follows another. Time is bounded, marked by separate and discrete steps or change events that are not necessarily designed with full cognizance of what went before them or of full consequence to what will follow. Detailed change plans are created, complete with roles, tasks, and mandated timelines. Change efforts are managed and controlled to adhere to these plans. Preconceived, predictable outcomes are expected. Variation is not tolerated, nor is deviation from the change plan. External force and control are used to prevent potentially chaotic processes from derailing or falling apart. In project thinking, people are often viewed as cogs in the machinery, neither asked nor encouraged to think outside the boundaries and constraints of their roles in the change plan. A project thinker's intent is to make the change effort "behave" as the leaders require to achieve results "on time and on budget."

Project thinkers run many, if not most, of today's organizations. In the quest to enhance short-term tangible results, competent project thinkers have *historically* stood out as the superstars. In the more stable environment of the past, they made things happen and, therefore, received the most frequent promotions, even though their people skills might have been lacking. Historically, an organization's succession plan has mostly been filled with its best project thinkers.

As today's leaders have had to expand their job responsibilities from improving operations (developmental change) to managing transitional change to leading transformational change, they have naturally applied their "reliable" project thinking tendencies to the job. Unfortunately, project thinking does not work as the only thinking style for leading transformation. As you will recall from our earlier discussion of types of change, transformation is not a linear or controllable process, which conflicts with the very nature of project thinking. In the future, succession plans will not be dominated by the best project thinkers unless they also possess systems thinking and process thinking skills. Project managers, who have traditionally been project thinkers, can and must expand their repertoire to include systems and process thinking orientations. The good news is that many of our young leaders possess these thinking skills. Growing up in a "connected" world made certain of that.

Systems Thinking

In the 1960s, Jay Forrester, at the Massachusetts Institute of Technology, broke away from this linear, sequential mode of project thinking and developed "systems dynamics" as a way of mapping the interconnected relationships between components of any system. Forrester (1961) developed the notion of reinforcing and balancing feedback loops to show the dynamic relationship between the parts of a system and how those relationships would impact the overall system through time.

Forrester's development of systems dynamics is indicative of the general direction of development toward greater span, especially as it relates to the principles of seeing the whole not just the part, and interdependencies across boundaries. However, even though Forrester spoke often to his students about the importance of their "quality of thinking" as a determinant in their evaluation of a system's dynamics, he did not overtly include mindset or internal reality in his diagnosis of systems. His was primarily an engineering view; he focused mostly on the surface structures of inanimate systems (external reality). He promoted expanded perception across space but neglected the depth component.

Peter Senge (2006), once a student of Forrester's at M.I.T., popularized the concepts of Forrester's systems dynamics by introducing systems thinking to organizational leaders through his book, *The Fifth Discipline*. A significant contribution of Senge's is his inclusion of mental models (mindset) as a valid and essential component of the diagnostic of any human system. Senge included the internal state of people and culture when mapping the forces at play within a system that influence an organization's current reality and the possible achievement of its vision. Senge brought in the depth factor.

Senge's approach to systems thinking is perhaps the most complete available because it attends to all four sights: (1) wholeness and interconnectedness across space (seeing systems); (2) continuous process through time (seeing process); (3) the dynamic relationship between internal and external realities (seeing internal/external); and (4) consciously attending to mindset (seeing consciously). All four sights are equally essential in his approach; none can be ignored. He and his colleagues have made a huge contribution in their work.[1] However, Senge's is only one of many approaches available today. Systems thinking is now taught by many different people in academic institutions, training companies, and consulting firms, and not all (few) embrace all four sights in their work.

The variation in what is meant by systems thinking can be huge, depending on whether proponents are focusing on all four sights or just on one or two. All teachers focus on the first, interdependencies of external variables (seeing systems); fewer add the effects of the system's dynamic relationships over time (seeing process); and fewer still include internal dynamics, operating consciously, or the full multi-dimensional aspects of change. Consequently, when most leaders refer to systems thinking, they consider only interdependencies between external variables and neglect the notions of continuous process and the validity of internal reality. They see the span across the space variable but not the time variable or the depth dimension. This limits the benefits that their systems thinking can deliver.

The good news is that leadership thinking is definitely evolving. In the 1980s, quality, TQM, process improvement, Six Sigma, and reengineering all contributed to leaders' understanding of business and manufacturing processes. These efforts applied project thinking and were mostly implemented through a linear, cause-and-effect approach applied to one *isolated* process. While most leaders still adhere to a project thinking orientation when operating unconsciously, over the past ten years, we have seen a significant increase in attention to cross-boundary interdependencies. Leaders are applying more systems thinking. We attribute this to the fact that many very expensive and very visible technology implementations (ERP, SAP, Electronic Health Records, CRM, etc.) demand attention to system dynamics, and many have failed as a result of this oversight. Failure is often the best catalyst.

LEAN methodologies model the direction of the evolution we are describing. Over the past ten years, advanced practitioners have moved from a very tool-oriented approach to a more systemic view, constantly attempting to expand the span of "process in scope." They often orient to the value stream rather than an individual process, include macro processes and their subprocesses, and encourage managers to think outside their own functional areas for interdependencies. They have migrated their orientation over the past decade to working not just at the organizational level but also with the causative force of culture within teams and relationships. While still applied predominantly to external reality, insightful LEAN practitioners are expanding their reach to attend more to interdependencies across processes and levels of the organization, and they are starting the journey inward toward mindset and culture.

We are moving toward a multi-dimensional perspective, but more complete attention to all quadrants and levels is required to achieve breakthrough results from transformation.

Conscious Process Thinking

In conscious process thinking, the word "conscious" denotes being *aware* of all aspects of the entire Conscious Change Leader Accountability Model. Conscious process thinking, then, means "seeing reality as a multi-dimensional process, part/wholes connected across space, continuously unfolding through time, affecting both internal and external dimensions at all levels of organizations, from the individual to the environment." Wow! What a mouthful. "Flow of the whole across time" is a bit more concise.

We believe that this definition of conscious process thinking is what is intended by the teachers who present the complete view of systems thinking that attends to all four sights. However, we use our term, "conscious process thinking," because it reinforces what we see are the next two critical steps in the evolution of change leadership skill—attention to consciousness and to multi-dimensional process.

APPLICATIONS OF PROJECT THINKING, SYSTEMS THINKING, AND CONSCIOUS PROCESS THINKING

PROJECT THINKING

- Creating project plans
- Project managing developmental or transitional change according to a timeline and budget, especially when the project can be sequestered from outside influence
- Assessing resource and time requirements for developmental and transitional change efforts
- Determining quantifiable and observable measurements
- Mapping sequential and parallel change activities

SYSTEMS THINKING

- Identifying the underlying structure that "causes" an organization's behavior
- Assessing the interconnected and interdependent relationships within a system and its environment when planning for change or assessing change impacts
- Assessing leverage points and blockages for change within a system and its environment
- Identifying key relationships within a system where energy and information currently flow, or must flow in the future, and in what critical directions
- Identifying possible breakdowns and breakthroughs within a system undergoing change
- Identifying cyclical patterns that may help or hinder the performance of a system as it changes

CONSCIOUS PROCESS THINKING

- Seeing the flow of actions within all quadrants and levels that will build momentum toward a result over time
- Designing conscious transformational change strategy and a change process that integrates content, people, and process

- Incorporating the mindset and cultural dimensions of transformation into change strategy
- Using historical and current reality or momentum to build the desired future
- Assessing and implementing course corrections to the transformation process as it unfolds
- Designing strategy for building an organization's capacity for change while it undergoes its current change, especially raising the level of conscious awareness about the breadth and depth of what is required to succeed
- Engaging in conscious process design and conscious process facilitation

To summarize, successful change leaders need to view organizations, people, and transformation from this process perspective. They must see their organizations as multi-dimensional, interconnected, conscious "living systems" in constant and perpetual motion. Although they may perceive that external change occurs in surges, they must attend to the often subtle, always continuous processes that drive those surges. This will enable change leaders to build momentum by creating appropriate plans for transformation that guide the "flow" of the change process, internally and externally, at all levels, to their desired outcomes.

Project thinking, systems thinking, and conscious process thinking all have their uses. The sidebar above lists valuable change leadership applications of each.

TOOLS OF THE THINKING ORIENTATIONS

Leaders who expand and deepen their awareness to embrace systems thinking and then conscious process thinking do not forgo their previous project thinking orientation. They carry it forward. Their evolved thinking does not replace the previous, but rather, they use all three capabilities and can apply them as appropriate.

Each thinking orientation has its own set of tools, all of which can be valuable in transformation when used in the correct applications. The more consciously aware you are, the more you can discern which tools to use when.

Project Management Methodologies

The basic tool of project thinking is a *project management methodology*. This is very common in organizations and is extremely effective at organizing discrete actions to achieve a tangible, specific goal on a specific timeline. Project management methodologies provide structured checklists and linear action plans outlining the sequence of what needs to be done. "On time, on budget" is the motto of project management. Traditionally, project management methodologies have required stable, "closed system" settings in which the project can be protected from the impact of change in its environment. Although dynamic transformational change efforts can use project management tools to manage relatively short, time-bound, tangible aspects of change, they should *not* be used as a guidance system for dynamic change processes. Project management methodologies are simply too linear and inflexible to drive the design of a transformational process. They do not provide adequate options for what to include in a comprehensive change process. However, after the change process is designed using a broader guidance system, project management tools can be very useful, if not essential, for mapping who does what, when, and the resources needed to implement.

Project management has also evolved over the past ten years to include far more focus on people, embracing and incorporating some of the tools and methods of change management in an attempt to better manage people's resistance. Project managers often include attention to communication, training, and stakeholder input in their change plans, which was neglected ten to fifteen years ago. The most progressive of today's project managers attend more to "value generation" (outcomes and ROI) than previously and are no longer solely focused on deliverables, time schedules, and project costs. The traditional, linear "waterfall" model is no longer recommended across the board for all types of projects. Project managers now work with "time-boxing," iterations, and "agile project management," meaning that they can run more phases of a project in parallel, which was unthinkable in the past. They direct resources to the activities with the best value-to-cost ratios, which means that timelines are more flexible as relates to both activities and deadlines, and they are no longer fixed in stone as they once were.

Keep in mind that this describes cutting-edge project managers. Most still, when the going gets tough, revert to the default mindset, and traditional, linear, control-oriented processes. But still, you can see the evolution. Project managers are beginning to perceive more broadly across space and time and attend more to human dynamics, albeit still shallowly.

Other tools and methods were originally developed on the foundation of project thinking, such as TQM, process improvement, Six Sigma, LEAN, and others. As we have mentioned, most, including change management, are evolving to incorporate aspects of systems thinking and conscious process thinking.

Systems Diagrams

The primary tool of systems thinking is a *systems diagram*. These identify the interrelationships that exist between phenomena in a system. Systems diagrams are comprised of reinforcing and balancing feedback loops that portray the causal effects that variables within a system have on each other and on the overall system. Feedback loops portray these effects across both space and time and can attend to internal dynamics as well, depending on the orientation of the person creating the diagram. For a superb introduction to systems thinking and systems diagrams, we refer you to Peter Senge's (2006) book, *The Fifth Discipline*. More detailed application can be found in *The Fifth Discipline Fieldbook*, written by Senge and others (1994).

In systems thinking language, the unique relationships among variables in a system create an underlying dynamic "structure." All systems have underlying dynamic structures that "cause" the behavior of the system. Systems thinking suggests that if leaders want to change the organization's behavior, then they must identify and alter these underlying structures. Furthermore, systems thinking suggests that within any system there are "leverage points," places where small, well-focused actions will produce larger desired results. Applying leverage is the concept of "maximum gain for minimum effort." Systems diagrams, which outline the organization's underlying dynamic structure, assist systems thinkers to identify the leverage points for change.

For change leaders attending to all quadrants and levels, identifying the leverage points for change is perhaps the greatest value of systems thinking and systems mapping. These leverage points will identify the critical content and people changes, revealing the most beneficial changes to the strategy, structure, systems, technology, or processes, as well as the required changes to mindset and culture.

Recall from the previous chapter that in our own approach to culture change, the fourth activity is to identify leverage points. The systems diagram is an extremely useful tool for this.

Become familiar with systems diagrams because they can be invaluable aids in identifying *what* must change. Their limitation is that they do not provide insight about *how* the change might occur. That is the job of a change process model.

Change Process Models

Change process models are tools of conscious process thinking. They are both action oriented and results producing. They organize the activities of the change process so the transformation's desired outcomes are achieved over time. Change process models possess varying degrees of effectiveness, based on how accurately and completely they reflect the actual process dynamics of transformation (all quadrants, all levels). Figure 10.3 (on page 240) portrays the phase level of Being First's own change process model for leading conscious transformation—The Change Leader's Roadmap.

A systems diagram can show change leaders what levers to pull to produce maximum change, whereas a comprehensive change process model organizes the activities to actually pull those levers. In other words, systems diagrams build *knowledge* about the systems dynamics, whereas a change process model organizes *action* to alter the systems dynamics. Each tool needs the other to deliver its full benefit.

There are a number of systems analysis tools that have been developed over the years to map work flow processes. These should not be confused with change process models. "Process mapping," as used in quality and continuous process improvement, is perhaps the most well known of these tools. Others exist in LEAN and Six Sigma.

Process maps denote the chronological sequence of steps within discrete processes. They can be highly detailed or extremely generic, as in W. Edwards Deming's famous process, "plan, do, study, act." First, you plan, then you do, then you study what occurred, and then you take subsequent action. You don't take the second action until you have completed the first (note again the influence of project thinking).

Process maps can outline steps in a process at any level—core enterprise processes that cross boundaries, their functional area subprocesses, or even detailed procedures or work steps in a team.

While process maps define the *prescribed sequential steps* in an isolated organizational process that will be *stable, consistent, and repeated over time*, a change process model provides a *suggested* plan of action for how to *change* an organization over time. Process maps outline what is meant to remain stable and consistent; change process models drive change.

These distinctions are critical. Transformation is dynamic and unpredictable. You cannot reliably map its process sequentially. In fact, you cannot predict its process with any level of certainty. Therefore, a change process model should not prescribe linear actions. Instead, it should offer a general guidance system for organizing actions that will catalyze the transformation toward desired outcomes. A change process model must be flexible and adaptable in real time to the emerging dynamics as they arise.

Process maps, systems diagrams, and change process models all have their place in transformation. Which of these tools are used, and how, should be a function of what is required.

SUMMARY

In this chapter, we defined the term *process* as "the natural or intentional unfolding of continuous events, within all dimensions of reality, toward a desired outcome." We said that all dimensions of the Conscious Change Leader Accountability Model are continually "in process" and that all are interdependent. We stressed that any one of them can surface as a significant force within an organization's transformation, making it imperative that change leaders attend to the process dynamics of all facets.

We differentiated among three different thinking orientations: project thinking, systems thinking, and conscious process thinking—and described the tools that each orientation relies on to produce change results. In particular, we identified the differences among project management methodologies, systems diagrams, process maps, and change process models.

In the next chapter, we will continue to explore the critical requirements of a comprehensive change process model and introduce our nine-phase Change Leader's Roadmap.

ENDNOTE

1. Society for Organizational Learning, www.solonline.org.

Change Process Models

I have never been lost, but I will admit to being confused for several weeks.

—Daniel Boone

Traveling into new territory centuries ago must have been extremely challenging and scary, to say the least. The first pioneers had no maps, no way to know whether food, water, or hostile enemies were around the next bend or over the next mountain. They assumed that opportunity lay ahead but had no way of knowing whether their route was going to get them there, wherever "there" was.

Navigating organizational transformation over the past few decades has been a similar experience for adventuresome leaders and consultants alike. Change leader pioneers have had few maps and little reconnaissance information to support their journey. Most of them traveled alone. A roadmap is invaluable for traveling in new territory. It minimizes confusion and keeps you from getting lost. Transformational change leaders especially need a roadmap to guide their journey as they move beyond the known territory of managing developmental and transitional change into the relatively unknown terrain of leading transformational change.

In the previous chapter, we began the introduction of change process models, which, when designed properly, are in fact roadmaps for transformation. In this chapter, we further explore process models, differentiate them from change frameworks, and explain why they must be "thinking disciplines," rather than prescriptions for action. We also introduce the notion of "fullstream" transformation, which any comprehensive change process model must embrace. We further develop our discussion of conscious process thinking, introducing conscious process design and facilitation, and reveal how an effective change process model supports both. We conclude the chapter with a conceptual overview of our own nine-phase change process model—The Change Leaders Roadmap.

We have developed our change process model as the result of taking numerous transformational journeys with our clients over the past thirty years. Because we have repeatedly scouted the territory as we looked for passable routes, our journeys have revealed much about the transformational terrain. First, we know that the trip is full of humility; success is never guaranteed, even if you do have a roadmap. Second, we know that a roadmap is highly beneficial because it can point out both obstructed and clear paths; specific obstacles always seem to be present around certain types of bends in the river, and clear paths can be repeatedly found by addressing the subtle dynamics present. Having a roadmap does not take the mystery out of the journey, but it certainly makes finding a workable route more likely.

CHANGE FRAMEWORK VERSUS CHANGE PROCESS MODELS

A scan of the literature and the practices of change leadership, change management, and organization development reveals many models designed to help organizations improve how they change and grow. These models seem to fall into two categories: *frameworks* and *process models*. The majority of models available today are frameworks. Some speak to process but at varying levels of specificity. Both frameworks and process models are valuable for leading change, but a process model is absolutely essential for leading transformation. Let's explore their differences.

Change frameworks present the types or categories of topics requiring leadership attention to effect change. For example, McKinsey's 7-S Framework (Peters & Waterman, 1982), Weisbord's Six Box Model (1978), Nadler and Tushman's Congruence Model (1977), Miles' Framework for Leading Corporate Transformation (1997), and our own Conscious Change Leadership Accountability Model, are all good examples.

In general, frameworks offer an organizing construct for what to pay attention to when undergoing change. Think of them as handy catalog indexes for selecting information and topics relevant to change. They can be useful as planning tools and checklists. For example, if you were looking to identify key areas you must address in transformation, you might choose to use the Conscious Change Leader Accountability Model (Figure 10.1).

Figure 10.1. The Conscious Change Leader Accountability Model[1]

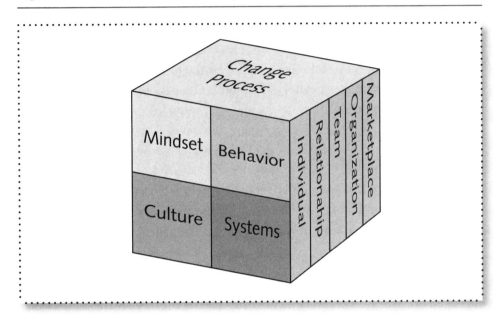

The model gives an accurate, albeit static representation of the four key areas in which you must work and the five levels in which that work must occur, shows that all quadrants and levels are interconnected, and highlights that change process occurs in all dimensions. As useful as the framework might be for pointing to the critical areas of transformation, it does not tell you what to do to accomplish your desired outcomes. It provides no guidance about how to sequence the items you may need to attend to nor does it explain what tangible actions to take to accomplish each. By itself, the Conscious Change Leader Accountability Model is insufficient for guiding the *process* of transforming your organization because it applies a still camera's view to a continuous process, much like incomplete systems maps do. Frameworks can be great educational or diagnostic tools but are less viable as application tools in the field. For that, you need a more dynamic model, a change process model.

While change frameworks are generally static, change process models demonstrate action, movement, and flow. They offer guidance on what to *do* to accomplish change and, *generally*, in what order. Think of process models as roadmaps for action that provide a potential path to follow for designing and implementing your future state. Because transformation requires getting from where you are to where you want to be, having a roadmap that portrays the *process* of the journey is essential.

Examples of process models include Conner's Cycle of Change (1998), Nadler's Cycle of Change (1998), and Kotter's Eight Stage Process of Creating Major Change (1996). Each provides unique process guidance, and several also function like frameworks by listing many important topics requiring attention. Kotter's model, in particular, appears to us to be a hybrid. The first four phases denote a process flow (one stage leads to the next), while the last four specify areas to nurture and give attention (as in a framework model).

From our perspective, the majority of current change process models are either too general or reflect only a partial picture of what is required to lead transformational change. Some focus exclusively on human behavior and neglect any attention to business content. Many more do the reverse, attending heavily to business and organizational imperatives but placing inadequate attention on human dynamics, neither behavior nor culture. Fewer still put adequate attention on mindset. Finding one that takes a complete "multi-dimensional process" view and attends to all quadrants and all levels is next to impossible.

Some process models are too conceptual and neglect guidance at the operational level of getting things done. For example, The Deming Cycle of "Plan, Do, Study, and Act" may represent a process, yet is of minimal help to leaders faced with the complex drama of orchestrating transformational change. More pragmatic guidance is necessary.

Other models we have investigated focus only on implementation and neglect the design phase, or the reverse. A comprehensive model will guide change leaders from conception to completion, even beyond design to integrating the new state into operations to achieve the complete set of results originally intended.

Some models are simply based on ill-conceived concepts of transformation; that is, they are too prescriptive for the dynamic realities of transformation or attend only to external realities and neglect the internal world of culture and the human psyche. The highly prescriptive ones act more like project management methodologies. Those focused solely on external dynamics are minimally useful, especially as the marketplace and change continue to become hyper-dynamic, triggering significant core human needs.

Leaders and consultants need an effective and comprehensive change process model that is fit for transformation. Such a model must attend to and integrate people and content needs. It must provide strategic guidance (30,000-foot view) to help change leaders find their path to success through the troubled and challenging terrain, and be pragmatic, offering on the ground tools to support accomplishing the work required. It must provide clear guidance to navigate and oversee the action required to create desired transformational outcomes.

This change process model should accurately portray how change actually takes place, giving leaders a map of the territory for tailoring, supporting, and accelerating their actual change efforts. Leaders need a change process model that expands their thinking and their conversations about both the internal and external dynamics of transformation, one that helps them observe what is really occurring in their live transformation and create discussion around it. Mostly, this model must provide "informed guesses" for designing in advance what has to occur for the transformation to succeed, as well as insight about how to course-correct when unexpected circumstances arise—as they will. The model must be flexible and adapt to emergent dynamics.

Leaders need a change process model that adequately attends to all quadrants and levels. It must help leaders view transformation consciously to perceive accurately the full range of multi-dimensional dynamics present in transformation. It must support them to think and respond to these dynamics with methods that actually influence them and guide them forward toward desired results. And, of great importance, this change process model must be a *thinking discipline* rather than a prescription for action. It also must be *fullstream*, guiding the entire journey of transformation, not just a piece of it. Let's address these two key points in greater detail.

THE CHANGE PROCESS MODEL AS A CONSCIOUS THINKING DISCIPLINE

This is perhaps the most significant message we can convey about ours, or anyone's, process model for transformation: Your roadmap should be a process model fit for the dynamic nature of transformation, attending to all its multi-dimensional aspects. It should be flexible, customizable, and able to respond in real time to emerging dynamics. Your roadmap can and should guide action but not mandate it. It can and should inform process design decisions but not prescribe them. It can and should organize your plan but not rigidify it. In other words, your change process model can be structured as long as it does not promote you to operate on autopilot and unconsciously follow its structure. Instead, it should trigger you to *think and talk* consciously about all quadrants and all levels and *choose* the change tasks from it that will deliver your desired level of success. It should be a "conscious thinking discipline," not a prescription for action.

On the other hand, just because your change is transformational does not mean that you cannot use a structured guidance system. You can and should. The key is that the guidance system must help to discipline your thinking, to trigger you into consciously addressing the full scope of content, people, and process dynamics you face. It must call you to attend to dynamics that you would otherwise neglect and, in doing so, make you more conscious of them and successful!

Prescriptive change process models expect you to operate on autopilot, but do not allow your guidance system to take over your planning process and make your decisions for you regarding what should be—and not be—in your change process. No two transformational change efforts are ever the same. Your change process model must honor that fact and help you choose your unique path through the territory ahead. It should promote you to consciously think through and uncover what is required given the complex dynamics before you. It should call your conscious awareness into the game and require you to choose from the model what is needed. Remember that the primary purpose of any change process model must be to *increase your conscious awareness* of key change tasks so you design and facilitate the best change process possible.

Transformation demands that you participate and co-create with your emerging dynamics, but it does not demand that you forego any structured support for how to expand your conscious awareness of the process dynamics at play and how to attend to them. A good change process model should assist you in this regard.

TRANSFORMATION AS A FULLSTREAM PROCESS

When leaders first hear the wake-up call that a transformational change is required, the thinking, planning, and communicating that takes place all have implications for how the change will occur and how employees will receive it. A comprehensive change process model must attend to designing the transformation from the initial wake-up call through achievement of the desired state and the Level Three results it is intended to produce. If you seek Level Four or Five Success, then your change process model should guide you all the way to their achievement. We call this entire process *fullstream transformation* (see Figure 10.2).

Transformation, as a continuous process, has an upstream component, a midstream component, and a downstream component, all of which need to be designed and led consciously for the transformation to succeed. The *upstream* stage is oriented to planning and setting the foundations for success. The *midstream* stage is

Figure 10.2. Fullstream Transformation Model

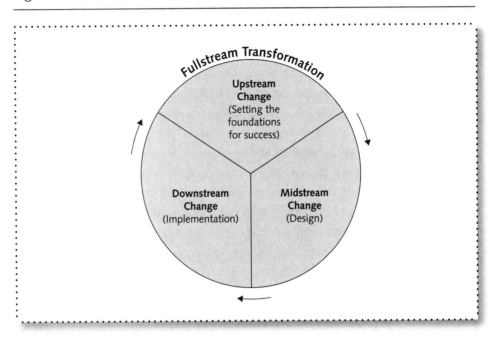

focused on designing the desired state, while the *downstream* stage is about implementation. Implementation, for us, does *not* mean simply installing a new system. Rather, it means completing all the work required to achieve the Level of Success (Three, Four, or Five) you intended from the beginning.

All change process models that are not fullstream neglect at least one of these critical stages, causing the transformation to fall short of expectations. If you do the research, you will find that few change process models are fullstream, which is another reason why 60–70 percent of change efforts fail to deliver their desired results. We will highlight what is in each stage, as perceived through the eyes of a conscious change leader, and point out some of the common challenges that occur within them. Keep in mind that our discussion is from the perspective of a conscious change leader; an autopilot leader would approach these stages very differently, with a narrower and shallower perspective.

Upstream

The upstream stage of transformation, setting the foundations for success, begins with hearing the wake-up call. In this stage, change leaders assess their drivers of change, determine the type of change occurring, and declare the Level of Success they are pursuing. They become clear about the case for change, assess their culture, and begin to clarify the desired culture they want to co-create along with their specified business outcomes. They develop shared vision across the organization regarding these outcomes and assess the organization's capacity to achieve this vision and succeed in the change. They decide who is leading the effort, develop their change strategy, and establish a governance system to minimize impact on operations and guide decision making. They identify conditions and infrastructures needed to support the change and the individual initiatives required to organize the work. They develop their communication and engagement plans, as well as other key support functions.

Leaders begin modeling the desired culture in this stage, and they lay the foundation for ensuring that the way the change is run (decisions, actions, levels of communication, and engagement) also models the desired culture. The upstream stage is the leaders' opportunity to get their heads, hearts, and hands aligned before engaging the rest of the organization in the change. Without such unity and commitment, the change and its leadership are usually seen by employees as disorganized and incompetent, which creates a significant hurdle to overcome. Building leadership alignment upfront sets the ideal conditions for positive employee involvement throughout the change. This is a fundamental requirement of success, and all effective change process models should provide the guidance to ensure this occurs.

Also during the upstream stage, the workforce is initially engaged in the transformation. Employees are informed about the rationale for the transformation and, in many cases, actually help build the case for change. They are fully supported to participate in the planning efforts early in the change process. This builds buy-in and commitment and sets the stage for minimal downstream resistance. Initiating the transformation in ways that are meaningful, positive, and well-received is a critical aspect of the upstream stage. All of this work *precedes* the actual design of the desired future state or the "solution." In other words, employees become involved long before design and implementation.

The upstream stage is critical because it establishes the possibility (or not) for breakthrough results. It sets up the rest of the change effort to run smoothly (or not), and creates a foundation for either commitment or resistance in stakeholders. It is where the climate, commitment, and runway for unleashing human potential throughout the entire transformation are established. It includes critical leadership decisions that are the primary acceleration rockets for the effort. The time and attention this stage takes pays off exponentially throughout the remainder of the change process. We cannot over-emphasize this point, especially if you want breakthrough. But to be honest, most of our clients want to skip critical tasks in this stage. When they do, it almost always comes back to haunt them downstream.

Attention to this stage models the operating principle, "Go slow to go fast." When leaders want to skip tasks in this stage, it is usually because they are trying to accelerate their efforts and want to quickly get to designing their content solution, which occurs in the midstream stage. What they neglect in this stage undermines the foundation for stakeholder commitment. Ultimately, negative human dynamics get triggered because of what they did not put in place (e.g., clear roles, decision making, support infrastructures, communication and engagement plans, etc.), which ultimately causes their efforts to stall at some point downstream. This occurs often when leaders operate predominantly on autopilot because they unconsciously think that speed is measured by how quickly they can get their change solution implemented (Level Two) and do not realize that it takes committed people to actually get the solution to generate real results (Level Three).

Attending to this stage well gives leaders the opportunity to walk their talk of the change right from the start, modeling their desired culture "as if it already existed." This often inspires stakeholders and is a primary enabler of breakthrough results, which, along with culture change and change capability, *demand* effective attention to this stage.

Midstream

The midstream stage of change is when the *actual* design of the desired state occurs. The design is developed, clarified, tested, and refined. Its impact is studied, and plans are created to pace and coordinate its implementation accurately. All of the conditions, structures, systems, and policies decided in the upstream stage are tailored and established to help prepare and support the organization for implementation. More readiness is built through significant two-way communication and employee engagement in the design as appropriate, all of which continues to model the desired culture. The organization's capability to succeed in the change is further developed. Change-relevant training for any or all key stakeholder groups occurs, such as how to lead breakthrough results, transformation, and the human dynamics of change.

Many organizations become stuck in midstream change, spending untold dollars, resources, and hours solely on the design of their desired future state. When this occurs, it is often because they are leaning too far toward a controlling style and place exclusive priority on developing the "right" answer, the right content of their change. These are usually high-compliance organizations with significant passive/defensive aspects to their culture, where little significant action occurs unless there is a very high certainty or predictability of success. Aggressive/defensive cultures can also get bogged down as their perfectionistic and oppositional nature keeps a highly charged debate raging about what is the best design solution. Whether the organization develops the design using internal expertise or an external consulting firm does not seem to matter. Either way, the limitations of the culture negatively influence decision making regarding the design.

The over-focus on design can create an under-focus on implementation. By the time the design is finalized, the leaders may be in such a rush to get the new state in place that they save little time to plan adequately for its implementation. Sometimes, the organization has run out of budget for downstream change activities as well. It is as if writing the perfect script for the change solution gets all of the leaders' attention, and no energy is given to what it takes to actually perform the play! In this all too common scenario, the leaders have focused on design or midstream change at the expense of implementation or downstream change. And to further complicate matters in this scenario, we usually find that such leaders have also neglected the upstream stage as well, as discussed.

When done well, this stage includes a formal impact analysis of the new state on the current organization. This surfaces the issues that need to be resolved to implement smoothly in the downstream stage. These issues are identified, categorized, and given to workstream to resolve. The resolution plans become the basis for the implementation master plan and ensure that implementation can occur without any major surprises. This also provides guidance regarding how best to engage stakeholders throughout implementation. This engagement continues to model the desired culture.

Downstream

The downstream stage includes implementation, integrating the new state fully into operational performance, and learning about and course correcting the new state. Stakeholders are highly engaged, and communication is frequent, with much listening. Implementation models the desired culture, which by now is beginning to formulate in certain areas of the organization. Skill training about how to operate in the new state occurs, as does building best change practices and dismantling the change infrastructure when it is no longer needed. This is also the time of celebration during which support for making the transformation a success is officially acknowledged.

A common mistake frequently occurs in this stage, especially when the pace of change has been mandated by leaders operating on autopilot and is unrealistic. In this scenario, leaders rush into implementation before they have adequately identified and created the upstream conditions for success or before they have adequately completed their desired state designs and tested them for feasibility. This makes implementation extremely difficult. As implementation begins, the need for the neglected yet necessary upstream and midstream work becomes apparent. Leaders are forced to stop implementation in order to clarify what is required for success, further flesh out the details of the desired state, or study its impacts. Employees become resistant because they feel jerked around by leaders' poor planning and the "stop and go" dynamic it creates.

When change management was first gaining speed as a legitimate practice in the early 1990s, we performed an informal research study to identify what "change management" meant to leaders and what they wanted and were ready to hear about leading change. We found that most leaders believed that change management meant the *implementation* of a desired outcome that had previously been designed and the need to overcome employee resistance. They recognized the need for change management only when they couldn't put their good solutions into action successfully, due largely to workforce opposition or emotional upheaval. Twenty years later, leaders often request change management support at the start of the effort, which helps tremendously.

However, in transformation, this is not making the difference it needs to because traditional change management does not adequately establish the upstream and midstream foundations for breakthrough and successful implementation. It misses key ingredients for success such as adequate executive and stakeholder alignment, clear assessment of the drivers of change and the business case for change, shared vision, change strategy, capacity assessment, governance and other change infrastructures, initiative integration, adequate testing of design solutions, impact analysis and resolution, and so on.

The net effect is that autopilot leaders still "rush to implement" before these critical foundations are established. They do not know what they do not know. They rely on change management to handle the people issues because they still view them as "issues." Change management does not help them understand that the upstream stage is not about containing resistance but establishing an environment where the full human potential of the organization can be released. Change management does not help them see the multi-dimensional nature of transformation and why and how they must attend to all quadrants and all levels right from the start. The leaders' requests to engage change management earlier are still based on their unconscious desires to rush to get the new state in place. Their hope that change management will salvage a shaky or resisted implementation is unrealistic because the seeds of a successful implementation are sown in the multi-dimensional treatment of the required upstream and midstream stages.

Implementation is essential, yet it is only one of the three necessary stages of the transformation process. Conscious change leaders, by addressing the fullstream nature of change using conscious process thinking to attend to all quadrants and levels from the start, not only ensure a smooth implementation but also maximize the possibility of breakthrough Level Three, Four, and Five results. Change process models that focus heavily on implementation planning and overcoming employee resistance are designed that way because they neglect the required upstream and midstream change activities. Make sure your process model is fullstream and multi-dimensional.

The Fullstream Transformation Model offers a conceptual overview of the process of change, but it has little value in actually guiding a live change effort because it is too general. The model's value is only in introducing leaders to an expanded view of the process of change—across time—so they begin to think fullstream. To actually lead transformation successfully, a more developed change process model is required.

THE CHANGE LEADER'S ROADMAP

The nine-phase Change Leader's Roadmap, shown in Figure 10.3, attends to what we believe is required of a comprehensive change process model fit for transformation.

The model represents a fullstream roadmap for getting your organization from where it is to where it wants to be. The nine phases represent the generic process of how change takes place in organizations over time. The model integrates the change strategy elements of content, people, and process, and it attends to all quadrants and all levels. A detailed description of The Change Leader's Roadmap is the focus of our companion book.

Figure 10.3. The Change Leader's Roadmap

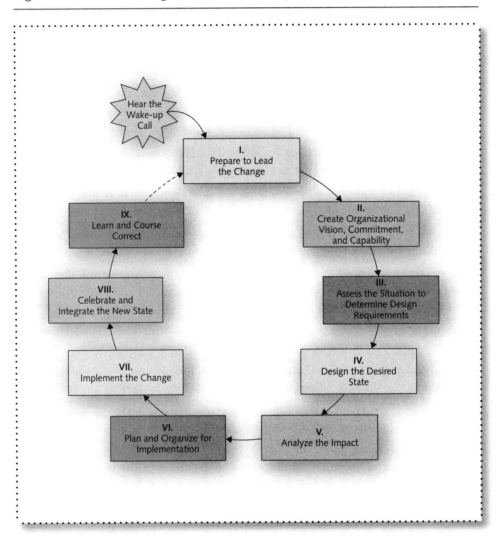

We have been working with The Change Leader's Roadmap for thirty years. In the early 1980s, we used it in a simpler form for guiding transitional change. In the early 1990s, we expanded it to specifically address the multi-dimensional process dynamics of transformation, assisting change leaders to take a conscious approach to leading transformation.

Although designed for transformational change, The Change Leader's Road-map can be tailored for all types of change, as well as any magnitude of change effort. Smaller, less complex transitional changes require selective tailoring of the activities in the model. Even more tailoring is required for developmental change applications, as the model attends to much more than is required in most developmental changes.

The model graphically represents the inherent logic and flow of the key phases of transformation. You may, however, mistakenly interpret the sequential graphic to mean that you must complete one phase before you proceed to the next. In actual practice, transformation is not linear, and you may be in two, three, or even four phases simultaneously. You may do the work of some phases in parallel with the work of other phases as your situation dictates. Remember that this model is a thinking discipline, a navigation system, not a project thinking oriented methodology. You can combine phases however you choose, given your circumstances.

The graphic representation may also cause you to think mistakenly that The Change Leader's Roadmap portrays cyclical change, where you end a cycle only to start over again from the same place. This graphic rendering is to clearly show the sequence of the nine phases. In reality, the model is a spiral. When your change effort is complete, you will likely continue on your journey with another change effort. After each "cycle" of change, you end at a future state that is transformed, improved, and better than where you started. Hence, the accurate portrayal of the model is as a spiral going continuously upward.

In a complex transformation, the enterprise is often going through an overarching nine-phase change process while simultaneously, individual change initiatives engage in their own processes within the overall transformation. Therefore, different change initiatives, business units, or regions of the enterprise may be in different phases. The key, of course, is to ensure adequate integration so that all individual initiatives support the overarching change of the enterprise. When each change effort is using the same change process model, integration becomes much easier. The reality of the complex, nonlinear dynamics of the model in action is shown in Figure 10.4.

Structure of The Change Leader's Roadmap

The roadmap incorporates the Fullstream Transformation Model (see Figure 10.5). Phases I to III are the upstream stage (setting the foundations for success), Phases IV to VI comprise the midstream stage (design), and Phases VII through IX denote the downstream stage (implementation).

Figure 10.4. The Change Leader's Roadmap in Action

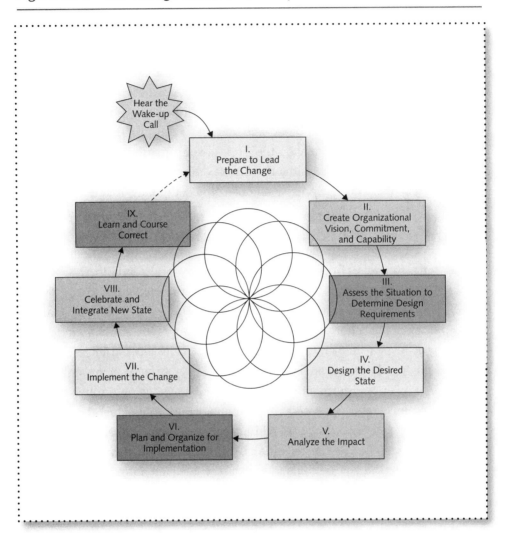

There are several levels of guidance available in the model, from conceptual to very detailed. Depending on your need, you can customize the application of the model to any level of detail for any stakeholder group, from executives to change team members to managers and employees.

The most conceptual level is the general description of the nine phases as shown earlier in Figure 10.3. Each phase is further organized into major activities, as outlined in Figure 10.6. Each activity is achieved through focused tasks.

Figure 10.5. The Change Leader's Roadmap As a Fullstream Process

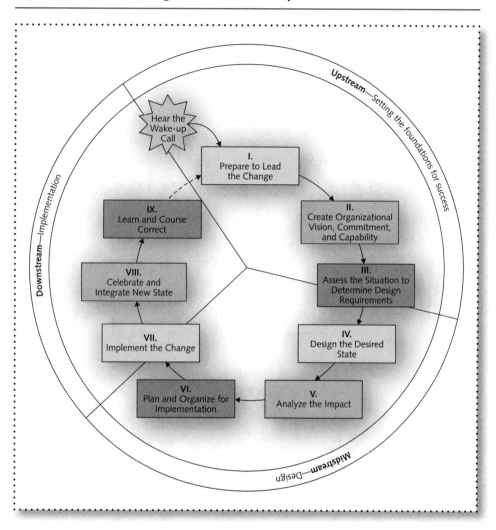

The tasks for each activity all have deliverables, which, at the most operational level, are accomplished through a series of suggested work steps.

The Change Leader's Roadmap is a task-driven process model, meaning that the work of change gets carried out through the tasks, and more procedurally, the work steps for each task. The activities are "rollups" of the tasks, and the phases are rollups of the activities. Phases and activities organize the model, making it easy to understand, follow, and navigate for practitioners. They also provide the greatest

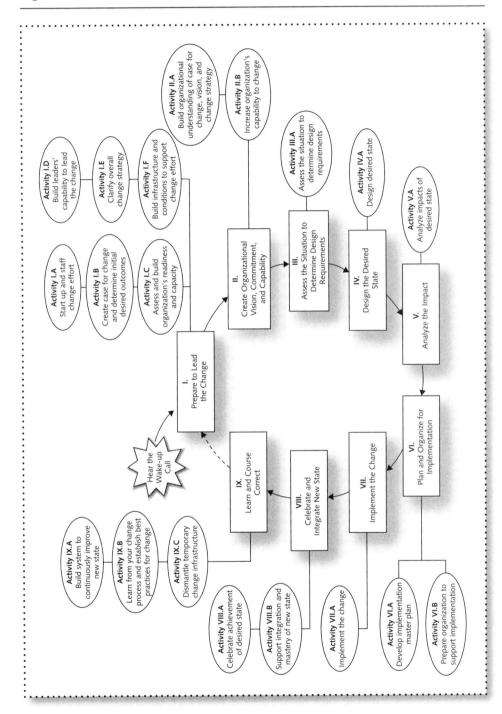

Figure 10.6. The Change Leader's Roadmap—Activity Level

versatility for the various people who use the model, be they executives who need only the conceptual phase level or change process leaders and consultants who benefit from the greater detail.

The work steps for each task are provided as guidance and suggestions. Most users of The Change Leader's Roadmap customize all aspects of its application to their need, including the work steps. Never is the model meant to be followed as a prescription, even at the work step level.

We have structured the material in this way—phase, activity, task, work steps—for ease of use for line managers who are familiar with similarly structured project thinking approaches, such as project management, LEAN, or Six Sigma. This structure gives them a familiar language and organizing construct for the material, which they then apply using their systems and conscious process thinking skills. This leverages the best of all three modes of thinking.

A full array of change resources and tools are included in each task in The Change Leader's Roadmap. Resources include information sheets, tools, checklists, assessments, process questions, potential problems, and articles. These are provided as educational and application support to ensure the successful use of the model. We have not included the tasks, work steps, or resources in this book, as that is the subject of our companion book, *The Change Leader's Roadmap*. Refer to it regarding how to use the model, or go to www.changeleadersroadmap.com. We introduce The Change Leader's Roadmap here to demonstrate how a comprehensive model can be multi-dimensional (all quadrants all levels), fullstream (all phases of change), complete (strategic guidance and pragmatic tools), and adaptable (structured but adjustable to emergent dynamics).

There Is No Cookbook for Transformation!

The Change Leader's Roadmap was designed to benefit both leaders and consultants by helping them *consciously* design and facilitate their change processes. Unconsciously applying the model can be hazardous to either.

Beware: The structure, detail, and logic of The Change Leader's Roadmap might create the impression that it is a cookbook—providing a prescribed course of action—for how to succeed at transformation. The structure of the model may give you the illusion that transformation can be carefully managed, sequenced, and controlled. As we have already said, this is not possible! There is no cookbook for transformational change. Anyone using The Change Leader's Roadmap must remember that it is a thinking discipline, not a prescription for action.

We created The Change Leader's Roadmap to be as complete and comprehensive as possible. We included everything that we have discovered over the past thirty years that can be essential to the success of your organization's transformation. That thoroughness is both a strength and a potential weakness of the model.

Remember, The Change Leader's Roadmap, in all its comprehensiveness, is designed to support you to consciously ask yourself which of its many activities are critical for *your* transformation's success. While it alerts you to what you *might* need in your transformation, application of the model must *always be tailored* to the outcomes, magnitude, change leadership style, pacing requirements, and resource constraints unique to your situation.

In any given transformation effort, we suggest that you consider all of what is offered in the model and then select *only* the work that is appropriate to your change effort and that will help you guide and accelerate your change. You want to choose as few tasks as possible and just enough to succeed. The fewer tasks you choose, the less burden you will place on operations to provide the resources to carry out those tasks. You should skip activities that have been completed or are of marginal or no value to your situation. However, if you skip critical tasks, you may either fail or delay success. You should combine tasks or run them in parallel whenever possible to accelerate your pace and achieve multiple deliverables simultaneously. And of course, you will always need to decide for yourself how you will actually design each chosen task in real time.

Using a complete change process model like The Change Leader's Roadmap enables you to monitor progress very closely. It not only gives you a process roadmap but also enables you to quickly course-correct and add other tasks as necessary if you hit roadblocks. This way, you can initially design a very streamlined, highly efficient change process, and expand it as you proceed if necessary. This is a key to effectively managing capacity during transformation.

Conscious Change Process Design and Facilitation

Transformation, ultimately, is the journey from where an organization is to where it chooses to be, when the change required to get there is so significant that it requires the people and culture of the organization to "transform," and the journey must begin before you can fully identify what your ultimate goal or desired state looks like.

Change leadership is the function of leading an organization through this journey. Change leaders are responsible both for designing the process of this journey and for overseeing and guiding that process as it unfolds. We refer to these change leadership responsibilities as process design and process facilitation. This is where conscious change leaders put their conscious process thinking skills to use.

Process design governs the advanced planning and creation of any process, whereas process facilitation pertains to real-time oversight and execution of that preliminary design. Process design is akin to the "game plan" that coaches of a sports team prepare *before* the game; it is how they want the game to go. Process facilitation entails the real-time play calling *during* the game; it requires the coaches to respond in the moment to what is actually happening on the field. Similarly, an architect uses process design to *conceive* a custom home, whereas the builder uses process facilitation to *construct* the house to both the plan's specifications and the client's changing desires. Some processes, such as house-building, require that you facilitate the process exactly as designed. Other processes, such as coaching a football game, demand that you continually improvise based on what is occurring in real time.

Throughout this book, we have referred to the need for change leaders to attend to the *actual* dynamics and requirements of transformation. Conscious process thinking enables change leaders to discover and see these dynamics and requirements. *Conscious change process design* is the preliminary strategy and process plan that conscious change leaders develop to attend to these dynamics, whereas *conscious change process facilitation* refers to change leaders' implementation of their process design, while responding to the actual dynamics and requirements that spontaneously arise.

In designing any transformational change process, use all "four sights" and keep in mind the conscious process design requirements outlined in Exhibit 10.1. Your change processes will always be more successful if you design them with these requirements in mind.

Change Leadership Styles and Their Influence on Change Facilitation

There are two basic types of change processes: planned and emergent. Conscious change leaders orient to both. We plan, and then we pay conscious attention to emerging dynamics and adjust our plan as necessary.

Three different change leadership styles exist that dictate the way change leaders facilitate their change processes: (1) Control (make it happen); (2) Facilitate (help it happen); and (3) Co-create (partner it into existence). It is important to be clear about your normal change leadership style because any time you are

Exhibit 10.1.   Conscious Change Process Design Requirements

Your change process must do the following:

- Model your desired culture, values, and mindset.
- Awaken people to greater conscious awareness and understanding.
- Unleash human potential and performance by minimizing resistance and maximizing commitment.
- Honor agreed-upon boundary conditions, including desired outcomes, resources and time availability, and stakeholders to engage.
- Integrate attention to content and people where possible.
- Address all quadrants and all levels as required to succeed.

operating on autopilot, you will make decisions about your change process that match your style. The resulting change process you facilitate will model and promote a certain type of culture. If you are not conscious of your change leadership style, you may inadvertently design and facilitate change processes that promote an undesired culture.

Change leaders with controlling styles design change processes that model command-and-control cultures. With this style, change leaders exert their personal control on the change process. They treat the change process as something "out there" that must proceed in a certain way, using power and control mechanisms to ensure that occurs. These leaders tend to plan their entire change process at the beginning and then force it into that timeline. As you can imagine, they tend to orient primarily to content and external dynamics. Their attention to people is minimal, mostly to attempt to minimize or contain resistance. Communication is often one-way, and if they engage the workforce at all, it is usually only after the change solution has been designed.

Facilitative styles tend to model cultures that are structured and planned but lean toward being more flexible and humanistic. With this style, change leaders attempt to work *with* rather than dominate the change process, guiding it as needed to assist it to proceed. These leaders use less force and are less oppositional when things don't go as planned, yet still focus on getting the change "out there" to roll out according to plan if possible. However, facilitative leaders are also open to course-correcting their plans as needed.

Facilitative change leaders often use two-way communications, and ask for greater workforce input and engagement earlier in the change process. They seek more input on key decisions, provide more local control of implementation plans to teams and departments that are highly impacted by the change, and consider the impacts of human needs and culture on their plans.

Change leaders with co-creative styles model cultures of empowered partnership, collaboration, learning, and course correcting. With this "partner it into existence" mindset, these change leaders put less of their own personal stamp on the structure of the change process. They engage the workforce upfront and sincerely seek and expect input. They share decision making and empower key stakeholders to own the overall design of the change. Communications is multi-directional, engagement is maximized, and they consciously use the transformation as a mechanism to call the workforce into greater self-actualization. They want people to participate in significant ways. (See premium content: How Command and Control as a Change Leadership Style Causes Transformational Change Efforts to Fail; www.pfeiffer.com/go/anderson.)

Co-creative change leaders see themselves as coach and "holder of the space" for their teams to design and facilitate the change. They support it with initial direction based on market needs but allow the actual change process to emerge in response to the initial direction they offer. Such change processes are a constant give and take between leaders and their change teams providing guidance and then responding to what is occurring. These leaders see their role as a direction setter and guide, as well as a listener and respondent to what is needed. Because of this, their project plans are generally shorter in time frame than facilitative leaders.

Co-creative change leaders see themselves as part of the change process and treat their own modeling of desired mindsets and behaviors as paramount. They operate consciously and engage stakeholders in ways that deepen their own insight and understanding of human and process dynamics. While seeking Level Five Success, they are also attempting to wake up their organization, unleash its full potential, and build a sustainable co-creative culture. The reason these leaders can take such an evolved, forward-thinking style is because they have done the personal development work that enables it.

Conscious change leaders use The Change Leader's Roadmap to consciously design and facilitate their change process to model their desired culture. The CLR can be used with any change leadership style, but it is built for facilitative and co-creative change leaders who possess the personal awareness and flexibility to align their personal style and the design of their change process to the desired culture they are seeking to create. Breakthrough results become possible when all three are in synch. The beauty of operating consciously and using such a multi-dimensional process methodology is that it enables you to get all three in synch, while attending to all the dynamics at play (all quadrants, all levels).

Comparing Your Experience with Other Change Models

When teaching the CLR to seasoned change leaders and consultants, we have found it useful to have them compare their experience with change frameworks and other change process models with using the nine-phase CLR. Our intention is to expand their view of how to lead transformation effectively and add to their existing expertise, not replace it. Exhibit 10.2 offers a series of questions to assist you in this comparison. After completing this worksheet, consider what you want to add to your current way of guiding your organization's transformation.

Exhibit 10.2. Comparing Other Change Models with The Change Leader's Roadmap

WORKSHEET

1. What change frameworks are you familiar with or have you used?
2. What other change process models are you familiar with or have you used?
3. What aspects of each of these frameworks and/or process models fall under each of the three stages of the Fullstream Transformation Model?

   ▸ Upstream stage:

   ▸ Midstream stage:

   ▸ Downstream stage:

4. Do aspects of any of these frameworks/process models address issues not within the three stages of change? If so, what are they?
5. For each of the preceding frameworks/process models, which focus your attention on building a change strategy for the overall transformation?
6. Which support the design and implementation of the content of the transformation?
7. Which address the deeper human dynamics of turning resistance into commitment?

(continued)

8. Which adequately address cultural transformation as part of the organization's transformation?
9. Which adequately address mindset change?
10. Of the change process models you listed, how would you compare their guidance against the nine phases and all of the activities of the Change Leader's Roadmap? Check the activities within each phase that you feel are adequately covered in the models you currently use:

PHASE I: PREPARE TO LEAD THE CHANGE

- ▶ Activity I.A Start-Up and Staff Change Effort
- ▶ Activity I.B Create Case for Change and Determine Initial Desired Outcomes
- ▶ Activity I.C Assess and Build Organization's Readiness and Capacity
- ▶ Activity I.D Build Leaders' Capacity to Lead the Change
- ▶ Activity I.E Clarify Overall Change Strategy
- ▶ Activity I.F Build Infrastructure and Conditions to Support Change Effort

PHASE II: CREATE ORGANIZATIONAL VISION, COMMITMENT, AND CAPACITY

- ▶ Activity II.A Build Organizational Understanding of Case for Change, Vision, and Change Strategy
- ▶ Activity II.B Increase Organization's Capability to Change

PHASE III: ASSESS THE SITUATION TO DETERMINE DESIGN REQUIREMENTS

- ▶ Activity III.A Assess the Situation to Determine Design Requirements

PHASE IV: DESIGN THE DESIRED STATE

- ▶ Activity IV.A Design Desired State

PHASE V: ANALYZE THE IMPACT

- ▶ Activity V.A. Analyze Impacts of the Desired State

PHASE VI: PLAN AND ORGANIZE FOR IMPLEMENTATION

- ▶ Activity VI.A Develop Implementation Master Plan
- ▶ Activity VI.B Prepare Organization to Support Implementation

PHASE VII: IMPLEMENT THE CHANGE

- ▶ Activity VII.A Implement the Change

(continued)

WORKSHEET (continued)

PHASE VIII: CELEBRATE AND INTEGRATE THE NEW STATE

▸ Activity VIII.A Celebrate Achievement of Desired State
▸ Activity VIII.B Support Integration and Mastery of New State

PHASE IX: LEARN AND COURSE-CORRECT

▸ Activity IX.A Build a System to Continuously Improve New State
▸ Activity IX.B Learn from Your Change Process and Establish Best Practices
▸ Activity IX.C Dismantle Temporary Change Infrastructure

11. For this question, set aside your attention to any change framework or change process model, including the CLR. What does your professional experience say about what is needed to lead the process of transformation successfully in real time? What guidance is essential?

12. What do you need to add, modify, or delete from your current way of guiding transformation?

SUMMARY

Transformation is a complex, multi-dimensional process that can be greatly served by a structured change process model to discipline your thinking and help you remain conscious of all of the dynamics to which you must attend. Such a model must honor the integral, process nature of transformation and provide a roadmap for navigating its complexities. Change frameworks, while valuable to identify critical areas of attention, do not suffice for designing and leading the *process* of transformation. A change process model is required.

This concludes our discussion of process dynamics. In Section Four, we address what it means and what it takes to answer the call of conscious change leadership.

ENDNOTE

1. Peters, T., and Waterman, R. H. *In search of Excellence*. New York: Harper & Row, 1982.

Answering the Call to Conscious Change Leadership

CHAPTER

11

Answering the Call

The price of greatness is responsibility.

—Winston Churchill

This book is a call to conscious change leadership, an invitation into a way of leading change that unleashes the greatest possibility we know for you, your people, your organization, and the world. In the Introduction, we said that we would keep our feet firmly on the ground as we stretched our heads into the stars, that we would chart new territory and deliver insights and methods for achieving breakthrough results from change. We hope we have done that.

But this is just the beginning, not the end. Now we must get to work.

In this chapter, we will explore what it means to answer the call to conscious change leadership. We will identify the commitment change leaders make when they choose to operate consciously and the natural direction this choice often takes them. We hope this chapter stirs you to inquire deeply of yourself—who you are and what you stand for in your life and leadership. We will begin this inquiry with a review of the journey we have taken throughout the book, highlighting the key insights, conclusions, and actions we have identified along the way. We will conclude by contemplating the profound possibilities our future holds when we have hundreds of thousands of conscious change leaders co-creating positive change in our organizations and the world.

A REVIEW OF OUR JOURNEY

In the book, we made the following key points. Our discussion began talking about results, in particular, breakthrough results. There are five different Levels of Success change leaders can pursue with their change efforts. Most leaders want Level Five Success, but they do not lead their change efforts in ways that will produce those results. Our premise is that conscious change leadership increases the probability of achieving superior business outcomes, cultural transformation, and change capability, all at the same time (Level Five). Conscious change leaders do not simply want their change efforts to run more smoothly with less resistance. Rather, they want to "break through" and unleash the full human potential of their people through their organization's transformation. On a foundation of commitment and alignment, they want the workforce and the organization to transform to achieve significant improvements in performance. They are not after average outcomes from change but truly extraordinary ones.

There are seven drivers of change, and transformation requires change leaders to address all of them. The pace and scope of change in the marketplace have increased over the past forty years, calling change leaders to attend to all of these drivers, including culture, behavior, and mindset, in many of their change efforts.

Three different types of change are occurring in organizations—developmental, transitional, and transformation. Transformation is the type occurring when all seven drivers are called into action. Transformation requires change leaders to begin the change process before the ultimate destination is known. The future state emerges and becomes clear as they proceed and gather information. Their change process will be nonlinear, taking numerous turns as they learn and figure out how best to respond to the market. This requires leaders and stakeholders to step into the unknown, which triggers significantly greater (and deeper) human dynamics in transformation, all of which must be "managed." Instead of attempting to "contain" these human dynamics, conscious change leaders provide opportunities to "invite them out" so they can be transformed, naturally generating greater commitment, support, and collaboration in their organizations. This creates in transformation a real opportunity for people and the organization to break old comfort zone barriers and achieve higher aspirations and outcomes.

Taking a conscious approach to transformation is key to achieving success. This requires understanding how human beings function, not just behaviorally, but mentally and emotionally. "Mindset is causative:" Beliefs, values, and assumptions dictate how change leaders perceive situations, which determines their internal state, including what they think and feel. Their mindset determines whether their behaviors are oriented to fighting, fleeing from, or working effectively with the situation. This then generates their actions and quality of performance, which determine their results. Mindset, then, causes not only the change leader's interpretation of events but also how much of their ability and potential they deliver in their response. Their level of personal performance and success is a direct reflection of their mindset. Taking a conscious approach means change leaders turn inward and address their mindset and emotional patterns, and seek to transform the aspects of their mental conditioning that limit their outcomes. Breakthrough starts on the inside.

Transformation requires change leaders to attend to both internal and external dynamics, in individuals as well as the collective. This "all quadrant, all level" orientation includes individual mindset and behavior, as well as collective culture and systems as they play out in relationships, teams, the organization, and the marketplace. All these dynamics, across quadrants and levels, are interdependent, causing a gravitational force for a system to remain stable until a "tipping point" occurs, and the whole interdependent system transforms. Conscious change leaders nurture all quadrants and all levels to catalyze that transformation.

Building organizational change capability is a twenty-first century strategic advantage. Change is so prevalent and significant to an organization's sustainability that change leaders need to elevate change to a "strategic discipline" within the organization and establish management protocols and best practices to maximize the results from change. There are five strategies for building organizational change capability: (1) identifying and managing an enterprise change agenda; (2) having one common change *process* methodology; (3) establishing change infrastructures; (4) building a strategic change center of excellence for all change practitioners; and (5) creating a strategic change office. These strategies enable change leaders to streamline, accelerate, and lower the cost of change while supporting both business and cultural outcomes.

We distinguished between two core inner human dynamics—ego and being—and saw that the ability of change leaders to develop conscious awareness of their internal world is foundational to transcending the limitations of their ego functioning. This maximizes the breakthrough possibilities inherent in operating from their beings, or higher selves. Conscious change leaders must "put their beings first."

Everyone has core needs of security, inclusion and connection, power, order and control, competence, and justice and fairness. These needs often get triggered during change, especially transformational change. These core needs come from the ego and its fear of not getting them met. When the ego interprets that our core needs are handled, we feel okay. When it perceives otherwise, we feel stress and fear. These "unmet core needs" are the underlying cause of most behavioral resistance. Overcoming resistance is a process of assisting people to "transform" their ego's issues, which naturally leads to greater commitment. Commitment gets generated not out of containing resistance, but rather by "allowing it into the space," dialoguing about it authentically in ways that nurture and honor people, and supporting people through the natural process of emotional transition.

Culture has a powerful impact on the success of change efforts. In fact, "culture is to an organization as mindset is to an individual." Just as individuals have different mindsets and ways of being, so do organizations. Constructive, co-creative cultures deliver the highest performance, and these cultures match the co-creative ways of being of effective individuals. Low-performing cultures play out ego dynamics at the scale of the collective, with people competing across boundaries rather than cooperating, being oppositional instead of supportive, worrying about power rather than serving customers, and holding back their contribution rather than expressing their full potential in the market. The ego dynamics that limit people personally are the same that limit people collectively, just as the dynamics of *being* that enable personal excellence also generate organizational excellence.

Change is the essence of life; nothing is static even when it appears that way. Life—like organizational change—is a multidimensional process, occurring always in all quadrants and levels, forever moving, and evolving forward. Process dynamics refers to the nature and laws of our forever-in-motion, multi-dimensional reality.

The physical domain often seems at a standstill, even though activity is always occurring in other quadrants that ultimately will cause the physical systems or behavior to surge forward in a "spurt" of change. The fundamental responsibility of a change leader is to support this positive direction by intervening in the appropriate, often internal, domains as needed. Change leaders can "make change happen," "help it happen," or "partner it into existence," and no matter what their change leadership style, using a change process model is far more effective than using a static change framework. An effective change process model for transformation attends to the "fullstream" of change and is a strategic thinking discipline rather than a set prescription for action.

Lastly, The Change Leader's Roadmap—our change process model—effectively organizes and supports the conscious design and facilitation of complex transformation, keeping users conscious of and attending to all the quadrants and levels they must focus on to succeed.

Change leaders and consultants of all types can take these insights of conscious change leadership and apply them to any content or type of change, no matter what their industry, organization, or change role. The application of this material is only limited by what the change leader chooses to change.

COMMITING TO BEING A CONSCIOUS CHANGE LEADER

Recall that leaders *choose* to become *conscious* change leaders. They are not anointed by someone else, such as a superior, peer, or subordinate. Their role, responsibilities, and level of authority do not matter in this choice. What matters is how they choose to be, work, and relate.

When you choose to be a conscious change leader, you commit to live and lead consciously, by doing the following:

▶ Pursuing greater awareness and your own self mastery; turning inward and observing your mindset in action; and continually transforming your ego's self-limiting conditioning so you can see the broader and deeper dynamics at play in transformation

▶ Putting your "being first" and operating from your higher self so you can perform optimally, express more of your potential, and bring your best to all that you do

▶ Serving others better by fulfilling and then transcending your ego's core needs and its inherent orientation to self-interests

▶ Helping others wake up and operate consciously themselves by modeling and engaging with them in conversation about the inner dynamics of mindset and culture and the breakthroughs they enable

▶ Being a voice, champion, and proponent in your change efforts for change leaders attending to the multi-dimensional process dynamics across all quadrants and levels

If you make this commitment, you hold *yourself* accountable for this way of being, working, and relating because it is what you stand for in your life and leadership. It is who you are, how you enable breakthrough change results, and ultimately, how you contribute to making the world a better place.

You are either compelled to take this journey and operate consciously or not. You can anoint yourself to the position of conscious change leader right now or reconfirm the choice you have already made. No one can do it for you, nor should anyone try. It is a personal decision about who you are, who you choose to be, and how you want to live and lead. And only you can ultimately hold yourself accountable for walking this path. You are accountable to your boss for performing your responsibilities as a change leader, but you are accountable only to yourself for doing so consciously.

As you consider making this commitment, first consider what commitment is. Commitment is not simply a thought, or a good idea that you *should* follow. It doesn't come from your ego, and it isn't generated from your conditioning. It is not some obligation you must make because of who your ego thinks you are.

Commitment comes from your being, your essential self. It can start in your mind as a good idea, but from there it grows as you weigh its pluses and minuses, its relevance and meaning to your life and leadership, and its alignment to your deepest values. A commitment is a possibility that profoundly moves and inspires you, and calls you to be something more. It is a promise of a future that is larger than your current identity. A commitment registers your aspiration for what you deem is most important in your life and work. And when you commit, you move mountains. The question is: to what do you commit?

CO-CREATING A BETTER WORLD

How wonderful it is that nobody need wait a single moment before starting to improve the world.

—Anne Frank

Committing to operate consciously puts you on a path of intentional personal development. This development has a direction. It is purposeful and naturally unfolds toward greater breadth and depth in your awareness. From a breadth perspective, as you transform your ego-driven needs, habits, and positions, you see more of life's interdependencies and how you, and they, are profoundly connected. From a depth perspective, you experience more deeply your essential self and witness the human condition in others with more compassion and understanding. This growth in your awareness causes a natural "turning of your attention" from your ego's myopic self-interests to pursuing what is best for others and causes larger than yourself. You forgive, cooperate, and serve more, not because they are good ideas, but because they are natural expressions of who you have become. You reach out and seek support from others when in need, just as you provide it to others across what you previously thought were adversarial boundaries. When you transform your personal identity as an ego, you naturally begin to identify more deeply with what is trans-personal, beyond your individual self.

This worldview and its way of being and behaving are called "co-creating." It is a natural outgrowth of the personal development from ego to being. It includes a shift in perspective and motivation from win-lose, or even win-win, to WIN-win-win.

In win-lose, the ego sees you and me as separate. The boundary between us is most critical, and we compete to get our maximum personal share. In win-win, the ego's perspective is often "If I compete, I may lose. Therefore, I'll compromise and give you half. That way there is no fight, and at least I get some of what I want." While the boundary between us is less rigid, it is still there, and self-interest is still at play, even though the ego employs a more collaborative strategy. In win-win, our motivation is often not as altruistic as it might seem.

In a WIN-win-win orientation, ego is not dominant, being is. Being sees across boundaries and seeks to serve the greater good, the larger wholes that are common to us—our relationship, team, organization, society, and world. WIN-win-win means the larger wholes win—you win, and I win. The first win is capitalized and we call it the Big Win, for in co-creating, we must not forget the levels larger than ourselves.

When operating from your being—your essential self—boundaries disappear. In this co-creative worldview, with its greater span and depth of awareness, you see and care for all of reality: all quadrants including people's feelings, motivations and needs, and all levels, from relationships, teams, and organizations to communities, societies, and the planet. This means all people, all races, and all genders, no matter what their religion, sexual preference, or favorite ice cream. You are naturally compelled to care and have compassion for others without condition because you are so in touch with your own human strengths and frailties, which you have become intimate with while traveling the humbling path of your own personal transformation.

From the perspective of your higher self, you come to care deeply for the natural environment. As you overcome your ego's inclination to exert power over and control of people and the environment, you begin to realize that you, as a human being, are actually part of the environment. There is no separation. You have the same atoms and molecules in your body; you return to the same dust as all organic matter; and you are enlivened by the same Spirit that infuses all of life. How could any of us not care for the earth when we realize that we are essentially connected to it and that we as individuals and societies can only be as healthy as it is?

Without the ego's boundaries and self-interest in control, you now see others as partners rather than competitors or adversaries. You reach across old dividing lines and seek to work together on the same team of humanity serving what is larger than your individual self and common to all. Your being's natural compassion, understanding, and care cause you to reach out in unconditional ways across all boundaries and you become compelled to take a stand for what is socially just and environmentally sustainable, for these are the fundamental values that support Life itself.

In your development as a conscious change leader, you become more than you thought you ever were, more in touch with your essential self and more capable of generating breakthroughs in thinking, acting, and achieving. What was once impossible becomes increasingly plausible because you see new possibilities in yourself and others. All this brings hope and inspiration for you to make a difference beyond simply achieving your ego's personal goals. With your new capabilities, these goals become relatively easy, and you begin to stand for something greater in the world.

Through the eyes of being, you see multi-dimensional process everywhere and begin to sense the fundamental process of Life—the evolutionary impulse to develop, grow, and make things better. You feel this impulse in yourself, and it drives you to co-create with others to make a positive, meaningful difference in the world, to assist Life's evolution by transforming and improving all you touch.

Ultimately, it is this stance within you to be your highest and best self, and your stand for it in the world that makes you a phenomenal change leader. By your own choice, you become accountable to support the multi-dimensional expression of process—the natural impulse to evolve and change—as it rolls through you, your organization, others, and the world. You now see the possibilities for breakthrough everywhere, in all quadrants and all levels. You know what to do and how to do it subtly and powerfully because of the understanding you have developed, who you have become, and what you are attuned to—the whole of Life in its broadest and deepest expressions.

You now know that your primary contribution as a conscious change leader is to stay awake and conscious, support process—Life in all its dimensions—to evolve, and assist others to wake up to this greater awareness, all on behalf of co-creating breakthrough results for the whole of multi-dimensional reality. As a conscious change leader, you become compelled to serve Life.

We would love to be on this journey of *conscious evolution* with you. Do you care to join us?

BIBLIOGRAPHY

Ackerman Anderson, L. (1986). Development, transition or transformation: The question of change in organizations. *OD Practitioner, 18*(4).

Ackerman Anderson, L., & Anderson, D. (1996). *Facilitating large systems change participant manual.* Durango, CO: Being First, Inc.

Ackerman Anderson, L., & Anderson, D. (2001). *The Change Leader's Roadmap.* San Francisco: Jossey-Bass/Pfeiffer.

Adams, J. (1984). *Transforming work: A collection of organizational transformation readings.* Alexandria, VA: Miles River Press.

Adams, J. (1986). *Transforming leadership: From vision to results.* Alexandria, VA: Miles River Press.

Adams, J., & Spencer, S. (2002). *Life changes: A Guide to the seven stages of personal growth.* New York: Paraview Press.

Alban, B., & Bunker, B. (1997). *Large group interventions: Engaging the whole system for rapid change.* San Francisco: Jossey-Bass.

Anderson, D. (1986). *Optimal performance manual.* Durango, CO: Being First, Inc.

Anderson, D., & Ackerman Anderson, L. (2001). *Beyond change management: Advanced strategies for today's transformational leaders.* San Francisco: Jossey-Bass/Pfeiffer.

Argyris, C. (1985). *Strategy, change, and defensive routines.* Marshfield, MA: Pitman.

Argyris, C. (1993). *Knowledge and action: A guide to overcoming barriers to organizational change.* San Francisco: Jossey-Bass.

Ashkenas, R., Ulrich, R., Jick, T., & Kerr, S. (1995). *The boundaryless organization: Breaking the chains of organizational structure.* San Francisco: Jossey-Bass.

Axelrod, R. (1992). *Terms of engagement: Changing the way we change our organizations*. San Francisco: Berrett-Koehler.

Balthazard, P. A., Cooke, R. S., & Potter, R. E. (2006). "Dysfunctional Culture, Dysfunctional Organization: Capturing the Behavioral Norms the Form Organizational Culture and Drive Performance." *Journal of Managerial Psychology*, 21(8), 709–732.

Beck, D., & Cohen C. (1996). *Spiral dynamics: Mastering values, leadership and change*. Cambridge, MA: Blackwell.

Beckhard, R. (1997). *Agent of change: My life, my practice*. San Francisco: Jossey-Bass.

Beckhard, R., & Harris, R. (1987). *Organizational transitions*. Reading, MA: Addison-Wesley.

Bennis, W. (1989). *Why leaders can't lead: The unconscious conspiracy continues*. San Francisco: Jossey-Bass.

Bennis, W. (1995). *On becoming a leader* (audio). New York: Simon & Schuster.

Bennis, W., & Nanus, B. (1985). *Leaders: The strategies for taking charge*. New York: Harper & Row.

Blanchard, K. (2006). *Leading at a higher level: Blanchard on leadership and creating high performing organizations*. Upper Saddle River, NJ: Prentice Hall.

Blanchard, K., & Hersey, P. (1982). *Management of organizational behavior: Utilizing human resources*. Upper Saddle River, NJ: Prentice Hall.

Blanchard, K., & O'Connor, M. (1997). *Managing by values*. San Francisco: Berrett-Koehler.

Block, P. (1999). *Flawless consulting: A guide to getting your expertise used* (2nd ed.). San Francisco: Jossey-Bass/Pfeiffer.

Block, P. (2003). *The answer to how is yes: Acting on what matters*. San Francisco: Berrett-Koehler.

Block, P. (2009). *Community: The structure of belonging*. San Francisco: Berrett-Koehler.

Bohm, D. (1980). *Wholeness and the implicate order*. New York: Routledge.

Bridges, W. (1980). *Transitions* (2nd ed.). New York: Perseus Publishing.

Bridges, W. (1991). *Managing transitions: Making the most of change*. Reading, MA: Addison-Wesley.

Bridges, W. (1994). *Jobshift: How to prosper in a workplace without jobs*. Reading, MA: Addison-Wesley.

Bridges, W. (2001). *The way of transition: Embracing life's most difficult moments*. New York: Perseus Publishing.

Bridges, W. (2003). *Managing transitions: Making the most of change* (2nd ed.). Cambridge, MA: Da Capo Press.

Briggs, J., & Peat, F. D. (1989). *Turbulent mirror: An illustrated guide to chaos theory and the science of wholeness*. New York: Harper & Row.

Briggs, J., & Peat, F. D. (1999). *Seven life lessons of chaos: Spiritual wisdom from the science of change*. New York: HarperCollins.

Brown, J. & Isaacs, D. (2005). *The World Café: Shaping our futures through conversations that matter*. San Francisco: Berrett-Koehler.

Bunker, B., & Alban, B. (eds.). (1992/December). Special issue: Large group interventions. *Applied Behavioral Science, (28)*4.

Canter, L., Ulrich, D., & Goldsmith, M. (eds.). (2004). *Best practices in leadership development and organization change: How the best companies ensure meaningful change and sustainable leadership*. San Francisco: Pfeiffer.

Capra, F. (1983). *The turning point: Science, society, and the rising culture*. New York: Bantam.

Capra, F. (1991). *The tao of physics: An exploration of the parallels between modern physics and eastern mysticism*. Boston: Shambhala.

Capra, F. (1996). *The web of life*. New York: Anchor Press.

Case, J. (1998). *The open-book experience: Lessons from over 100 companies who successfully transformed themselves*. Reading, MA: Addison-Wesley.

Collins, J., & Porras, J. (1994). *Built to last: Successful habits of visionary companies*. New York: HarperCollins.

Combs, A. (2002). *The radiance of being: Understanding the grand integral vision: Living the integral life*. New York: Paragon House.

Combs, A. (2009). *Consciousness explained better: Towards an integral understanding of the multifaceted nature of consciousness*. New York: Paragon House.

Conger, J., Spreitzer, G., & Lawler, E., III (1999). *The leader's change handbook: An essential guide to setting direction and taking action*. San Francisco: Jossey-Bass.

Conner, D. (1993). *Managing at the speed of change: How resilient managers succeed and prosper where others fail*. New York: Villard Books.

Conner, D. (1998). *Leading at the edge of chaos: How to create the nimble organization*. New York: John Wiley & Sons.

Cooperrider, D., Whitney, D., Stavros, J., & Fry, R. (2008). *Appreciative inquiry handbook: For leaders of change*. Brunswick, OH: Crown Custom Publishing.

Csikszentmihalyi, M. (1990). *Flow: The psychology of optimal experience*. New York: Harper & Row.

Csikszentmihalyi, M. (2004). *Good Business: Leadership, flow and the making of meaning*. New York: Penguin.

Dalai Lama. (2006). *The universe in a single atom: The convergence of science and spirituality*. New York: Broadway.

De Chardin, P. (1962). *Human energy*. New York: Harcourt Brace Jovanovich.

Deal, T., & Kennedy, A. (1982). *Corporate cultures: The rites and rituals of corporate life*. Reading, MA: Addison-Wesley.

Devane, T., & Holman, P. (eds.). (1999). *The change handbook: Group methods for shaping the future*. San Francisco: Berrett-Koehler.

Dowd, M. (2009). *Thank god for evolution: How the marriage of science and religion will transform how you live and our world*. New York: Plume.

Drucker, P. (1999). *Management challenges for the 21st century*. New York: HarperCollins.

Drucker, P. (2006). *The effective executive: The definitive guide to getting the right things done*. New York: Harper Paperbacks.

Drucker, P. (2008). *The five most important questions you'll ever ask about your organization*. San Francisco: Jossey-Bass.

Dym, B. (1995). *Readiness and change in couple therapy*. New York: HarperCollins.

Ferguson, M., & Naisbitt, J. (1980). *The aquarian conspiracy*. Los Angeles: Jeremy P. Tarcher.

Forrester, J. (1961). *Industrial dynamics*. Cambridge, MA: MIT Press.

Francis, D., & Woodcock, M. (1990). *Unblocking organizational values*. Glenview, IL: Scott, Foresman.

Frenier, C. (1997). *Business and the feminine principle: The untapped resource*. Boston: Butterworth-Heinemann.

Friedman, T. (2002). *Longitudes & attitudes: Exploring the world after September 11*. New York: Farrar, Straus, Giroux.

Friedman, T. (2005). *The world is flat: A brief history of the twenty-first century*. Vancouver, CA: Douglas & McIntyre.

Fullan, M. (2008). *The six secrets of change: What the best leaders do to help their organizations survive and thrive*. San Francisco: Jossey-Bass.

Galbraith, J., Lawler, E., & Associates. (1993). *Organizing for the future: The new logic for managing complex organizations*. San Francisco: Jossey-Bass.

Gleick, J. (1987). *Chaos: Making a new science*. New York: Penguin.

Gleick, J. (1999). *Faster: The acceleration of just about everything*. New York: Pantheon.

Goldsmith, M. (2009). *Mojo: How to get it, how to keep it, how to get it back if you lose it*. New York: Hyperion.

Goldstein, J. (1994). *The unshackled organization: Facing the challenge of unpredictability through spontaneous reorganization*. Portland, OR: Productivity Press.

Goleman, D. (1995). *Emotional intelligence: Why it can matter more than IQ*. New York: Bantam.

Greenleaf, R. (1977). *Servant leadership: A journey into the nature of legitimate power and greatness*. Mahwah, NJ: Paulist Press.

Grof, S. (1993). *The holotropic mind: The three levels of human consciousness and how they shape our lives*. New York: Harper Collins.

Gross, T. (1996). *The last word on power: Executive re-invention for leaders who must make the impossible happen*. New York: Doubleday.

Hagberg, J. (1984). *Real power: Stages of personal power in organizations*. Minneapolis, MN: Winston Press.

Hall, B. (1995). *Values shift: A guide to personal & organizational transformation*. Rockport, MA: Twin Lights Publishers.

Hammer, M., & Champy, J. (1993). *Reengineering the corporation: A manifesto for business revolution*. New York: HarperCollins.

Hammond, S. (1996). *The thin book of appreciative inquiry* (2nd ed.). Plano, TX: Thin Book Publishing.

Hammond, S., & Royal, C. (1998). *Lessons from the field: Applying appreciative inquiry*. Plano, TX: Practical Press.

Hawkins, D. (2002). *Power vs. force: The hidden determinants of human behavior*. Carlsbad, CA: Hay House.

Heisenberg, W. (1958). *Physics and philosophy*. New York: Harper Torchbooks.

Henricks, G., & Ludeman, K. (1996). *The corporate mystic: A guidebook for visionaries with their feet on the ground*. New York: Bantam.

Herbert, N. (1985). *Quantum reality: Beyond the new physics*. New York: Doubleday.

Herman, S. (1994). *The tao at work: On leading and following*. San Francisco: Jossey-Bass.

Hesselbien, F., & Goldsmith, M. (2006). *The leaders of the future 2: Visions, strategies and practices for the new era*. San Francisco: Jossey-Bass.

Hesselbein, F., Goldsmith, M., & Beckhard, R. (1996). *The leader of the future: New visions, strategies, and practices for the next era*. San Francisco: Jossey-Bass.

Holman, P., Devane, T., & Cady, S. (eds.). (2007). *The change handbook: The definitive resource on today's best methods for engaging whole systems (2nd ed.).* San Francisco: Berret-Koehler.

Huxley, A. (1956). *The doors of perception and heaven and hell.* New York: Harper Colophon.

Jacobs, R. (1994). *Real time strategic change: How to involve an entire organization in fast and far-reaching change.* San Francisco: Berrett-Koehler.

James, W. (1999). *The varieties of religious experience: A study in human nature.* New York: The Modern Library.

Jantsch, E. (1980). *The self-organizing universe.* New York: Pergamon Press.

Jaynes, J. (1990). *The origin of consciousness in the breakdown of the bicameral mind.* Boston: Houghton Mifflin.

Johnson, B. (1996). *Polarity management: Identifying and managing unsolvable problems.* Amherst, MA: HRD Press.

Joiner, W. B., & Josephs, S. A. (2007). *Leadership agility: Five levels of mastery for anticipating and initiating change.* San Francisco: Jossey-Bass.

Jones, J., & Bearley, W. (1996). *360-degree feedback: Strategies, tactics, and techniques for developing leaders.* Amherst, MA: HRD Press.

Jones, Q., Dunphy, D., Fishman, R., Larne, M., & Canter, C. (2007). *In great company: Unlocking the secrets of cultural transformation.* Sydney, Australia: Human Synergistics.

Jung, C. (1963). *Memories, dreams, reflections.* New York: Random House.

Jung, C. (1973). *Synchronicity: An acausal connecting principle.* Princeton, NJ: Princeton University Press.

Kanter, R. (1983). *The change masters: Innovation for productivity in the American corporation.* New York: Simon & Schuster.

Katz, J., & Miller, F. (2008). *Be big: Step up, step out, be bold.* San Francisco: Berrett-Koehler.

Katzenbach, J., & Smith, D. (1993). *The wisdom of teams: Creating the high performance organization.* Boston: Harvard Business School Press.

Katzenbach, J., & Smith, D. (2001). *The discipline of teams: A mindbook-workbook for delivering small group performance.* New York: Wiley.

Kay, B., & Jordan-Evans, S. (2005). *Love 'em or lose 'em.* San Francisco: Berrett Koehler Publishers.

Klein, E., & Izzo, J. (1998). *Awakening corporate soul: Four paths to unleash the power of people at work.* Lions Bay, BC, Canada: Fairwinds Press.

Koestenbaum, P. (1991). *Leadership: The inner side of greatness.* San Francisco: Jossey-Bass.

Kotter, J. (1996). *Leading change.* Boston: Harvard Business School Press.

Kotter, J. (2008). *A sense of urgency.* Boston: Harvard Business School Press.

Kotter, J., & Cohen, D. (2002). *The heart of change: Real-life stories of how people change their organizations.* Boston: Harvard Business School Press.

Kouzes, J., & Posner, B. (1995). *The leadership challenge: How to keep getting extraordinary things done in organizations.* San Francisco: Jossey-Bass.

Kouzes, J., & Posner, B. (1999). *Encouraging the heart: A leader's guide to rewarding and recognizing others.* San Francisco: Jossey-Bass.

Kouzes, J., & Posner, B. (2006). *A leader's legacy.* San Francisco: Jossey-Bass.

Kubler-Ross, E., & Kessler, D. (1997). *On grief and grieving.* New York: Scribner.

Kuhn, T. (1962). *The Structure of Scientific Resolutions* (1st ed.). Chicago: The University of Chicago Press.

Land, G., & Jarman, B. (1992). *Breakpoint and beyond: Mastering the future today.* San Francisco: HarperCollins.

Laszlo, E., Grof, S., & Russell, P. (1999). *The consciousness revolution.* Boston: Element Books.

Lebow, R., & Simon, W. (1997). *Lasting change: The shared values process that makes companies great.* New York: John Wiley & Sons.

Leider, R. (2010). *The power of purpose: Creating meaning in your life and work.* San Francisco: Berrett-Koehler.

Liebau, P. (1985). *Thoughts on relationships.* London, Ontario, Canada: P.S.A. Ventures.

Lipnack, J., & Stamps, J. (1993). *The teamnet factor: Bringing the power of boundary crossing into the heart of your business.* Essex Junction, VT: Oliver Wright.

London, M. (1988). *Change agents: New roles and innovation strategies for human resource professionals.* San Francisco: Jossey-Bass.

Lovelock, J.E. (1987). *Gaia.* London, England: Oxford University Press.

Ludema, J., Whitney, D., Mohr, B., & Griffin, T. (2003). *The appreciative inquiry summit: A practitioner's guide for leading large-group change.* San Francisco: Berrett-Koehler.

Maslow, A. (1964). *Religions, values, and peak experiences.* New York: Penguin.

Maslow, A. (1999). *Motivation and personality* (2nd ed.). New York: Harper and Row.

Maslow, A. (1999). *Toward a psychology of being* (3rd ed.). New York: John Wiley & Sons.

Maynard, H., & Mehrtens, S. (1993). *The fourth wave: Business in the 21st century*. San Francisco: Berrett-Koehler.

McFarland, L., Senn, L., & Childress, J. (1994). *21st century leadership: Dialogues with 100 top leaders*. Los Angeles: The Leadership Press.

McIntosh, S. (2007). *Integral consciousness and the future of evolution*. New York: Continuum.

Miles, R. (1997). *Leading corporate transformation: A blueprint for business renewal*. San Francisco: Jossey-Bass.

Miles, R., Miles, G., & Snow, C. (2005). *Collaborative Entrepreneurship*. Stanford, CA: Stanford University Press.

Mink, O., Mink, B., Downes, E., & Owen, K. (1994). *Open organizations: A model for effectiveness, renewal, and intelligent change*. San Francisco: Jossey-Bass.

Morton, C. (1984). *Managing operations in emerging companies*. Reading, MA: Addison-Wesley.

Nadler, D. (1998). *Champions of change: How CEOs and their companies are mastering the skills of radical change*. San Francisco: Jossey-Bass.

Nadler, D, Shaw, R., & Walton, A. (1995). *Discontinuous change: Leading organizational transformation*. San Francisco: Jossey-Bass.

Nadler, D., & Tushman, M.L. (1977). A diagnostic model for organizational behavior. In J.R. Hackman, E.E. Lawler, & L.W. Porter (eds.), *Perspectives on behavior in organizations*. New York: McGraw-Hill.

Naisbitt, J., & Aburdene, P. (1985). *Re-inventing the corporation: Transforming your job and your company for the new information society*. New York: Warner Books.

Nevis, E., Lancourt, J., & Vassallo, H. (1996). *Intentional revolutions: A seven-point strategy for transforming organizations*. San Francisco: Jossey-Bass.

Oakley, E., & Krug, D. (1994). Enlightened leadership: Getting to the heart of change. New York: Fireside.

O'Donovan, G. (2007).*The corporate culture handbook: How to plan, implement and measure a successful culture change*. Dublin, Ireland: Liffey Press.

Ogle, R. (2007). *Smart world: Breakthrough creativity and the new science of ideas*. Boston: Harvard Business Press.

Oshry, B. (1992). *The possibilities of organization*. Boston: Power & Systems.

Oshry, B. (1995). *Seeing systems: Unlocking the mysteries of organizational life*. San Francisco: Berrett-Koehler.

Pascarella, P., & Frohman, M. (1989). *The purpose-driven organization: Unleashing the power of direction and commitment*. San Francisco: Jossey-Bass.

Peat, D. F. (1987). *Synchronicity: The bridge between matter and mind*. New York: Bantam.

Penfield, W. (1975). *Mystery of the mind: A critical study of consciousness*. Princeton, NJ: Princeton University Press.

Peters, T., & Waterman, R. H. (1982) *In search of Excellence*. New York: Harper & Row.

Pribram, K. (1971). *Languages of the brain: Experimental paradoxes and principles in neuropsychology*. New York: Brandon House.

The Price Waterhouse Change Integration Team. (1995). *Better change: Best practices for transforming your organization*. New York: Irwin.

Prigogine, I. (1997). *The end of certainty: Time, chaos, and the new laws of nature*. New York: The Free Press.

Prigogine, I., & Stenger, I. (1984). *Order out of chaos*. New York: Bantam.

Puccio, G., Murdock, M. & Mance, M. (2006). *Creative leadership: Skills that drive change*. Thousand Oaks, CA: Sage Publications.

Quinn, R. E. (1996). *Deep Change: Discovering the leader within*. San Francisco: Jossey-Bass.

Ralston, F. (1995). *Hidden dynamics: How emotions affect business performance & how you can harness their power for positive results*. New York: American Management Association.

Rapaille, C. (2006). *The culture code: An ingenious way to understand why people around the world live and buy as they do*. New York: Broadway Books.

Ray, M., & Rinzler, A. (1993). *The new paradigm in business: Emerging strategies for leadership and organizational change*. New York: Tarcher/Pergee.

Reder, A. (1995). *75 best business practices for socially responsible companies*. New York: Tarcher/Putnam.

Renesch, J. (ed.). (1992). *New traditions in business: Spirit and leadership in the 21st century*. San Francisco: Berrett-Koehler.

Renesch, J. (1994). *Leadership in a new era: Visionary approaches to the biggest crisis of our time*. San Francisco: New Leaders Press.

Rogers, R., Hayden, J., Ferketish, B., with Matzen, R. (1985). *Organizational change that works: How to merge culture and business strategies for maximum results*. Pittsburgh, PA: Development Dimensions International.

Ross, G. (1994). *Toppling the pyramids: Redefining the way companies are run*. New York: Times Books.

Russell, P. (1995). *The global brain awakens: Our next evolutionary leap*. Palo Alto, CA: Global Brain, Inc.

Russell, P. (2008). *Waking up in time: Finding inner peace in times of accelerating change*. Novato, CA: Origin Press.

Ryan, K., & Oestreich, D. (1991). *Driving fear out of the workplace: How to overcome the invisible barriers to quality, productivity, and innovation*. San Francisco: Jossey-Bass.

Schein, E. (1969). *Process consultation: Its role in organization development*. Reading, MA: Addison-Wesley.

Schein, E. (1999). *The corporate culture survival guide: Sense and nonsense about culture change*. San Francisco: Jossey-Bass.

Schein, E. (2004). *Organizational culture and leadership*. San Francisco: Jossey-Bass.

Schwartz, P. (1996). *The art of the long view*. New York: Doubleday.

Schwartz, T. (1996). *What really matters: Searching for wisdom in America*. New York: Bantam.

Senge, P. (1990). *The fifth discipline: The art and practice of learning organization*. New York: Doubleday.

Senge, P. (2006). *The fifth discipline: the art and practice of the learning organization*. Broadway Business; revised edition.

Senge, P., Kleiner, A., Roberts, C., Ross, R., & Smith, B. (1994). *The fifth discipline fieldbook*. New York: Doubleday.

Senge, P., Kleiner, A., Roberts, C., Roth, G., Ross, R., & Smith, B. (1999). *The dance of change: The challenges of sustaining momentum in learning organizations*. New York: Doubleday.

Senge, P., Scharmer, C., Jaworski, J., & Flowers, B. (2005). *Presence: An exploration of profound change in people, organizations and society*. New York: Broadway Business.

Senge, P., Scharmer, C., Jaworski, J., & Flowers, B. (2008). *Presence: Human purpose and the field of the future*. New York: Doubleday.

Sheldrake, R. (1995). *A new science of life: The hypothesis of morphic resonance*. Rochester, VT: Park Street Press.

Sieler, A. (2007). *Coaching to the human soul: Ontological coaching and deep change: Volume 2: Emotional learning and ontological coaching*. Blackburn, AU: Newfield Austrailia.

Singer, J. (1994). *Boundaries of the soul: The practice of Jung's psychology*. New York: Doubleday.

Smith, H. (1992). *Forgotten truth: The common vision of the world's religions*. San Francisco: HarperCollins.

Spencer, S. A., & Adams, J. D. (1990). *Life changes: Growing through personal transitions.* San Luis Obispo, CA: Impact Publishing.

Stacey, R.(1992). *Managing the unknowable: Strategic boundaries between order and chaos in organizations.* San Francisco: Jossey-Bass.

Stiglitz, J. (2006). *Making Globalization Work.* New York: Norton.

Talbot, M. (1986). *Beyond the quantum.* New York: Bantam.

Tart, C. (1975). *States of consciousness.* New York: E.P. Dutton.

Tart, C. (2001). *Mind Science: Medication training for practical people.* Novato, CA: Wisdom Editions.

Tichy, N., with Cohen, E. (1997). *The leadership engine: How winning companies build leaders at every level.* New York: HarperCollins.

Waldrop, M. (1992). *Complexity: The emerging science at the edge of order and chaos.* New York: Touchstone.

Walsh, R., & Vaughan, F. (1993). *Paths beyond ego: The transpersonal vision.* New York: Penguin/Putnam.

Waterman, R. (1987). *The renewal factor: How the best get and keep the competitive edge.* New York: Bantam.

Watkins, J. M., & Mohr, B. (2001). *Appreciative inquiry: Change at the speed of imagination.* San Francisco: Jossey-Bass/Pfeiffer.

Weisbord, M. R. (1978). *Organizational diagnosis: A workbook of theory and practice.* Reading, MA: Addison-Wesley.

Weisbord, M., & Janoff, S. (1995). *Future search: An action guide to finding common ground for action in organizations.* San Francisco: Berrett-Koehler.

Weisinger, H. (1998). *Emotional intelligence at work: The untapped edge for success.* San Francisco: Jossey-Bass.

Wheatley, M. (1994). *Leadership and the new science: Learning about organization from an orderly universe.* San Francisco: Berrett-Koehler.

Wheatley, M., & Kellner-Rogers, M. (1995). *A simpler way.* San Francisco: Berrett-Koehler.

Wilber, K. (1977). *The spectrum of consciousness.* Wheaton, IL: Theosophical Publishing House.

Wilber, K. (1982). *The holographic paradigm and other paradoxes.* Boston: Shambhala.

Wilber, K. (1996). *A brief history of everything.* Boston: Shambhala.

Wilber, K. (1996). *Up from Eden, new edition: A transpersonal view of human evolution.* Wheaton, IL: Quest Books.

Wilber, K. (1998). *The marriage of sense and soul.* New York: Random House.

Wilber, K. (1999). *One taste: The journals of Ken Wilber*. Boston: Shambhala.

Wilber, K. (2000). A theory of everything. Boston: Shambala, p. 70.

Wilber, K. (2000). Integral psychology: Consciousness, spirit, psychology, therapy. Boston: Shambala.

Wilber, K. (2001). *Sex, ecology, spirituality: The spirit of evolution* (2nd ed.). Boston: Shambhala.

Wilber, K. (2001). *No Boundary: Eastern and western approaches to personal growth*. Boston: Shambhala.

Wilber, K. (2006). *Integral Spirituality: A startling new role for religion in the modern and postmodern world*. Boston: Shambhala.

Williamson, M. (1992). *Return to love*. New York: HarperCollins.

Wilson, J. (1994). *Leadership trapeze: Strategies for leadership in team-based organizations*. San Francisco: Jossey-Bass.

Wolf, F. (1988). *Parallel universes: The search for other worlds*. New York: Touchstone.

Wolf, F. (1989). *Taking the quantum leap: The new physics for nonscientists*. New York: Harper & Row.

Young, A. (1976). *The reflexive universe*. Englewood Cliffs, NJ: Prentice Hall.

Zaffron, S. & Logan, D. (2009). *The three laws of performance*. San Francisco: Jossey-Bass.

Zukav, G. (1979). *The dancing Wu Li master*. New York: Bantam.

ABOUT THE AUTHORS

Dean Anderson is CEO and co-founder of the consulting, training, and publishing company, Being First, Inc. Mr. Anderson consults to and coaches senior executives of Fortune 500 companies, government and large nonprofit organizations, specializing in organizational and personal transformation and optimal performance. He helps senior executives achieve breakthrough results from change, release the human potential in their organizations, and build high performing co-creative cultures.

Mr. Anderson has co-authored more than 50 articles on organizational and personal transformation. His first two books, the first editions of *Beyond Change Management* and *The Change Leader's Roadmap*, which he co-authored with Linda Ackerman Anderson, were the second and third best sellers in the Jossey-Bass/Pfeiffer "Practicing Organization Development" Series.

Mr. Anderson's interest in human performance and transformation began at an early age. He was the first ten-year-old boy in the world to swim 100 yards under a minute, and the first to ever swim 200 yards under two minutes. On this foundation, Mr. Anderson founded the Optimal Performance Institute in 1980, where he developed the *OPtimizing System for Personal Excellence*, training elite athletes, actors, singers, and other performers, some of whom went on to win Olympic gold medals.

Mr. Anderson is the co-developer of *The Change Leader's Roadmap* methodology, creator of Being First's renowned leadership breakthrough training, *Leading Breakthrough Results: Walking the Talk of Change*, and is the central developer of *The Co-Creating System*.™ He is the co-author of Being First's comprehensive set of change tools and the developer of the *Co-Creative Partnering and Team Development* processes.

Mr. Anderson has two degrees from Stanford University, a bachelor of arts in communications and a master's degree in education, where he was an All-American swimmer and water polo player. His current passions are fly fishing, whitewater rafting, horseback riding, learning guitar, and being in the wilderness with his wife, Linda, and daughter, Terra.

Linda Ackerman Anderson is a co-founder and principal of Being First, Inc, a consulting, training, and publishing company specializing in facilitating transformational change in Fortune 500 businesses, government, and the military. Over the past thirty years, her work has focused on change strategy development for transformational changes and the development of change consultants and leaders. Linda speaks about leading conscious transformation at national and international conferences and is known as an inspiring model of her message. In the past twenty years, she and her partner, Dean Anderson, have established themselves as thought leaders on leading conscious transformation and changing organizational mindset and culture as drivers of transformational change. She drove the thirty-year development of Being First's renowned change process methodology, The Change Leader's Roadmap. Linda also devotes herself to supporting women as leaders of change.

Ms. Ackerman Anderson was a founding creator of the organization transformation field, and she chaired the Second International Symposium on Organization Transformation in 1984. To help define this field, she has published more than 50 articles, including "Development, Transition or Transformation: Bringing Change Leadership into the 21st Century," "Awake at the Wheel: Moving beyond Change Management to Conscious Change Leadership," "The Flow State: A New View of Organizations and Leadership," and "Flow State Leadership in Action: Managing Organizational Energy." She was one of the first to articulate the notion and use of organizational energy as a tool for transformation.

In 1981 Ms. Ackerman Anderson formed Linda S. Ackerman, Inc., then merged it in 1988 with the Optimal Performance Institute, headed by Dean Anderson to form Being Fist, Inc. Prior to forming her first business, Ms. Ackerman Anderson spent four years working at Sun Company, Inc. and one of its subsidiaries, Sun

Petroleum Products Company, as both an organization development consultant and manager of human resources planning and development.

Ms. Ackerman Anderson's professional education includes Columbia University's Advanced Organization Development and Human Resources Management Program (1978–1979) and University Associates' Laboratory Education Internship Program (1977–1978). She has served on the faculty for the UA Intern Program and other UA conferences and many university professional development programs.

Ms. Ackerman Anderson received her master's degree in interdisciplinary arts from Columbia University's Teachers College and her bachelor's degree in art history and education from Boston University.

For further information, contact:

Being First, Inc.
1242 Oak Drive, DW2
Durango, CO 81301
USA
(970) 385–5100 voice
(970) 385–7751 fax
www.beingfirst.com
e-mail: deananderson@beingfirst.com
lindasaa@beingfirst.com

INDEX

Conscious awareness; Conscious Change Leader Accountability Model; Conscious change leaders

Change Leader's Roadmap (CLR): activity levels, 244; as fullstream process, 241–243; overview, 239–240; structure of, 241–244; as thinking discipline, 233–233, 241, 245; use by conscious change leaders, 247; worksheet comparing with other models, 250–252

Change Leader's Roadmap: How to Navigate Your Organization's Transformation, The (Ackerman Anderson and Anderson), 24

Change leadership: change management compared, 45, 49–50; focus areas in, 4, 11, 24–25; people strategies of, 69; resistance to change and, 12, 18, 45; role of, 249, 258; transforming to conscious change leadership, 3, 93–94, 99–101

Change management: change leadership compared, 45, 49–50; history of, 42–43; implementation stage role, 234–238; transitional change and, 56–59. *See also* Conscious Change Leader Accountability Model

Change management leaders. *See* Change leaders

Change process, 52, 57–61, 65, 67, 69, 72, 75, 78–79, 86, 94, 99, 108

Change process models: change framework compared, 228–230; as conscious thinking discipline not prescriptions, 12, 228; The Deming Cycle, 226, 231; elements needed, 239; Kotter's Eight Stage Process of Creating Major Change, 231; overview, 228–229; as tools of conscious process thinking, 223. *See also* Change Leader's Roadmap (CLR); Fullstream Transformation Model

Chaos leading to order, 61–62

Chief Change Officers (CCO), 120, 126–127

Churchill, Winston, 254

CLR. *See* Change Leader's Roadmap (CLR)

Co-creative ways of being, 180, 191–192, 257

Cohen, C., 160n

Collins, Jim 16

Command-and-control leadership style, 43, 46, 48, 63, 99, 199, 205, 248–249

Commitment. *See* Resistance changing to commitment

Common change process methodology, 20, 28, 114, 115, 117, 124–126, 128, 256

Competence core need, 141, 145–149, 257

Competency Model for learning, 88, 90

Connection and inclusion core need, 141, 144, 146–149, 257

Conner, Daryl, 44, 99, 231

Conscious awareness: cycling in and out of, 103; defined, 84; development of, 86–87, 89; flow or zone and, 86–87, 165; four sights, 87–88; importance of, 84; levels of, 93; overview, 84–85

Conscious Change Leader Accountability Model, 5–7, 11, 24, 74, 78, 162, 197, 212, 221, 227, 229–230

Conscious change leaders: approach to being, 82–83, 91, 93, 94, 99, 101, 103–104; autopilot leaders compared, 82–85; building change capability by, 124–125; commitment and accountability by, 254–255; core needs and, 133,140–148; defined, 2–4; downstream stage role, 233, 237–238; feeling your feelings, 153; midstream stage role, 233–234, 236–237; mindset awareness by, 164–165; moving from resistance to commitment, 152–156; multi-dimensional nature and process, 211–212, 214; personal responsibility of, 178–179, 182, 185; process facilitation by, 210, 223, 246–247; process orientation of, 214, 217; self-actualization issues and, 148–149, 160; self-assessment for, 102; self-awareness, 92; self-mastery by, 173–175; Strategic Change Office and, 121; styles of, 247–249; transformation to, 3–5, 99–101; upstream

Strategic Change Office (SCO): Chief Change Officer role, 120–121, 123; executive interactions with, 119–121; functions and benefits of, 122–125; overview, 120–121; staffing of, 120, 124–125; Strategic Change Center of Excellence and, 119

Strategic discipline for change: Center of Excellence for, 117–120; common change process methodology, 114–115; enterprise change agenda, 108–110; infrastructure for change, 116–117; overview, 108–111; requirements for success, 108; Strategic Change Office for, 115–122

Stevenson, Adlai, 132

Subconscious mind, 168

Subcultures, 76

Subprocesses, 209, 217, 221, 226

Success: ability and, 96, 164–165, 171; assessing level sought worksheet, 27; culture change and, 190, 195–197; enterprise change requirements for, 108–110; Fundamental Laws for, 170, 171, 189; Levels of, 21–23, 27; marketplace requirements for, 32; return on investment and, 21

Systems: culture change and, 186–187; diagrams, 225–226; dynamics, 219–220; quadrant of the Conscious Change Leader Accountability Model, 5–6, 24, 78; as reflecting culture, 187; seeing consciously, 88; thinking, 209, 218–220, 222–223

Team culture, 76, 191–192

Technological revolution, 44

Theory of everything. *See* All Quadrants, All Levels (AQAL)

Thinking, mindset compared, 163

Thinking orientations: applications of, 222–223; conscious process thinking, 221, 223; project thinking, 218–219; systems thinking, 219–221; use of multiple, 223

Thomas, Debbie, 172

Three States of Change Model, 56–57

Tipping points, 77, 197, 199, 256

Training. *See* Learning

Transformational change: compared with other types, 51–55; complexity of, 83; core issues triggered by, 142; culture change as critical to, 183; defined, 36, 59; determining types of change worksheet, 75; Drivers of Change Model for, 32; history of, 11; human dynamics of, 67–70; journey of, 65–66, 228–230, 246–247, 255; multi-dimensional nature and process, 4–7; overview, 59–61, 255; personal introspection during, 71–73; process nature of, 214; project management methodology limitations for, 224–225; requirements for, 2–3; uncertainty in, 65, 68, 70; wake-up calls for, 93–94. *See also* Conscious Change Leader Accountability Model; Course correcting in transformational change; Fullstream Transformation Model

"Transition state" of change, 53, 56–57

Transitional change: compared with other types, 51, 53–54, 49–50, 60, 65; effecting only content, 40; overview, 56–58; strategies for managing, 58–59

Uncertainty in transformational change, 65, 68, 70–72

Unconscious awareness. *See* Autopilot approach to awareness

Unconsciously competent, 91

Unconsciously incompetent, 88

Upstream stage of fullstream transformation, 233–236

Values, maintaining during change, 70

Victim mentality, 178–179

Wake-up calls, 53, 64, 66

Walking the talk, 95, 149, 181–182, 185, 215

Wall Street Journal, 44

Pfeiffer Publications Guide

This guide is designed to familiarize you with the various types of Pfeiffer publications. The formats section describes the various types of products that we publish; the methodologies section describes the many different ways that content might be provided within a product. We also provide a list of the topic areas in which we publish.

FORMATS

In addition to its extensive book-publishing program, Pfeiffer offers content in an array of formats, from fieldbooks for the practitioner to complete, ready-to-use training packages that support group learning.

FIELDBOOK Designed to provide information and guidance to practitioners in the midst of action. Most fieldbooks are companions to another, sometimes earlier, work, from which its ideas are derived; the fieldbook makes practical what was theoretical in the original text. Fieldbooks can certainly be read from cover to cover. More likely, though, you'll find yourself bouncing around following a particular theme, or dipping in as the mood, and the situation, dictate.

HANDBOOK A contributed volume of work on a single topic, comprising an eclectic mix of ideas, case studies, and best practices sourced by practitioners and experts in the field.

An editor or team of editors usually is appointed to seek out contributors and to evaluate content for relevance to the topic. Think of a handbook not as a ready-to-eat meal, but as a cookbook of ingredients that enables you to create the most fitting experience for the occasion.

RESOURCE Materials designed to support group learning. They come in many forms: a complete, ready-to-use exercise (such as a game); a comprehensive resource on one topic (such as conflict management) containing a variety of methods and approaches; or a collection of like-minded activities (such as icebreakers) on multiple subjects and situations.

TRAINING PACKAGE An entire, ready-to-use learning program that focuses on a particular topic or skill. All packages comprise a guide for the facilitator/trainer and a workbook for the participants. Some packages are supported with additional media—such as video—or learning aids, instruments, or other devices to help participants understand concepts or practice and develop skills.

- *Facilitator/trainer's guide* Contains an introduction to the program, advice on how to organize and facilitate the learning event, and step-by-step instructor notes. The guide also contains copies of presentation materials—handouts, presentations, and overhead designs, for example—used in the program.

- *Participant's workbook* Contains exercises and reading materials that support the learning goal and serves as a valuable reference and support guide for participants in the weeks and months that follow the learning event. Typically, each participant will require his or her own workbook.

ELECTRONIC CD-ROMs and web-based products transform static Pfeiffer content into dynamic, interactive experiences. Designed to take advantage of the searchability, automation, and ease-of-use that technology provides, our e-products bring convenience and immediate accessibility to your workspace.

METHODOLOGIES

CASE STUDY A presentation, in narrative form, of an actual event that has occurred inside an organization. Case studies are not prescriptive, nor are they used to prove a point; they are designed to develop critical analysis and decision-making skills. A case study has a specific time frame, specifies a sequence of events, is narrative in structure, and contains a plot structure—an issue (what should be/have been done?). Use case studies when the goal is to enable participants to apply previously learned theories to the circumstances in the case, decide what is pertinent, identify the real issues, decide what should have been done, and develop a plan of action.

ENERGIZER A short activity that develops readiness for the next session or learning event. Energizers are most commonly used after a break or lunch to stimulate or refocus the group. Many involve some form of physical activity, so they are a useful way to counter post-lunch lethargy. Other uses include transitioning from one topic to another, where "mental" distancing is important.

EXPERIENTIAL LEARNING ACTIVITY (ELA) A facilitator-led intervention that moves participants through the learning cycle from experience to application (also known as a Structured Experience). ELAs are carefully thought-out designs in which there is a definite learning purpose and intended outcome. Each step—everything that participants do during the activity—facilitates the accomplishment of the stated goal. Each ELA includes complete instructions for facilitating the intervention and a clear statement of goals, suggested group size and timing, materials required, an explanation of the process, and, where appropriate, possible variations to the activity. (For more detail on Experiential Learning Activities, see the Introduction to the *Reference Guide to Handbooks and Annuals*, 1999 edition, Pfeiffer, San Francisco.)

GAME A group activity that has the purpose of fostering team spirit and togetherness in addition to the achievement of a pre-stated goal. Usually contrived—undertaking a desert expedition, for example—this type of learning method offers an engaging means for participants to demonstrate and practice business and interpersonal skills. Games are effective for team building and personal development mainly because the goal is subordinate to the process—the means through which participants reach decisions, collaborate, communicate, and generate trust and understanding. Games often engage teams in "friendly" competition.

ICEBREAKER A (usually) short activity designed to help participants overcome initial anxiety in a training session and/or to acquaint the participants with one another. An icebreaker can be a fun activity or can be tied to specific topics or training goals. While a useful tool in itself, the icebreaker comes into its own in situations where tension or resistance exists within a group.

INSTRUMENT A device used to assess, appraise, evaluate, describe, classify, and summarize various aspects of human behavior. The term used to describe an instrument depends primarily on its format and purpose. These terms include survey, questionnaire, inventory, diagnostic, survey, and poll. Some uses of instruments include providing instrumental feedback to group members, studying here-and-now processes or functioning within a group, manipulating group composition, and evaluating outcomes of training and other interventions.

Instruments are popular in the training and HR field because, in general, more growth can occur if an individual is provided with a method for focusing specifically on his or her own behavior. Instruments also are used to obtain information that will serve as a basis for change and to assist in workforce planning efforts.

Paper-and-pencil tests still dominate the instrument landscape with a typical package comprising a facilitator's guide, which offers advice on administering the instrument and interpreting the collected data, and an initial set of instruments. Additional instruments are available separately. Pfeiffer, though, is investing heavily in e-instruments. Electronic instrumentation provides effortless distribution and, for larger groups particularly, offers advantages over paper-and-pencil tests in the time it takes to analyze data and provide feedback.

LECTURETTE A short talk that provides an explanation of a principle, model, or process that is pertinent to the participants' current learning needs. A lecturette is intended to establish a common language bond between the trainer and the participants by providing a mutual frame of reference. Use a lecturette as an introduction to a group activity or event, as an interjection during an event, or as a handout.

MODEL A graphic depiction of a system or process and the relationship among its elements. Models provide a frame of reference and something more tangible, and more easily remembered, than a verbal explanation. They also give participants something to "go on," enabling them to track their own progress as they experience the dynamics, processes, and relationships being depicted in the model.

ROLE PLAY A technique in which people assume a role in a situation/scenario: a customer service rep in an angry-customer exchange, for example. The way in which the role is approached is then discussed and feedback is offered. The role play is often repeated using a different approach and/or incorporating changes made based on feedback received. In other words, role playing is a spontaneous interaction involving realistic behavior under artificial (and safe) conditions.

SIMULATION A methodology for understanding the interrelationships among components of a system or process. Simulations differ from games in that they test or use a model that depicts or mirrors some aspect of reality in form, if not necessarily in content. Learning occurs by studying the effects of change on one or more factors of the model. Simulations are commonly used to test hypotheses about what happens in a system—often referred to as "what if?" analysis—or to examine best-case/worst-case scenarios.

THEORY A presentation of an idea from a conjectural perspective. Theories are useful because they encourage us to examine behavior and phenomena through a different lens.

TOPICS

The twin goals of providing effective and practical solutions for workforce training and organization development and meeting the educational needs of training and human resource professionals shape Pfeiffer's publishing program. Core topics include the following:

Leadership & Management

Communication & Presentation

Coaching & Mentoring

Training & Development

E-Learning

Teams & Collaboration

OD & Strategic Planning

Human Resources

Consulting

What will you find on pfeiffer.com?

- The best in workplace performance solutions for training and HR professionals

- Downloadable training tools, exercises, and content

- Web-exclusive offers

- Training tips, articles, and news

- Seamless on-line ordering

- Author guidelines, information on becoming a Pfeiffer Partner, and much more

Discover more at www.pfeiffer.com

The CHANGE LEADER'S ROADMAP

How to Navigate Your Organization Transformation

Second Edition

ISBN: 978-0-470-64806-3 | US $55.00
Available October 2010

This second edition of **The Change Leader's Roadmap** provides the most comprehensive guidance available for building transformational change strategy and designing and implementing successful transformation. Includes updated information on a wealth of topics including the critical path tasks and how to use CLR to change minds and cultures. The new edition also includes new activities, steps for changing capacity to capability, guiding principles to first phase, and advice for creating an organizational vision. This book is written for leaders, project managers, OD practitioners, change practitioners, and consultants.

DEAN ANDERSON is co-founder and president of Being First, a change leadership development and transformational change consulting firm. He is a powerful speaker, writer, coach, consultant and master trainer. He co-authored with Linda Ackerman Anderson of *Beyond Change Management* and *Change Leader's Roadmap*.

LINDA ACKERMAN ANDERSON is a co-founder and vice-president of Being First. She specializes in planning for and facilitating transformational change in Fortune 1000 businesses and the military. Linda has spoken about her work on conscious transformation at national and international conferences, and is known as a thought leader and inspiring model of her message. During the past 25 years, her practice has focused on strategy development for major organizational change using Being First's renown nine-phase Change Leader's Roadmap.

To order or for more information,
visit www.pfeiffer.com
For bulk orders, e-mail specialsales@wiley.com

Pfeiffer™
An Imprint of ®WILEY
Now you know.